lonely planet

EPIC BIKE TRIPS *of the* WORLD

Explore the world's most thrilling cycling routes

CONTENTS

Manuel Glira; Stefan Amato; Miles Arbour

SIMON
ELEMENT

An Imprint of Simon & Schuster, LLC
1230 Avenue of the Americas
New York, NY 10020

Food stylist: Cyd McDowell

Food stylist assistant: Tommy McKiernan

Food stylist assistant: Debbie Kim

Prop stylist assistant: Ashleigh Sarbone

Prop stylist: Maeve Sheridan

Prop stylist assistant: Fabi Arce

Prop stylist assistant: Tsering Dolma

Studio: Blue Salt Studio

First Simon Element hardcover edition August 2026

SIMON ELEMENT is a registered trademark of Simon & Schuster, LLC

Interior design by Farzana Razak and Jan Derevjanek

Manufactured in China

10 9 8 7 6 5 4 3 2 1

Library of Congress Control Number: 2025945933

ISBN 978-1-6680-8212-6
ISBN 978-1-6680-8213-3 (ebook)

Stefan Amato

Easy Harder Epic

INTRODUCTION

The first person to cycle all the way around the world was Thomas Stevens, who departed from San Francisco in 1884 and returned to the US in 1886. Annie Londonderry, the first woman to pedal around the planet, left Boston some 20 years later. The bicycle has been a great liberator for travellers for more than a century but never more so than today. Over recent years, regional and national organisations plus many enterprising individuals, such as some of the contributors to this book, have been busy creating more cycling routes for enthusiasts to follow. You might not be ready to pedal around the world but there are countless rides, from one day to a month or more, that will be immensely rewarding to complete.

This collection of epic cycling adventures focuses mostly on multiday trips (with a few shorter rides thrown in) and we've tried to capture every flavour of cycling. Whether you're into road cycling at speed or taking your time on a touring bike, hitting gravel tracks across distant plains or holding on to your handlebars on a mountain-biking descent, there are stories here to inspire everybody to try something new. A lot of the trips fall under the umbrella of 'bikepacking', which is essentially backpacking, but carrying your luggage on your bicycle instead of on your back. What they have in common is that these trips will teach you more about yourself than you'd expect – and most of the time you'll surprise yourself with the situations you can manage. There are few better ways of gaining resilience, confidence and the ability to think on your feet.

Awe-inspiring scenery is a given. Riding through Australia's forests of giant karri trees or across Bolivia's mesmerising salt flats are otherworldly experiences. Many of the rides in this book venture into extraordinary landscapes, such as the Dolomite mountains of Italy, the Andes of Peru or the Annapurna range in Nepal. With those extreme environments comes challenge and there's a lot to be said for leaving your comfort zone momentarily. Where appropriate, these rides are flagged as requiring experience and expertise at being self-sufficient.

Joining a group trip, whether a bunch of friends or with a tour operator, is also a great way of mitigating risk and picking up skills that you can later employ solo. And there are great beginner bikepacking routes that are close enough to civilisation to offer a confidence boost, for example the Pirinexus in northeast Spain and the Heart of the Octopus in northern New Zealand. Writers with their families in tow recommended accessible rides from a flat pedal following the Loire river in France to a more ambitious expedition along South Australia's Mawson Trail (they all survived).

Cycling can offer time out from daily routines for reflection and healing, as described in Sarah Pendergrass's bread-fuelled bike ride around Tasmania's Bruny Island and Betsy Welch's circumnavigation of Hawaii's Big Island. We know the benefits of being in nature for our mental health – couple that with the physical exercise of cycling and it's clear that these rides do wonders for our wellbeing.

Hopefully, this book will prove that there's no better way of experiencing a place, a culture and its people than by bicycle. We are independent, immersed in our surroundings and forever pondering the question 'I wonder what's over there?' And, as some of these tales tell, arriving on a bicycle opens doors, literally and figuratively. .

HOW TO USE THIS BOOK

The main stories in each chapter, organised by continent, feature first-hand accounts of fantastic cycling adventures. Each includes a toolkit to help plan the trip – when is the best time of year to ride, how to get there, and what to take. On the contents page, the rides have been colour coded according to their difficulty, which takes into account not just distance but also logistics and local conditions. Some of the included routes are signposted and safe for novice cyclists to attempt but others require a degree of experience and expertise. And the 'more like this' sections following each story, offer other ideas along a similar theme.

Mark Watson; Andrew Bain; Sam Rice

Clockwise from left: cycling through the karri forests of Western Australia on Munda Biddi; refreshments on the Tiger Head Mountain route in Thailand; crossing the Andes on the Peru Divide.

Opening spread from left: climbing into Italy's Dolomites; a picnic of Cornish pasties on the West Kernow Way; the Alberni Bam Bam on Vancouver Island; taking a break in Nepal's Annapurna

AFRICA

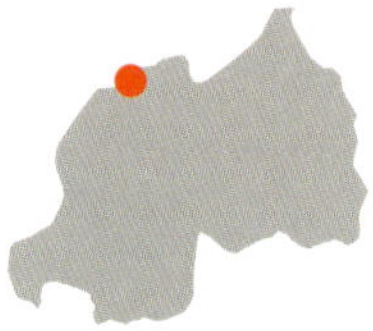

RWANDA VIA THE CONGO NILE TRAIL

A jewel in Africa's cycling crown, Rwanda celebrates the creation of the Congo Nile Trail, a multiday bikepacking route full of challenging terrain and jaw-dropping views.

I added the Congo Nile Trail (CNT) to my must-ride list the minute I heard about it. Like an earworm you can't stop singing, once the idea was in my head I had to find a way to get there. At 141 miles (227km), the CNT bikepacking trail makes it possible to ride clear across Rwanda, that small landlocked country in east Africa. The thought of being able to see so much of this beautiful land by bike was a tantalising prospect. Starting on the border of the Democratic Republic of the Congo, in the mountainous north and close to the Virunga Mountains and their resident gorillas, the trail runs southwest along shimmering Lake Kivu, through the populous Kivu Belt region, before terminating near the tropical splendour of Nyungwe Forest National Park.

Not for nothing is Rwanda dubbed the Land of a Thousand Hills. I'd ridden the hills around Kigali before, so I knew that riding the CNT would be anything but easy. Yet the memories that had stayed with me from that Kigali ride were not of

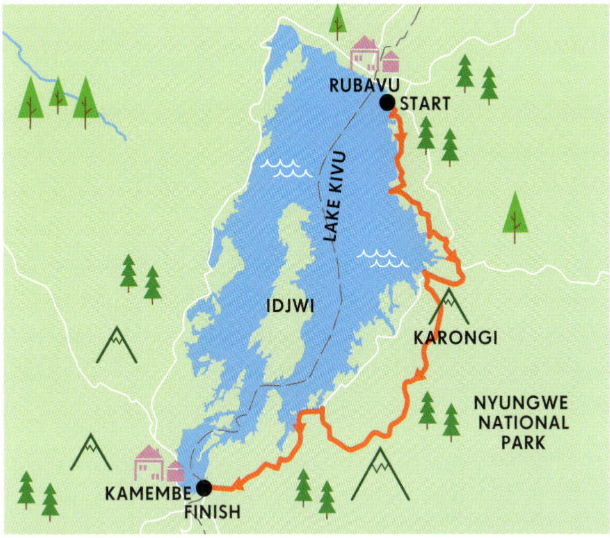

Tetyana Dotsenko/Shutterstock

"Peering through this window into daily Rwandan life was my favourite part of the journey"

punishing climbs. Instead, they were of the mesmerising sights, of the morning mist rising from valleys to reveal agricultural terraces, with neatly planted rows of beans and potatoes; of the vibrant greens of the banana and tea plantations, and of the fascinating to-and-fro of daily life. Rwanda is a land of hypnotising beauty. The CNT offered the chance to revel in those landscapes all the more, not just to see but to smell and hear them up close.

Rwanda may not be on every cyclist's radar, but it should be. Infamous for the genocide of 1994, some political tensions still exist but Rwanda is, at the time of writing, a safe and stable country with good infrastructure and services. It's also a country of cyclists. Travel anywhere in this nation and you'll pass people pedalling heavy steel bikes, the preferred mode of daily transport for millions of Rwandans. More recently, Rwanda has become a destination of choice for elite riders, both road cyclists and mountain bikers. Annual events such as the Tour du Rwanda (road), and Race Around Rwanda (bikepacking; p18) have been drawing increasingly international pelotons. In 2024, the country's Gorilla Gravel race became part of the UCI's Gravel World Series; and in 2025, Rwanda became the first African country to host the UCI Road World Championships, one of the biggest events in the sport outside of the Grand Tours.

The profile of the CNT has been on the up, too. Developed for tourists by the Rwandan government in 2011, it was named the Congo Nile Trail because it runs along the continental divide that separates the drainage basins of the Nile and Congo rivers. The valleys on the west side drain into the Congo, those on the east end up in the Nile. Today, a handful of excellent outfitters offer tours along on the trail and, helpfully, rent both bikes and guides. My guide, Albert, came courtesy of Rwandan Adventures and we were also joined by another guide, Casimu, whom we met out on the trail.

Albert and I hopped on the CNT at Rubavu, the northern terminus, riding Giant Fathom hardtails specced with 29-inch rims and 2.4-inch tyres. The sign at the trail junction told us the altitude was 5000ft (1524m), and I could certainly feel it. It was Sunday, and the songs of church choirs drifted out from nearby buildings. Kids ran alongside us, swinging their sandalled feet and trying to catch our rear mudguards. It was early but the sun was already burning the mist from the fields. On Lake Kivu, one of Africa's Great Lakes, fishermen headed out in search of tilapia, catfish and sambaza, a type of sardine. The air was fragrant with aromas; of tea, coffee and eucalyptus. Within minutes I was utterly absorbed. Then the climbing started.

The riding on the CNT is rough. Near Rubavu, the trail is a couple metres across and mostly hard-packed dirt, with deep ruts and jutting boulders. The trail's profile and conditions change as you head south, narrowing to grassy singletrack in some areas, with slick rock and shale in others. The section of the trail between Kibogora and Kamembe, meanwhile, has been paved. On some parts of the trail, washouts are common after heavy rains, and while there are bridge crossings sympathetic to two wheels, other sections are more hike than bike. The cumulative elevation gain over the entire trail is 26,247ft

Christina Palassio; Cavan Images/Alamy;. Cavan Images/Alamy

NATIONAL PARKS

A spectacular conservation area, in Volcanoes National Park it's recommended you book a gorilla trek and encounter these magnificent creatures up close. An experience you'll never forget, you can also choose from a range of challenging hikes, all with incredible vistas. In Nyungwe Forest National Park, experience the region's awe-inspiring diversity. The park is home to 13 species of monkey, including the charismatic and elusive golden monkey, along with a dazzling assortment of tropical birds and flora.

Left to right: a glimpse of Lake Kivu through tropical foliage; prepare to cross obstacles on the route; much of the route comprises dirt trails; but there are signposts. Previous spread: looking over Lake Kivu

(8000m), with the highest point at 8530ft (2600m). As Albert had told me enthusiastically on our eight-mile (13km) climb out of Rubavu, there's not a flat stretch of more than six miles (10km) on the whole CNT.

Many who ride the trail break it into five stages, travelling between 25 miles (40km) and 37 miles (60km) a day, with an average of 3281ft (1000m) of elevation per day. Invariably, this means stops in Kinunu, Karongi, Mugonero, Kigaga, and Kamembe. Albert's favourite part of the trail runs over the mountains between Kibuye and Mugonero, a preference he attributes to the changing elevation and cooler temperatures high up. 'There's a big climb and a big descent,' he says. 'It makes you feel something you've never felt in your life.' A sentiment, of course, which could stand for the trail as a whole.

If, to cyclists, the CNT is a bikepacking adventure, to the residents of the Kivu Belt region, it's a thoroughfare like any other. Peering through this window into daily Rwandan life was my own favourite part of the journey. Mothers with children strapped to their backs, farmers hauling bushels of bananas and sugar cane, all set against the most beautiful scenery. Even when trying to catch my breath and dripping sweat and sunscreen, I'd look around and marvel at my luck to be riding there. **CP**

Christina Palassion

TOOLKIT

Start // Rubavu
Finish // Kamembe
Distance // 141 miles (227km)
Getting there // Check visas prior to departure; fly to Kigali for a few days' acclimatisation. Bike rental, guides and shuttles: Kingfisher Journeys or Rwandan Adventures.
When to go // June–September/December–February are drier. Avoid rainy season in November.
What to wear // Breathable gear, plus hike-a-bike shoes. A rain jacket and layers; conditions vary with elevation.
What to pack // Rent a bike with suspension. Pack parts and tools you might need. Also a bladder, plus hydration and fuelling options. Local provisions include a lifetime supply of bananas but not electrolyte drinks, gels or bars.
Where to stay // Guest houses are plentiful; book in advance. Most have electricity and some wi-fi.
More info // www.ridewithgps.com/routes/41017228

Opposite: vines growing on the German side of Lake Constance

MORE LIKE THIS ROUTES AND LOOPS WITH A WATERY THEME

BIWAICHI ROUTE, LAKE BIWA

This popular 118-mile (190km) route circles Lake Biwa, Japan's largest freshwater lake, located in Honshū's Shiga Prefecture. Many cyclists tackle the trail in a couple of days, reaching the lake by car or train; the closest station to the water's edge is Ōtsu, 10 minutes from Kyoto. Sights along the way include the Shirahige Jinja, a Shinto shrine whose famous *torii* gate rises from the lake. The ride has views of several mountain ranges, a patchwork of rice paddies and Japanese gardens. Stop by the 17th-century Hikone Castle, an historic treasure, the tranquil Omi-Hachiman canals, or take the ropeway up Mt Uchimi, for panoramic views of the lake. Early May is cherry-blossom season, while autumn is when the maple leaves change colour. Post-ride, stop by a local *konbini*, the Japanese convenience stores stocking an incredible range of snack-food options, including tuna *onigiri* and matcha ice-cream bars.
Start/finish // Ōtsu; various
Distance // 118 miles (190km)

SIMCOE COUNTY LOOP TRAIL

The Simcoe County Loop Trail is a 99-mile (160km) spin through southern Ontario in Canada, and which touches three different bodies of water: Georgian Bay, Lake Simcoe, and Lake Couchiching. The trail is mainly flat and runs on hardpacked gravel, human-made bike paths and quiet roads. It's possible to do it in one day but most split it over two. Either way, submit the required information – social media tags mostly – and Cycle Simcoe will send you a free-shirt proclaiming: 'I Rode the 160-km Simcoe County Loop Trail.' Free tees aside, highlights of the ride including Georgian Bay's rock-and-pine landscape, a beloved Canadian scene popular with nature-lovers and artists. The section between Orillia and Coldwater is notable, as is Penetanguishene to Tiny. Ride in late September for a bug-free experience, with views of early-autumn foliage. Stop in at Creemore Springs, or Side Launch breweries for a pint, or at Birch Farms for one of their irresistible butter tarts.
Start/finish // Barrie
Distance // 99 miles (160km)

LAKE CONSTANCE CYCLE PATH

The Lake Constance Cycling Trail is one of Europe's finest. The 168-mile (270km) trail around the 'Bodensee' passes through three countries – Germany, Austria, and Switzerland – with views of the Alps. The three islands that lie just off the shore are all accessible by their respective bridges: UNESCO-designated Reichenau is home to an abbey founded in 724; Lindau Island, is also renowned for medieval architecture; while Mainau Island is a botanical reserve stocked with giant sequoias and extensive rose gardens. Back on shore, the route passes picturesque Konstanz, and Stein am Rhein, neither of which were bombed during WWII and thus are home to timber houses dating to the 15th century. Off the bike, visit the Zeppelin Museum in Friedrichshafen, or the 200 or so Barbary macaque monkeys in Affenberg Salem. The cycling season here is long, so plan a trip anytime from April to October.
Start/finish // Konstanz, Bregenz or Meersburg
Distance // 168 miles (270km)

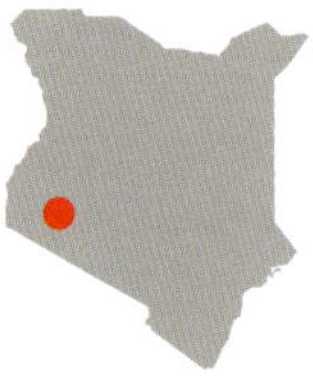

KENYA'S MIGRATION GRAVEL RACE

Cycling through Kenya's Masai Mara, journalist Betsy Welch learns that the Migration Gravel Race is less about podiums and more about people, places and adventure.

The first thing you should do, when you travel anywhere, is learn how to say 'hello' and 'thank you.' When your language skills limit you, those few words open doors. In Swahili, they sing. *Jambo. Asante.*

I didn't come to Kenya to sing, however, I came to ride. I used to cover the sport for a living and was always looking for stories in unexpected places. When I heard about the Migration Gravel Race – a 400-mile (644km) four-day stage ride through the Maasai Mara – I knew I wanted to be there. Held annually in mid- to late June, the race's mission is twofold: to bring people from all over the world to ride in one of Africa's largest game reserves; and to give aspiring East African pros the chance to compete against the world's best without leaving the continent.

Months later, in late June, I'm crammed into a minibus bumping along dirt roads cobbled with stones the size of melons. In the back, a cardboard box of bananas has sparked a spirited debate between visiting Rwandan cyclists and local Kenyans – the Rwandans are adamant that Kenyan fruit is inferior. I share a seat with Skylar, a photographer from Portland who's spent years documenting gorillas in Rwanda. He grins but won't take sides.

Three flat tyres later, our caravan rolls into camp. I've been to a lot of bike races, and although I know this one will be different, nothing can prepare me for the welcome. As riders stumble across the grass looking for their luggage and bike bags, a low hum rises from near the lodge. Two dozen Maasai men, barefoot or in sandals, cloaked in red and pink shukas, hop in unison. It's mesmerising, this ritual of welcome. We're supposed to queue up for our race-plates, but that can wait. We learn that these men will be our course staff, marshalls, cooks and aid-station support. They have all been recruited by Salaton, the Maasai elder responsible, in a place where

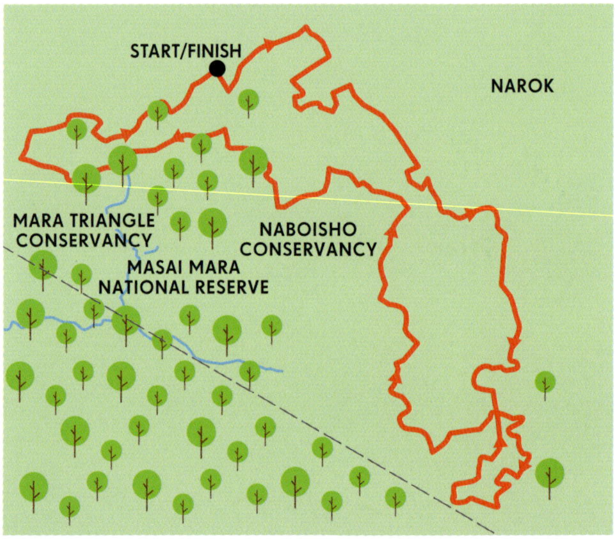

Wango Alfred courtesy of Migration Gravel Race

MIGRATION
GRAVEL RACE

livestock grazing provides an unsustainable income.

Race morning dawns chilly and damp. Excited, I pedal too hard, too early. We revisit the cobbles of the access road, truly brain-rattling, but hard to object to because of the kids. For the first half an hour, uniformed schoolchildren run to the roadside to yell at us. 'Jambo,' we shout back and they dissolve in laughter.

The day stretches across a patchwork of rough gravel, red dirt, and bush-lined tracks. I'm mostly alone, not fast enough for the front but quicker than the back. Fine by me, as long as there's no wind. The pros aren't stopping to take pictures of zebras – zebras! – but I am. I stop again to give a small girl my smashed energy bar after she quietly asks for my 'biscuits.' At the next river crossing, Mikel, the race organiser, tells me I've just missed a hippo. Incredible. I stuff a few Oreos in my mouth and roll on.

That night, at the Maji Moto Maasai Cultural Camp – the only camp where we have running water and electricity – I write my stage-report nursing a frosty Tusker beer from the cooler. Later, Salaton and a few others gather round our fire to teach us about Maasai culture. Their audience is rapt, until fatigue takes hold and people drift off to bed.

The next morning, I resolve to race less and observe more. On a stretch of singletrack, former WorldTour pro Ian Boswell rolls up behind me. He's taken a wrong turn and now, rather than racing, he's just riding. We spend the next hour talking about the Amani Project (see panel), whose mission it is to raise the profile of cycling in East Africa. It won't be easy, we agree, but it's worth it.

THE AMANI PROJECT

The Amani Project (*amani* is Swahili for 'peace') rewrites the story of African cycling. Based in East Africa, it supports riders from Kenya, Rwanda, Uganda and Ethiopia with coaching, gear, and race resources. The Migration Gravel Race (and the Safari Gravel Series), gives these athletes world-class competition closer to home, proving that talent runs deep across the continent and hinting that gravel racing could serve as an entry point for local riders seeking cycling's world stage.

Clockwise from top: watch out for wildlife on the course; athletes ready to roll; pro racer Lachlan Morton competing in the 2025 edition. Previous spread: crossing the start line; the race takes shape across the Masai Mara savannah

Wango Alfred courtesy of Migration Gravel Race

That night's bush camp feels far from anywhere. Our tented village sits under the sprawling limbs of an umbrella acacia; the massive dung piles on the approach are, it's confirmed, from elephants. We're also told not to wander, which I keep in mind as I stand on a small rise trying to find cell service to file my story. I give up and watch the sunset instead.

By the third day, I am wrecked. My forearms are useless, my back aches, my speed has evaporated. Two new, Dutch friends, Mieke and Dorien, pass me on a climb, all smiles, and I wave them on. Eventually, I find myself riding with Marc, a physio from Spain who has lived in Kenya for 20 years. He has a wife and three girls and speaks Swahili like a local. A marathon runner too, this is his first big bike race. That evening, it's a struggle even to type on my keyboard. When I finally finish my recap of the day, I realise the experience has been less riding and more about the people I've met.

The final day is a relief. The roads are smoother, the wildlife sightings frequent, and the end a mere 99 miles (160km) away. We arrive at the camp where we started, and I immediately lay down on the cool, concrete patio and elevate my legs against a wall. Another Dutch friend, Dennis, brings me a Tusker and snaps my picture. Later that evening, I stand on the second step of the podium, as race organisers drape a custom-made shuka over my head; without doubt it's the most meaningful prize I've ever won. The Maasai guys, by now friends, holler and yip beside me. After the prizegiving, they form a tunnel with their arms and invite every single rider to walk through it. 'Asante sana,' I repeat, over and over. I came here to cover a bike race. I left with a song. **BW**

Wanga Alfred courtesy of Migration Gravel Race

"At the next river crossing, Mikel, the race organiser, tells me I've just missed a hippo. Incredible!"

TOOLKIT

Start/finish // Masai Mara National Reserve
Distance // 404 miles (650km)
Getting there // Fly to Jomo Kenyatta International Airport in Nairobi, where organisers will transfer riders to/from base camp in the Mara.
When to go // The race is held in June, dates vary
What to wear // Highly breathable, lightweight race kit, plus whatever else you'll need for long days with hot weather and in remote country (water bladder, lights etc). You'll also need packable layers, the Mara sits at 4921ft (1500m), so mornings and evenings are chilly.
What to pack // Tubeless repair kit (including plugs), power bank, and plenty of electrolyte mix. On-course support is adequate, but if you have food preferences, bring extra snacks. GPS navigation is essential, as markings are minimal. Don't forget a headlamp for camp.
More info // migrationgravelrace.com, including GPX files and route details.

Opposite: Mt Kilimanjaro from the Tanzanian side; flamingos take flight from Lake Natron

MORE LIKE THIS
OFF-ROAD IN AFRICA

GRAVEL BURN, SOUTH AFRICA

Launched by Kevin Vermaak, founder of the Cape Epic mountain bike race, the Gravel Burn brings the stage-race spirit to South Africa's extensive gravel networks. Starting in Knysna, on the Garden Route, the 497-mile (800km) route is split across seven stages, traversing the Western Cape and linking wine country and coastal cliffs, as well as Great Karoo backroads and lively farming towns. Expect long days and big climbs, with an overall elevation gain of 34,875ft (10,630m). Like the Migration Gravel Race, the Gravel Burn attracts both elite riders and adventurous amateurs, all eager to explore South Africa's extremely picturesque off-road scene. Top-notch logistics help ease aching limbs; in addition to meticulous luggage transfers and exceptional on-course support, there's also a strong social element each evening. If that's not enough to keep you riding, the race ends in the private Shamwari reserve in the Eastern Cape, one of South Africa's most chichi safari destinations.

Start // Knysna
Finish // Shamwari
Distance // 497 miles (800km)

RACE AROUND RWANDA

One for endurance enthusiasts, Race Around Rwanda is a self-supported 621-mile (1000km) 'ultra' bikepacking event that circles the 'Land of a Thousand Hills'. Thanks to the burgeoning scene here, in 2024 the country's Gorilla Gravel race was accepted into the UCI's Gravel World Series, just reward for the Rwandan government's long-term investment in its cycling infrastructure. None of which is likely to bring much comfort to the riders who tackle this event's relentless mix of tarmac, dirt roads and climbs that seem to go on forever. The scenery is a feast for the senses, nonetheless, as the race passes tea plantations, volcanic lakes and bustling towns. Unlike the Migration Gravel Race, there's no nightly camp or support crew – just you, your bike and whatever fits in your frame bags. You'll also need to be aware of time, with 163 hours to complete the route, including four checkpoints and a punchy 62,336ft (19,000m) of elevation.

Start/finish // Kigali
Distance // 621 miles (1000km)

TRAVERSE TANZANIA

This supported, multiday journey sees riders power their way from the slopes of Mt Kilimanjaro to the shores of Lake Natron. Starting in the Enduimet Wildlife Management Area, the five-stage, 255-mile (410km) event includes 17,388ft (5300m) of climbing, as participants navigate the tourist-lite north of this vast country. Conceived to be culturally immersive, each stage is a manageable 37 to 68 miles (60–110km), passing through Maasai villages, reserves home to elephants and giraffes, and across acacia-dotted plains. Nights are spent in comfortable lodges or camps, with hearty meals and stories shared around the fire. Perfect for riders who like their races served sociable, with a side of adventure, the moderate distances and friendly atmosphere make this a great introduction to gravel riding on the continent. Reasonably priced for a range of budgets, the route ends in Engikaret, a region popular for birdwatching.

Start // Enduimet
Finish // Engikaret
Distance // 255 miles (410km)

Mahir Rustemov/Shutterstock; Pandora Pictures/Shutterstock

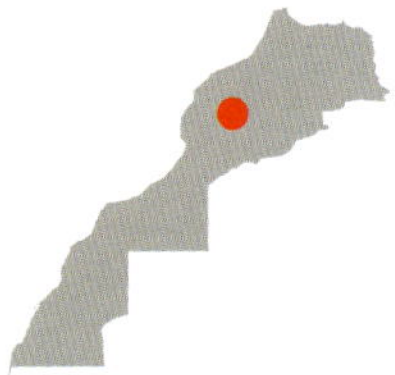

BIKEPACKING MOROCCO: MARRAKESH TO TAMRAGHT

Six friends, four days, 200 miles (320km). Following the Atlas Mountains from Marrakesh to the coast proved a journey of sisterhood, new experiences and a little Moroccan magic.

Touchdown in Marrakesh. After spending the previous night on the cold, hard floor of a Tenerife airport, the warmth of a Moroccan morning was a relief. The ride I was about to embark on had been conceived a year prior, with a phone call to my good friend, Tegan Phillips, in Girona. I'd mentioned Morocco was sitting pretty at the top of my cycling bucket-list and, before the call had even ended, it was decided.

Next to arrive was Magan, followed soon after by Tracy, and the usually quiet airport was filled with our joy. In addition to us, another three riders waited ahead on the trail; my original co-conspirator, Tegan, along with Remy, and Juanita.

Bike bags and parts littered the airport floor as we set about the builds. Eventually, with everything attached correctly, it was time to explore and we rolled out towards our accommodation for the evening. A mere 4 miles (7km) from the airport, it took three hours to get there. Why? The Marrakesh medina.

Located at the heart of the city and a UNESCO World Heritage Site, every square inch of the medina was alive; with music, bartering, and activity. Rich colours seemed to drip from shops, while perfumes and spices filled the air. Our wandering, and subsequent midnight-feasting, meant heads finally hit pillows at 2am. Tomorrow, we'd begin the journey to the Atlas Mountains and the rest of our crew.

With body clocks out of whack, we hit the road out of Marrakesh at 11am, bound for Ouirgane, a Berber village west of Toubkal, Morocco's highest peak at 13,671ft (4167m).

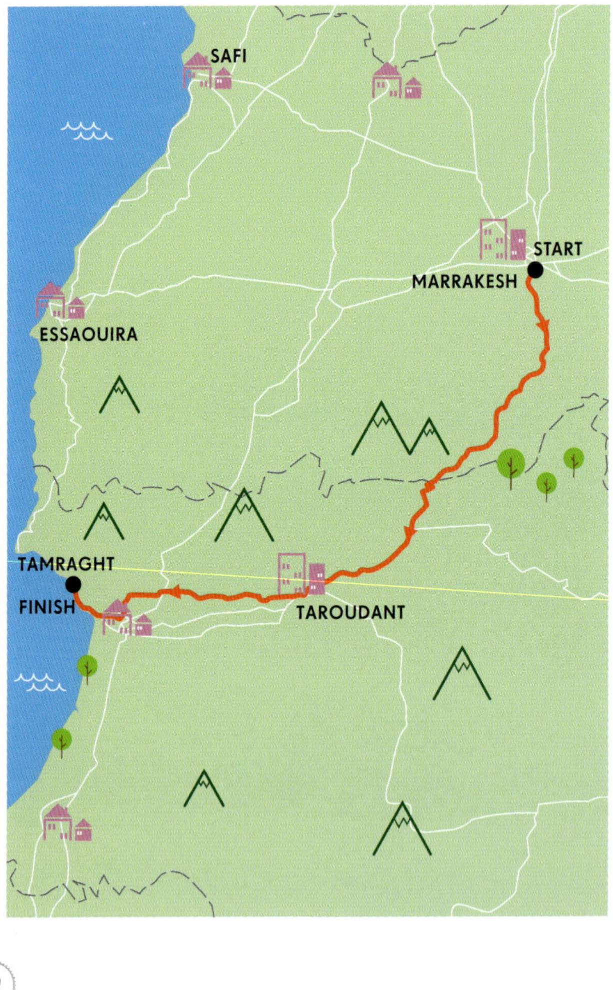

imagoDens/Shutterstock; Youssef Douib/Shutterstock

"Another icy dip, this time in the lake at Barrage Ouirgane, ensured everyone kept their sense of humour just about intact"

Riding on little sleep but fuelled by *ftour*, the abundant traditional breakfast, we made it all the way to Aghouatim before stopping for lunch. Seated on a Berber-woven *hanbel* rug beneath a stretch-tent, we ordered three spicy lamb tagines and couscous full of flavour.

Thirty-eight miles (61km) later, we pedalled into Ouirgane Ecolodge; an oasis of green, the grass and trees were in marked contrast to the rust-red buildings. This natural colouring comes from the iron-rich Moroccan earth that is used in construction. At the centre of the lodge sat an enticing but icy pool. The same deep blue as the interiors of our rooms, it was the perfect way to soothe weary limbs. That evening, having finally met up with Tegan, Remy and Juanita, our group sat united in the fading light beneath olive trees.

It was easy to slip into the Moroccan way of life, especially when it seemed to have the same priorities as we touring cyclists. Simple pleasures, such as shared meals, became special occasions, invariably rounded off with refreshing mint tea. 'The tea is poured from a height to aerate and mix the ingredients,' explained our host, Mohamed, of a ritual intended to aid digestion but which also symbolises hospitality. 'I call it Moroccan whiskey,' he added, as our group headed for bed.

Our destination on day two was a hostel based at the highest point of the Tizi n'Test pass. A distance of 47 miles (75km) was manageable, but the elevation of 5653ft (1723m) was spicy, something our muscles would have to digest without mint tea to offer relief. Things got off to a rocky start, thanks to technical issues that required some 'bush mechanics'. Another icy dip, this time in the lake at Barrage Ouirgane, ensured everyone kept their sense of humour just about intact.

On we rode, through the sparse, thorny scrub. For all its beauty, life in the high Atlas remains challenging. Following the Marrakesh-Safi earthquake, in 2023, many of the buildings here remain damaged, but occupied through necessity. With the epicentre located 45 miles (73km) southwest of Marrakesh, the quake killed close to 3000 people. So while laughter carried us to the top of the pass, where our hotel welcomed us with heated rooms and cold beers, we were only too aware of our good fortune.

The next morning was spent following a path to a yet higher vantage, above our accommodation. One sketchy

AFRICA ON WHEELS

Drawing cyclists, surfers and triathletes from around the globe, MojaSurf camp is run by the famous adventurer, Othmane Zolati. A dedicated bikepacker, in 2014, Zolati set out from his home in Morocco bound for South Africa, a journey of 18,600 miles (30,000km). Aged just 20, and with US$80 to his name, he spent four years travelling through 24 countries by bike, on foot and by skateboard. His quest later became the subject of a documentary, Africa and I.

Clockwise from top: the bracing lake at Barrage Ouirgane; meeting in Marrakesh's Jemaa el-Fnaa; delicious Moroccan meals keep the riders fuelled. Previous spread: the Atlas mountains loom over Taroudant; facing the daunting Tizi n'Test pass

Cally Silberbauer; RedonePhotographer/Shutterstock

scramble later and we all agreed: for climbing, bikes were better. By midday it was time to descend the Atlas, on a beautiful, flowy downhill that spat us back on to tar roads and into more well-inhabited areas. Day three, to Taroudant, spanned 54 miles (87km), and featured a mere 230ft (70m) of elevation. The wind, however, picked up and not in our favour. Luckily, Juanita volunteered for some extra 'training' and courageously carved a path through the headwind.

Taroudant follows a similar layout to Marrakesh, its unassuming streets holding hidden gems, including Riad le Jasmin, our extraordinary accommodation for the night. That evening found us by another palm-tree encircled pool. The next morning would bring our last day on the bikes and we reminisced about the journey. Swapping highs and lows, the conversation veered to the occasional teary eye.

There's a bittersweet feeling when a group-journey ends, the sadness of impending departure offset by the satisfaction of seeing it through. Before setting off on our final day together, Tegan, our 'content queen', had an idea for an Instagram Reel. Thus we spent a blissful hour remixing Mambo No. 5 into a film about coffee stops – cue some ridiculous dancing.

Our final 65 miles (105km) continued to be punctuated with giggles. All too soon, we were riding along the coastline, the sun setting on this last section of our adventure. At our final accommodation, MojaSurf camp, we raised beers into the salty air of Tamraght and toasted our friendship. It made me think of the late Christopher McCandless, an adventurous spirit if ever there was one, and who believed happiness was only real when shared with others; while I don't necessarily agree, it sure is sweeter. **CS**

Magan Hanekom

TOOLKIT

Start // Marrakesh
Finish // Tamraght
Distance // 204 miles (328km)
Getting there // Fights to Marrakesh Menara from major hubs. You ride from the airport, although taxis are plentiful should you wish to start further out of the city. Getting back is as simple as catching a bus, from Agadir. The CTM bus network is phenomenal, allowing fully packed bikes in cargo spaces.
When to go // Springtime is preferable, as you'll miss most of the rain and the intense heat of summer.
What to wear // Morocco is conservative in both religion and culture, so dress accordingly. Dress codes are more relaxed in tourist areas, especially surfing spots such as Tamraght.
What to pack // While it's not necessary to be fully self-sufficient along this route (shops and restaurants are many), bear in mind that during weeks-long Ramadan, these may be closed. Bring warm layers, the Atlas Mountains get cold.
More info // Though not an established route, bikepackers ride it regularly. Variations are covered in the Atlas Mountain Race GPX download.

Opposite: start-line anticipation at the Atlas Mountain Race; Ameln Valley in the Anti-Atlas mountains

MORE LIKE THIS
MAGICAL RIDES IN MOROCCO

ROUTE OF CARAVANS: MOROCCO TRAVERSE (SOUTH)

Using ancient trade thoroughfares dating back to the third century, the Route of Caravans is designed to be ridden south to north. Originally designed in 2024 by Logan Watts and Virginia Krabill of bikepacking.com, this route forms half of the full Moroccan Traverse. Beginning within the old Tiznit medina, this route heads out via the Anti-Atlas mountains, on mainly gravel roads towards the mighty Atlas range. As remote as it is beautiful, here you'll encounter aromatic wildflower meadows and high red-granite peaks. While there are a few steep, rocky climbs, the overall route is not especially technical. With a few sandy sections as you dip close to the Sahara Desert, chunkier tyres are advisable and sandstorms can be an issue. As always when bikepacking, but especially here, best be prepared with enough drinking water. Where possible, check in with locals, particularly ahead of sketchier sections.

Start // Tiznit
Finish // Imilchil
Distance // 768 miles (1236km)

ATLAS MOUNTAIN RACE (AMR)

The Atlas Mountain Race (AMR) is an unsupported bikepacking event designed to test mental and physical endurance. Launched in 2020, the route changes slightly from year to year. Originally beginning in Marrakesh and ending in Essaouira, a new start was announced for the 2026 edition, in Beni-Mellal. From here, the latest route climbs towards Tizi n'Ait Imi, at 9547ft (2910m) the highest pass yet included in the AMR. Dropping into the narrow, winding gorges of M'Goun, the route then reconnects with more familiar AMR territory: the colonial piste to Afra; the climb to Aguinane; and CP2, the old Colonial Rd, which serves as the final run to Essaouira. Expect both rugged terrain and a daunting elevation gain of up to 82,000ft (25,000m). Even allowing for the AMR's 1350km distance, that's a lot of up. Recent AMRs have seen close to 300 riders line up at the start, of which only half finished. Extreme conditions, extreme discomfort, and spectacular scenery.

Start // Marrakesh
Finish // Essaouira
Distance // 838 miles (1350km)

ROUTE OF CARAVANS: MOROCCO TRAVERSE (NORTH)

The northern section of the Route of Caravans northern completes the Moroccan Traverse, covering the remaining 520 miles (837km) from Imilchil, in the Atlas Mountains, to Tangier. This part of the route takes you through the heart of the traditional territories of the indigenous Amazigh (Berber) people. Winding across riverbeds, following donkey trails and backroads through small villages, this section of the Traverse is less technical than its southern counterpart, with more access to food and accommodation, although you can still expect to see nomadic camel herders and mud-brick kasbahs. This section also has rolling green hills, with a couple of steep climbs and descents, although all very much worth it for iconic destinations such as Chefchaouen, the 'Blue City'. As you ride, you'll appreciate the views, as the northern stretch of the Traverse has some of the finest scenery in all Morocco. Bikepacking.com offers extensive trail notes for the Morocco Traverse, often updated, so well worth reading before departure.

Start // Imilchil
Finish // Tangier
Distance // 520 miles (837km)

WitR/Shutterstock; Imago/Alamy

205

AMERICAS

BRITISH COLUMBIA'S ALBERNI BAM BAM

A new route around the south of Canada's Vancouver Island sees the best-laid bikepacking plans come to fabulous fruition, thanks to old-growth forests and mystical swim spots.

The Alberni Bam Bam was born after several years of plotting: speaking with locals, asking questions in Facebook groups and short, route-scouting trips. The result is a 272-mile (438km) loop that starts and ends in Nanaimo, on Vancouver Island, and is specifically designed for easy access from the mainland. Beginning at the ferry terminal in Departure Bay, this challenging but straightforward week-long ride takes you round the southern part of an island that is already well established as bikerpacker's haven.

Having spent substantial time planning, poring over maps and making revisions, I had a pretty good idea of what I was getting into ahead of the inaugural ride. Plus, living just across the water on British Columbia's Sunshine Coast, I've got to know the maze of roads that wend their way across the island. All the same, I needed a final ride to ensure my various theories held together, and that meant a 'big trip'.

Arriving in Nanaimo with six other friends, we rolled off the ferry and headed south, to the Cowichan Valley. In addition to the forest service roads that comprise much of the route, other sections run along decommissioned logging roads or doubletrack, both of which are more comfortable on either a rigid mountain bike, or one with a drop-bar. With the ride conceived very much as an all-terrain outing, I'd also added some shorter sections of smooth gravel roads and pavement, on a route that features 27,030ft (8239m) of climbing.

Central to my plans was an awareness that Canadian forestry regulations are among the strictest in the world. In some locations, forestry gates open only rarely, during shoulder seasons or when the fire risk is low, for example. Hence the need for local knowledge in my planning.

Having made the 46 miles (75km) to Lake Cowichan in good time, we stopped at Honeymoon Bay's general store for lunch. Like many locations en route, it's used to both hikers and bikers and so well-stocked for provisions on the fly. From there we made our way to Port Renfrew, in the island's southwest corner, and a 37-mile (60km) ride.

The traditional territory of the Pacheedaht First Nation, Port Renfrew is also home to some of Canada's tallest trees,

Miles Arbour

including the wonderfully named 'Big Lonely Doug', a towering 'old-growth' Douglas fir topping out at 230ft (70m) tall, and which some estimates put at a staggering 1200 years old. It's a welcoming, quirky town and a good option for a rest day.

Next morning, the Coastal Kitchen Cafe provided much-needed breakfast, including excellent coffee, cakes and pastries. Sufficiently fuelled, our next stop was the Walbran Valley. Marking the halfway point of the route, the valley is at the centre of ongoing environmental campaigning to preserve its ancient ecosystems. As logging companies seek to 'harvest' what they see as abundant resources, the Walbran is one of the last remaining old-growth forests on the island, home not just to Douglas fir but also Sitka spruce and cedar.

None of us knew quite what to expect from the Walbran Valley; photographs online make for grim viewing, with industrial-scale logging rendering bare vast areas of previously pristine woodland. The six-mile (10km) descent into the valley ended at a makeshift campground, whose residents included plenty of environmental activists. A short walk from our tents, however, we found stunning emerald pools; accessed by boardwalks and surrounded by old-growth forests, it felt positively mystical.

Our swim spot in the Walbran was one of many. Riding during a particularly warm week, whenever long gravel climbs in the heat wore us out, there was usually a swimming hole to cool us off. From the valley, the route skirts Carmanah Walbran Provincial Park to Nitinat Lake, itself an ecological reserve (and another swim spot, if a windy one). A lower-key highlight of this route is the various small coastal communities, linked by gravel

THE OTHER FIR TRADE

Not for nothing is Big Doug 'lonely'. The giant Douglas fir now stands in less than splendid isolation, due to the heavy logging that has taken place on Vancouver Island, around Port Renfrew, the Walbran Valley and beyond. The subject of extensive press coverage, Doug has come to symbolise not just the rich diversity under threat from 'Big Logging', but also the plight of the region's First Nations peoples, whose rights can be overlooked in favour of commercial interests.

Clockwise from top: research suitable camping spots; Pachena Bay, south of Bamfield; Pacific Rim National Park. Previous spread: enjoy off-road riding

Danita Delimont/Shutterstock; Miles Arbour

roads and doubletrack. Happening upon a small store was invariably a cause for excitement, such as the gas station on Nitinat Lake, whose well-provisioned fridge was an unexpected delight on a hot day.

From Nitinat Lake, the route rolls on to Barkley Sound and the small town of Bamfield. Much like Port Renfrew, it's another good option for a rest day, although the bikepacker's main business here is leaving. The MV Frances Barkley, a 65-year-old heritage ship built in in Norway, departs from Bamfield three days a week, year-round. Terminating at Port Alberni, the four-hour voyage north along the Alberni Inlet isn't speedy but that's the point. As our group took the chance to catch their collective breath before the final leg of riding, the views of Barkley Sound were worth every dollar. The final 62 miles (100km) of the route wound its way along logging roads and doubletrack as it passed two waterfalls – Little Qualicum and Englishman River – both worth a break to admire.

As the end of our time loomed, the prospect of finishing this trip brought a mix of emotions. I was looking forward to a shower and a home-cooked meal, but I wasn't quite ready to trade this routine for my usual one. Bikepacking is repetitive by nature but, for me, that repetition is addictive. The process of waking up, packing up camp and just riding your bike is much simpler (and more fun) than paying bills and meeting deadlines. While the Alberni Bam Bam more than lived up to my expectations, riding it was a good reminder that all the route-planning in the world is no substitute for getting out there to experience a ride for yourself. **MA**

Miles Arbour

TOOLKIT

Start/Finish // Nanaimo (BC)
Distance // 272 miles (438km)
Getting there // Nanaimo is accessed via ferry from Vancouver. BC Transit has routes that run between Victoria and Nanaimo, and most bikes can be accommodated. Call ahead. Air Canada and West Jet have flights into Nanaimo Airport from Calgary, Vancouver and Kelowna.
When to go // May to September, as the majority of stores and resupply points operate during these months. Spring and autumn have lower daily temperatures.
What to wear // Conditions vary; summers are traditionally mild but grow increasingly hot. Coastal locations bring wind, so bring warm layers, especially for evenings. Rainier months are October to March.
What to pack // Bikepacking staples: tent, cookset, toolkit and spares. And, crucially, swimmers.
Where to stay // Options for a range of budgets, from campgrounds to cabins and more.
Where to eat // Local general stores; the island's cafes.
Things to know // Bears and cougars live here; learn what to do in an encounter.
More info // www.bikepacking.com

Opposite: cross the Kinsol Trestle on the Cowichan Valley bikepacking route

MORE LIKE THIS
PEDAL PERFECT IN THE PACIFIC NORTHWEST

TREE TO SEA LOOP

Coastal British Columbia is home to several established off-road bikepacking routes with a similar flavour to the Alberni Bam Bam. For something even longer, check out the Tree to Sea Loop, a 621-mile (1000km) circuit on the north end of Vancouver Island. The route starts and ends in Comox, on the eastern shore. Along the way you'll ride through massive valleys and oceanside villages, past towering mountains and deep fjords, via an impressive patchwork of forest service roads. In addition to some of the best gravel riding in the area, there are opportunities for spelunking, whale-watching, waterside camping and more. I first scouted the Tree to Sea Loop in the autumn of 2021, and it has since experienced a surge in popularity. Over the last few years, businesses along the route have reported hundreds of bike riders passing through each season, a welcome addition to the island's growing bikepacking community.
Start/finish // Comox
Distance // 621 miles (1000km)

COWICHAN VALLEY 8

At the southern end of Vancouver Island, the Cowichan Valley 8 has proven to be very popular among newer bikepackers seeking an approachable route, and those starting from Victoria. The 118-mile (190km) ride follows several regional trails along a figure of eight, including the Galloping Goose Trail, Sooke Hills Wilderness Trail and The Great Trail (part of the Trans Canada Trail). A mix of gravel, doubletrack and paved paths creates a scenic and rewarding route that can be easily ridden in a weekend or less, with fantastic camping along the Cowichan River; there are also options for pleasure/ferry rides, because who doesn't like a trip in a boat? Resupply points are spread across the route, including in Victoria, Shawnigan Lake, Lake Cowichan and Duncan, so it's an excellent chance to ride slowly, eat well and introduce yourself to the joys of bikepacking on Vancouver Island.
Start/finish // Victoria (BC)
Distance // 118 miles (190km)

TEXADA RIDGE RUNNER

My all-time favourite bikepacking overnighter in the Pacific Northwest. Texada Island is a 40-minute ferry ride from Powell River, which is a half-day's drive from North Vancouver. If you're coming from Vancouver Island, Powell River can be reached by ferry from Comox. The Texada Ridge Runner is an 89-mile (144km) gravel route that traverses Texada Island from north to south and back again, following a mix of quiet gravel roads and pavement. The route is designed to visit some of the must-see spots on the island, including Bob's Lake, Shingle Beach and the communities of Gillies Bay and Van Anda, all accessible via some of the best gravel – and largest climbs – around. The ascents can be challenging, notably the approach to Anderson Bay, at the route's southernmost point. With epic descents to compensate, the Texada Ridge Runner also offers (usually) bear-free camping and friendly locals.
Start/finish // Blubber Bay
Distance // 89 miles (144km)

achinthamb/Shutterstock

CHILE'S CARRETERA AUSTRAL

Experience the ancient forests, fjords and mountains of Patagonia, via one of the world's most classic cycle touring routes as it journeys through the Chilean Andes.

Crossing a pass from Argentina, we join the Carretera Austral at Villa Santa Lucia. We've exchanged the high, dry pampa of the Patagonian Steppe for the lowland humidity of Chile's densely forested valleys. Here, the human footprint is confined to the easily tamed land of the valley floors. Beyond the small farms or fincas, with their rustic buildings and grazing cattle, beech-clad slopes launch up through strands of mist, beyond which I can just spot the white of the névé and the yawning blue seracs of a glacier.

Occasional traffic – mostly tourists – hums past on the highway. The activity on this central section of the Carretera belies the fact that this 808-mile (1300km) road is one of the world's remotest highways. Squeezed between the Andes and the deeply incised fjords of Chile's mountainous southwest coast, the Carretera Austral is the only longitudinal highway in southern Chile, providing a vital link to some of the country's most isolated settlements. For much of the 20th century this

Mark Watson

"The open pampa of Valle Chacabuco is a great place to see herds of guanaco"

province of Aysén was only accessible by boat or plane, until the initiation of an ambitious project to forge a road south to the town of Villa O'Higgins, at the Argentinian border. Some of the allure of the legendary Carretera Austral is that it ventures into regions of Patagonia that were inaccessible by road until as late as 2000.

Like many cyclists, we intend to camp as much as possible during our ride south. Tonight we have the perfect spot, a kilometre from the main road. Alone, we pitch our tent on a wide, sandy riverbank, alongside crystal-clear water and surrounded by verdant forest. While this region is popular for tourism, it's not hard to find peace if you escape the beaten track.

After a few days we become familiar with the Carretera's casual rhythm of small towns once or twice a day, separated by moderate riding, gentle climbs and exceptional views of the snow-capped Andes.

A popular stop along the Carretera is the Cascada Ventisquero Colgante, in Parque Nacional Queulat. One of the tallest in South America, this ethereal waterfall courses off a huge cliff from a hanging glacier. The 1.9-mile (3km) hiking trail to access the viewpoint is well worthwhile, with awe-inspiring views right from the start as it crosses a roaring glacial river choked with house-sized boulders. Between the entrance to the park and Rio Cisnes, the road turns to *ripio* (gravel), climbing a series of switchbacks through forest over a 1900ft (580m) saddle. It's a beautiful stretch of road with epic views of Queulat ice cap.

Three days later we arrive in Coyhaique, the largest town on the Carretera. It has all the services and we take a couple of days off to rest, eat well, service our bikes and stock up with food. Beyond Coyhaique, we climb away from the rolling plains into the mountains of Parque Nacional Cerro Castillo. Above the small village of Villa Cerro Castillo, the region's namesake peak lords over the land. A condor circles high above as we hike the steep trail to a turquoise lake at the base of the mountain's towering upper ramparts. I'm captivated by the ribbon-like waterfalls and torrents of ice which cascade down the sheer face from the glacier above.

Shortly beyond Villa Cerro Castillo the Carretera's pavement stops. Between here and Villa O'Higgins at the end of the road is 280 miles (450km) of *ripio* and, as the road deteriorates, the land becomes more untamed. A fjord-like arm of the mountain-ringed Lago General Carrera leads us to Puerto Río Tranquilo, where we take a side trip from the highway, following Valle Exploradores for 34 miles (55km) to gain our first view of the mythical Northern Patagonian Ice Field. It's a fantastic ride to

BEECH LIFE

Notable among Chile's distinctive flora and fauna is the dozen varieties of southern beech which clad the valleys and mountain slopes on both sides of the Andes. This forest is of the genus Nothofagus – an ancient gift from the former supercontinent of Gondwana, which is found only in the Southern Cone of South America, Australia, New Zealand, New Guinea, and New Caledonia. Watch for their spectacular colour as the leaves turn in the cool of the Patagonian autumn.

Clockwise from top: Cascada Ventisquero Colgante; wild guanacos; southern beech forest and Andean peaks near Villa Amengual. Previous spread: Riding towards Lago General Carrera

Mark Watson

the viewpoint, between towering peaks, hanging glaciers and thick lowland forest. Across the vast Exploradores Glacier, the icy summit of Chilean Patagonia's highest mountain, Monte San Valentin (13,353ft/4070m) is visible between occasional gaps in the cloud. Outside of Antarctica, this remote ice-cap peak is the highest mountain south of the 37th parallel.

Two more days' riding finds us in Cochrane, the last resupply town on the Carretera. Aside from small farms, there are no settlements between here and Villa O'Higgins, 136 miles (220km) away. Sitting just inside the rain shadow of the mountains to the west, Cochrane has a frontier-town feel, with its ranching heritage and buildings clad in the distinctively Patagonian style, with small wooden tiles. From here, another side trip takes us into Valle Chacabuco, within Parque Nacional Patagonia. Nicknamed the 'Serengeti of the Southern Cone', the open pampa of the valley is a great place to see herds of guanaco, a wild camelid related to the llama.

For the final four days of our ride we have the road almost to ourselves. Few make it this far south. Our sense of solitude increases – as does the challenge of the route – as we cycle through the wild austral landscape, with just the crunch of our tyres on the gravel interrupting the peace. This far south the forest is more stunted, and the treeline is lower. Travel off-road looks slow and perilous, with frigid rivers, vast swamps and endless lakes, while on the road the climbs are steeper and the turns tighter. It's the raw and wild Patagonia of my imagination.

Carretera Austral is deserving of its status as the most popular cycle-touring route in South America. It's a unique journey through one of the most dramatic and unspoiled environments on Earth. **MW**

Mark Watson

TOOLKIT

Start // Puerto Montt
Finish // Villa O'Higgins
Distance // 770 miles (1240km)
Getting there // There are regular flights or buses to Puerto Montt from Santiago. The Carretera is also commonly accessed from Argentina, via Paso Futaleufú or Huemules. It can be cycled in either direction, but Villa O'Higgins is only accessible via ferry from Argentina, or by air.
When to go // The austral summer (December to March) is the best time to ride. Early autumn (March and April) is quieter, and towards mid-late autumn the beech forest turns a spectacular red and orange, but temperatures cool.
What to wear // Chilean Patagonia experiences periods of rain year-round, so bring good waterproofs and clothes for summer hiking, including a puffer jacket.
What to pack // A three-season tent, and sleeping bag rated to -5°C (23°F).
More info // www.epicroadrides.com/cycling-blog/cycling-the-carretera-austral-chile/

Opposite: ride to Llaima volcano in Chile's Conguillío National Park

MORE LIKE THIS BIKEPACKING EPICS IN PATAGONIA

FORGOTTEN RUTA 41, ARGENTINA

For a more complete experience of bikepacking in Patagonia, it's essential to spend time on the eastern side of the Andes, where Argentina occupies the vast and windy Patagonian Steppe. Unlike the often-sheltered valleys and rainforests of Chile in the west, the Andes' east is swept by dry Foehn winds which vigorously blow down from the heights of the Andes. The result is the famous pampa grassland, pocketed with stunted beech forests. It's a landscape that once lay beneath a massive ice cap, which flowed into the western valleys of Chile and to the sea. The Ruta 41 can be reached from the Carretera Austral via Valle Chacabuco and Paso Roballos and followed over Andean foothills to one of Argentina's most peaceful and beautiful reserves, Parque Nacional Perito Merino. Come prepared for long climbs and sometimes rough off-road riding.
Start // Paso Roballos
Finish // Parque Nacional Perito Merino
Distance // 92 miles (148km)

PASO LAS PAMPAS, AND LAGO VERDE TO LA TAPERA

Crossing the Andes via a seldom-used pass, this off-road route can be used to connect Trevelin in Argentina with the Carretera Austral at its midpoint, near Villa Amengual. The route transitions from the pampa of the steppe to Chile's denser forests, following gravel and dirt roads via Corcovado and the village of Doctor Atilio Oscar Viglione (Argentina) to Paso Las Pampas and the town of Lago Verde (Chile). From here an unmaintained 4WD track hugs the border towards the village of La Tapera, where a gravel road joins the Carretera Austral. Unlike the Carretera, this route is steep and rough in places, making it appropriate only with a light-to-moderate touring load and knobbly tyres. It is a challenge but the reward lies in fun mountain biking on a route that takes you deeper into the Patagonian wilderness.
Start // Trevelin, Argentina
Finish // Villa Amengual, Chile
Distance // 178 miles (287km)
Info // www.highlux.co.nz/category/argentina

CORREDOR DE LOS VOLCANES

Chile is famous not only for the glacier-sculpted mountains of its south, but also for its high concentration of volcanoes, some of which reach over 19,500ft (5944m). Starting in the scenic region of Araucania, a mountainous route through a corridor of conical stratovolcanoes can be used to connect to well-known bikepacking routes, the Monkey Puzzle Trail (Chile) and Patagonian Beer Trail (Argentina), or else ridden as a standalone tour. From Melipeuco, under the shadow of nearby Volcan Llaima, this route rises steadily into the backcountry surrounding Nevados de Sollipulli (a recommended climb), to follow 4WD tracks and then pavement and dirt roads past Currarehue to Parque Nacional Villarrica, where it climbs over a pass high on the side of active Volcan Villarrica, to Coñaripe. Good quality paved and dirt roads are then followed over the border via Paso Carirriñe to Argentina and Parque Nacional Lanín.
Start // Melipeuco, Chile
Finish // San Martín de los Andes, Argentina
Distance // 195 miles (314km)
Info // www.ridewithgps.com/routes/52602652

Vicente Fernandez/Shutterstock

THE GREAT DIVIDE MOUNTAIN BIKE ROUTE

One of the world's top gravel rides, the Great Divide Mountain Bike Route begins in the heights of the Rockies and ends in the heat of New Mexico.

The sun wasn't even at quarter-strength when I stumbled off my bike and crawled under a rocky overhang, digging in my handlebar-bag for my Sour Patch Kids. I was just 150 miles (240km) into our northbound expedition on the Great Divide Mountain Bike Route (GDMBR), and New Mexico was testing my mettle with every mile ridden.

'I can't do this,' I groaned, shovelling a fistful of candy into my mouth. My partner took a photo of the distant buttes framed against the blue sky. 'You're fine,' he said, tossing me his water bottle.

And I was. The day ended with a swooping downhill, overlooking flat-topped mesas bathed in golden-hour light, the wind whipping my hair as I careened around the switchbacks. By the time we coasted into a dispersed campsite near a stock tank (a common desert water source), our morale was replenished.

First mapped by the Adventure Cycling Association in 1997, the Great Divide is one of the premier gravel rides in the world. Clocking in at around 3084 miles (4963km), the route will astound you. Stretching from the Canadian Rockies, though rugged Montana backcountry into Idaho and Wyoming, it climbs Colorado's high-mountain passes before entering the remoteness of the New Mexico desert.

It's also a roller-coaster, not just of terrain but also emotions. Each state, each week, each day – all offer something different; from tailwind-coasting past snow-capped peaks, to route-cursing exhaustion as you push your bike up a 10% grade.

Though 90% of the route is off-pavement, very little qualifies

Nick Fitzharding/Getty Images

as 'technical' and many riders (myself included) do it on a rigid bike. Each year, thousands of people complete either sections of the GDMBR or its entire length. Wherever you ride it, you'll encounter everyone from elite racers to amateur riders to couples on tandem bikes.

Direction also matters. Most people ride southbound, starting at a northern terminus, either Jasper or Banff, and making their way, eventually, to the US-Mexico border at Antelope Wells. It's a direction supposedly offering more favourable tailwinds. Despite the fact we live in Montana, we chose to ride northbound, but encountered sufficiently strong headwinds to corroborate the southbounder's view. Like most cyclists on a long-distance route, our timing was determined by work schedules, as well as the seasonality that inevitably influences such an extended endeavour.

Whether starting north or south, riders must time their trip to tackle the high-mountain passes of Colorado when the snow is in retreat. Similarly, it's best to avoid melting yourself when finishing at – or in our case, starting from – the route's southern tip.

From Antelope Wells, it took time to settle into our riding. Yes, New Mexico was hot, but I was blown away by the range of terrain. From sandy deserts to pine-shaded passes, the 700 miles (1120km) in that state both challenged and toughened us. By the time we crested the final pass in New Mexico, we'd established a rhythm. All the same, I was intimidated by Colorado's extended ascents, but the grades and surfaces proved quite rideable, the water sources plentiful.

I was surprised, too, by how much Wyoming felt similar to New Mexico; again, riding there was characterised by both deserts and mountain passes. We strapped bear spray to our handlebars and rode through the notorious Great Basin in just a few days, battling headwinds that were worth it thanks to the wild horses that visited our campsites at night.

Passing through our 'home' territory of Montana, I rode distant passes I'd previously only dreamed of, and where brilliant sunsets backlit tall peaks. The final few hundred or so miles, into Canada, might have seemed scant reward for crossing the entire United States. Except that, whichever way you ride, cyclists will encounter such a wide range of environments (and emotions, did I say emotions?), that the experience will sustain them long after they finish.

On the Tour Divide (see panel), the self-supported endurance event that follows the GDMBR, the fastest racers can complete the entire route in 14 days. My partner and I rode 50 to 70 miles (80–115km) per day, bringing us home in a little over six weeks. To me, it was more than fast enough. We made decent time but were able to admire the landscape and stop in picturesque towns along the way.

Tom Tietz/Shutterstock

AMATEUR DRAMATICS

A high point in the ultra-distance cycling calendar, the dramatic Tour Divide is one of the most prestigious self-supported bike races. Each year, hundreds of racers congregate in Banff, Canada, in the second week of June ahead of the race's Grand Depart. The event's amateur credentials (no entry fees or prizes), are amplified by its lack of registration process. Organisers encourage 'letters of intent' to be sent in advance but competitors can turn up on the day.

Left to right: a wild stallion in Wyoming's Great Basin; epic scenery entering Wyoming. Previous spread: summer wildflowers in Banff National Park, starting point of the route south.

We camped behind small-town bars and on lakeshores deep in the national forest. We filtered water from both stock tanks and clear glacial springs, biked through a herd of antelope and climbed a tree to escape a cranky bull. We rode uphill for 20 miles (32km), then sailed downward for 2000ft (610m) beneath a canopy of shimmery aspen. I slept under trees in New Mexico to beat the midday sun, ate three cheeseburgers in one sitting (thank you, Steamboat Springs), and set 4am alarms to evade Wyoming's headwinds. Because, generally, conditions on the GDMBR lived up to their reputation. We melted in New Mexico and hauled our bikes through snow in Colorado. In my home state of Montana, not once did I feel warm at night; but then I never have, no matter the season.

Sometimes we went days without seeing another rider. On other occasions, we met kindly hostel owners and Tour Divide racers. The relief I felt at seeing a road-crossing gas station was equalled only by the relief of fixing my shattered derailleur in the middle of a deserted, national-forest road. I never remembered which side of my handlebar-bag I'd stashed my water filter but I did become proficient at drying stream-rinsed bike shorts on my handlebars. The overall experience is one I'll never forget, and the GDMBR has become the basis for how I measure all other long-distance cycling routes. No matter how you ride the Divide, you'll never be the same. **MS**

TOOLKIT

Start // Jasper, Alberta
Finish // Antelope Wells, New Mexico
Distance // 3084 miles (4963km)
Getting there // Northern terminus via the Trans-Canada Hwy or Rocky Mountaineer train. The closest bus station to southern terminus is Lordsburg, New Mexico; cyclists can hire a shuttle from there.
When to go // Northbound riders start in late May / early June to avoid the worst heat without hitting too much snow in Colorado. Southbound riders start in late July to get through Colorado before the snow returns.
What to wear // Cycling shorts, sun-shirt, mid-layer, rain gear, insulated jacket.
What to pack // Tent, sleep system, cookset, repair kit, extra layers, water filter, headlamp, first-aid kit.
Where to stay // Camping, bike hostels and hotels.
Where to eat // Resupply at gas stations and in towns.
More info // www.bikepacking.com

Maggie Slepian

Opposite: crossing San Francisco's Golden Gate Bridge on its dedicated bike path; cycling Going-to-the-Sun Road in Glacier National Park on the Northern Tier route

MORE LIKE THIS
LONG-DISTANCE GRAVEL GRINDS

PACIFIC COAST ROUTE

From deep forests to urban cycling, this route has a little bit of everything as you cross the United States top to bottom along the Pacific Coast. The route begins in Vancouver, British Columbia, and heads through farmlands before crossing into Washington and through quaint towns on the Olympic Peninsula. Attractions abound through Oregon, including a short detour to the Mt St Helens Visitor Centre and plenty of state parks along the majestic shoreline. California brings towering redwoods and curved coastal roads; be aware of traffic but also keep an eye out for elk herds in the woods, and seals offshore. Take advantage of the warm weather with a dip in the Pacific, as you cycle south to the finish near San Diego.
Start // Vancouver, British Columbia
Finish // Imperial Beach, California
Distance // 1852 miles (2980km)

LEWIS AND CLARK TRAIL

Originally developed to celebrate Lewis and Clark's expedition, in the early 1800s, across what is now the western United States, this trail travels from Illinois to Oregon, following the general courses of the Columbia and Missouri rivers. The route has more variation than many other cross-country journeys, with plentiful opportunities to visit historic sites made famous by the Corps of Discovery. During this two-month journey you'll crest rolling hills and flat tablelands in the Midwest, cycle through Montana's cowboy country, and ride through the Columbia River Gorge to the western terminus. Since this route goes east-west, you can conceivably ride it from May to September, although snow in the Rocky Mountains bookends both seasons.
Start // Hartford, Illinois
Finish // Pacific County, Washington
Distance // 3961 miles (6374km)

NORTHERN TIER

An ambitiously long route crossing the entire United States along the Canadian border, the Northern Tier is known for the variety of its terrain and challenging climbing in both the northwest and northeast. This route can be ridden eastbound or westbound and offers everything from lush rainforest to open plains and climbs (without a switchback in sight). You'll ride remote dirt tracks and bike paths, busy roads and rail trails, pedalling through cities and small towns at frequent intervals. A highlight will be following the Mississippi River, with plenty of historical signage, before continuing into the eastern states and their hilly, forested roads. You'll finish at the Atlantic Ocean, in Maine, where you can celebrate with a jump in the water and a well-earned lobster roll.
Start // Anacortes, Washington
Finish // Bar Harbor, Maine
Distance // 4000 miles (6437km)

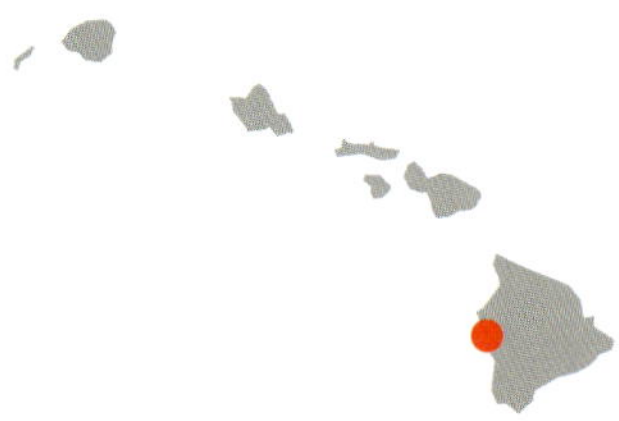

BIG ISLAND BIG RIDE

Volcanoes, rainforests and roadside 'malasadas' – Betsy Welch's 320-mile (515km) ride around Hawaii's Big Island reveals the rugged beauty hiding beyond the beaches.

The woman at the Pineapple Park Hostel outside Kona looks sceptical when I tell her I'm planning to ride around the island. She doesn't say much, just shrugs and points to a corner where I can stash my bike bag. I prop my phone and FaceTime my mechanic back in Colorado; something's shifted in transit and I need help realigning my fork. 'Looks rough,' he says sarcastically, squinting into the tropical light. When I finally get the fork in place, everything feels possible again. Three days, 300-plus miles (480km), and the Big Island all to myself.

The next morning, I start early. The road is quiet, washed in the soft pink light of dawn. It's Thanksgiving, which feels like the right day to begin a long ride. The Queen Ka'ahumanu Hwy isn't exactly romantic but is strangely beautiful; the ocean unfurls to my left in endless shades of blue and I crane my neck to look for *koholā* (whales).

By the time I reach Kawaihae, a small coastal settlement where the road splits – north toward Hawi, east to Waimea – the wind is up and the sun higher. I'm elated to find the Kawaihae Marketplace still open and, after a Thanksgiving breakfast, I pedal first toward Hawi (pronounced hah-vee), the island's northernmost town.

As I ride, palms bow sideways in the wind, and my ponytail whips across my face. From Hawi the road climbs, flanked by stout ironwood trees. There's no shoulder but no traffic, just cows, mist and the inescapable sense I'm suddenly in the mountains. By the time I descend into Waimea, 20 miles (32km) later, I'm shivering.

I roll into the Foodland parking lot and ask the man wrangling carts if he'll keep an eye on my bike. I re-emerge with

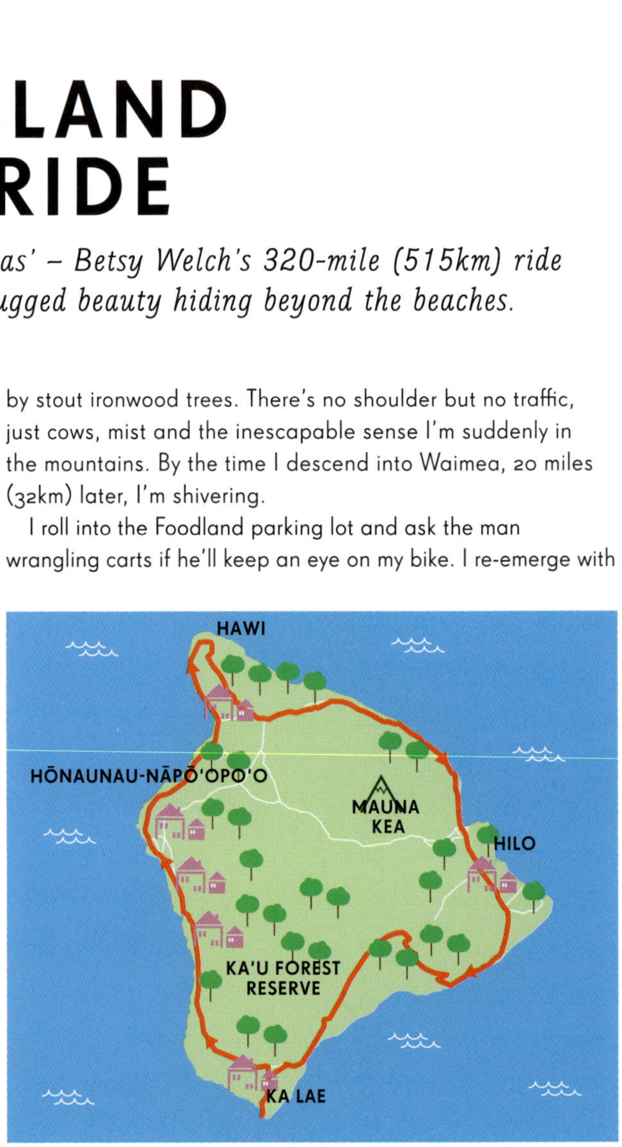

mhgstan/Shutterstock; Anadolu/Getty Images (M. Zoeller / United States Geological Survey (USGS)) handout

my haul and head toward Honoka'a on the Old Mamalahoa Hwy, where the pavement ripples with age, and fallen guavas pop beneath my tyres. I reach the guesthouse, everything I own now damp, but I'm thrilled. Day one, done.

The next morning dawns bright and dry, a rare miracle on the island's wet eastern side. I hug the coastline, the road dipping in and out of rainforests so green they almost hum. In Hilo I'm torn, wanting to stop but knowing these hundred-mile days can soon stretch away. I compromise by taking photos.

Twenty miles (32km) south of Hilo I do stop, in Pāhoa, at Island Naturals grocery. Another nice man says he'll watch my bike. I linger inside, partly because I want everything but partly because of the memories. A few years earlier, I was here with Andy, my boyfriend, who's gone now. After much convincing (he stubbornly said that Hawaii was for surfing, riding was for home), we rented bikes one windless day in the middle of a surf trip and rode up the Mauna Loa Observatory Rd. The air, warm at 6600ft (2012m), turned thin and cold by 11,000ft (3353m). We took a selfie at the top, shivering and laughing through the graupel.

On our next trip, he wanted to go higher – the 13,803ft (4207m) Mauna Kea, of course. As soon as the surf flattened, we rented bikes. After a night in our minivan, we started riding from Hilo. As the sun began to sink toward the horizon, we summited. I think of Andy atop Mauna Kea as I pedal away from it, the volcano's shimmering white peak jutting above the clouds.

"From Hawi the road climbs, flanked by stout ironwood trees, and I'm suddenly in the mountains"

My destination for the night is Volcano Village, gateway to the Hawai'i Volcanoes National Park. South of Hilo, the road rises and falls gently as the lushness gives way to black fields of lava from nearby Kīlauea, the same flow that, in 2014, swallowed homes near Pāhoa. After an otherworldly seven miles (11km) on a gravel road laid down by the park service, I begin the biggest climb of the day, the 3700ft (1128m) from the island's lip to Volcano Village. By the time I reach the tiny town, fog hangs in the trees. My guesthouse smells like mildew and ferns. I hang my wet kit by a weak heater, falling asleep to the sound of rain on the roof.

On the final morning, I tuck a white plumeria into my handlebar strap and point my bike south. The road skirts Mauna Loa, and in Pāhala I detour onto the more scenic

Alvis Upitis/Getty Images

ROAD FUEL, HAWAIIAN-STYLE

Cycling the Big Island means snacking local, with treats that trace the island's multicultural history and conveniently offer some of the best mid-ride fuel you'll find anywhere in the Pacific. Swap energy gels for Spam musubi, Hawaii's beloved grab-and-go combo of rice, seaweed and salty-sweet Spam. Also look out for roadside stands selling fresh banana bread still warm from the oven, and family-run bakeries frying up Portuguese *malasadas*.

Left to right: Hawi, on the north side of the island; the southernmost point of the US. Previous spread: Kilauea volcano erupting in 2025; ohia flowers blooming in Volcano National Park

Cane Haul Rd. It dumps me into Nāʻālehu, where I happily wait in line for a sugary *liliko'i* (passion fruit) *malasada* at the Punalu'u Bake Shop. From there, I make my way to South Point, or Ka Lae, the southernmost point of the entire US. The wind is relentless, ripping across the cliffs where the Pacific crashes below. I take a selfie, my heart hitching as I remember another photo from a year earlier, someone else grinning beside me. As I pedal away, a giant *honu* (green sea turtle) rises in a wave.

The miles after South Point are the worst. A busy highway, narrow shoulder, and aggressive drivers keep me moving steadily. My last stop is at the Fujihara Store, one of those perfectly Hawaiian general stores where time has stood still. Eventually I reach the small roads of South Kona, ducking off the highway into Hōnaunau-Nāpōʻopoʻo, where huge hibiscus droop, and avocado trees drop fruit onto the road.

When I roll back into Pineapple Park, the same woman is on the porch. She doesn't seem impressed I made it back but doesn't seem surprised either. After a shower, I walk over to the taco truck. The sun has set and the sky is a similar shade of pink to the one I set out under two days ago. I raise a Big Wave beer in a toast; to myself, to adventure and to the notion that Andy, once a cycling-in-Hawaii sceptic, would have loved this ride, too. **BW**

TOOLKIT

Start/finish // Just south of Kona.
Distance // 320 miles (515km)
Getting there // There are international airports in Kona and Hilo. A rental car is the quickest way to get around, or the Hele-On bus service is free.
When to go // The weather is consistently good. Peak tourist times are late December to early January, and mid-June to mid-August.
What to wear // Road gear, preferably quick-drying, packable insulation for higher elevations.
What to pack // Spares (multitool, chain lube etc), but also sunscreen, board shorts, mask and snorkel.
Where to stay // Pineapple Park Hostel, Kona
What to eat // Classics include *poke*, diced and marinated raw fish with a range of toppings; and *saimin*, a clear, noodle-packed broth.
More info // Big Island Bike Tours in Waimea offers rentals.

Opposite: sunrise at Mauna Kea

MORE LIKE THIS HAWAIIAN VOLCANOES FROM SEA TO SUMMIT

HALEAKALĀ, MAUI

Hawaii's volcanoes offer some of the most spectacular climbs on Earth. From sea level, riders follow ribbons of tarmac through lava fields and rainforests to summits routinely above 10,000ft (3048m). Weather can change in minutes, with sun, rain, wind and snow all possible. Few places combine such adventure and beauty as Maui's Haleakalā, the ride that started the 'world's biggest climb' conversation. Starting in the surf town of Pā'ia, the route climbs 36 miles (58km) to the 10,023ft (3055m) summit of Maui's dormant volcano, the island's highest paved road. Smooth pavement, gentle switchbacks and steady gradients wind through tropical forest, pastureland and, above 6562ft (2000m), a barren moonscape. Start early to avoid afternoon weather and pack a jacket for the descent. Return via the same route, giving yourself time for a *poke* bowl in Makawao and a post-ride beach beer back in Pā'ia.
Start/finish // Pā'ia
Distance // 70 miles (113km); elevation gain 14,314ft (4363m)

MAUNA KEA

Sacred to Native Hawaiians as a realm of the gods, Mauna Kea is more than just a mountain – it's a spiritual summit, the highest point in the Pacific Ocean, and one of the hardest paved climbs in the world. From Hilo, the route gains nearly 13,780ft (4200m) over 42 miles (68km), following Saddle Rd before turning onto the Mauna Kea Access Rd, where gradients steepen further (yes, really). Most cyclists stop at the Visitor Information Station at 9186ft (2800m), but those who continue to the 13,796ft (4205m) summit, which includes 5 miles (8km) of rough gravel and an adventure in itself, earn rare bragging rights. For those who do make it to the top, the view – clouds below, ocean beyond – is worth every pedal stroke. Those riders choosing to start from Waikoloa, on the west side of the volcano, face a slightly longer route but the same cumulative gain.
Start/finish // Hilo (eastern approach); Waikoloa (western)
Distance // 85 miles (137km); elevation gain 13,799ft (4206m)

MAUNA LOA

Although Mauna Kea's snow-capped summit claims the glory as Hawai'i's toughest climb, its bigger sibling, Mauna Loa, actually holds the record for sheer size. As with Mauna Kea, there are two main approaches: from Hilo via Saddle Rd to the Observatory Rd turnoff, a section that covers 47 miles (75km); or from Waikoloa along the northern Saddle Rd to the turnoff, practically across the highway from the Mauna Kea Access Rd. The final 17 miles (27km) of the Mauna Loa climb traverse barren, black lava fields, with views stretching to Mauna Kea. The road dead-ends at 10,991ft (3350m), where temperatures can be near-freezing. Bring layers, food and water, for a remote climb that is stark, otherworldly and unforgettable.
Start/finish // Hilo or Waikoloa
Distance // 64 miles (102km); at 10,991ft (3350m)

Wirestock Creators/Shutterstock

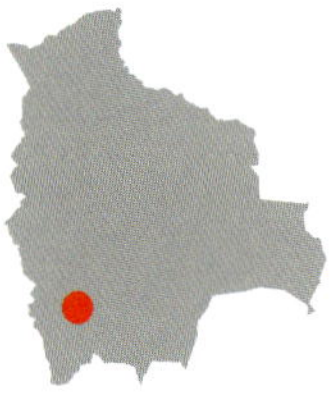

BOLIVIA'S LAGUNAS ROUTE

The Central Andean Dry Puna holds the world's largest salt flat, tallest volcanoes and unique wildlife. Experience this Mars-like region from the saddle of your bike.

Superlatives abound when describing the vast evaporated lakes and arid puna region of south-west Bolivia. Salar de Uyuni isn't just the largest salt flat on earth, it's the flattest place period, covering 6575 sq mi (17,032 sq km) in an off-white expanse that varies by less than three feet (1m) in vertical relief. In fact, it's so level and cloudless that it's favoured for calibrating satellites. We've just spent two and a half days cycling across the *salar*: camping one night on the 'beach' of a cactus-covered rock island, surrounded by an ocean of salt; and another on the rock-hard salt itself, our tent alone under a dome of stars.

Crossing Bolivia's *salars* is usually near the top of the list of must-have experiences for cyclists in western South America. But they are also the gateway to the most scenic region of the 1243-mile (2000km) Altiplano–Puna plateau. The second largest plateau on earth, this high-altitude steppe is studded with volcanoes, pocked with lakes and *salars* and scoured by winds that blow unimpeded across its sandy basins. Stretching south to the Atacama Desert of Chile, and including the Puna de Atacama of Argentina, this desert environment is also the location of many of the world's tallest volcanoes.

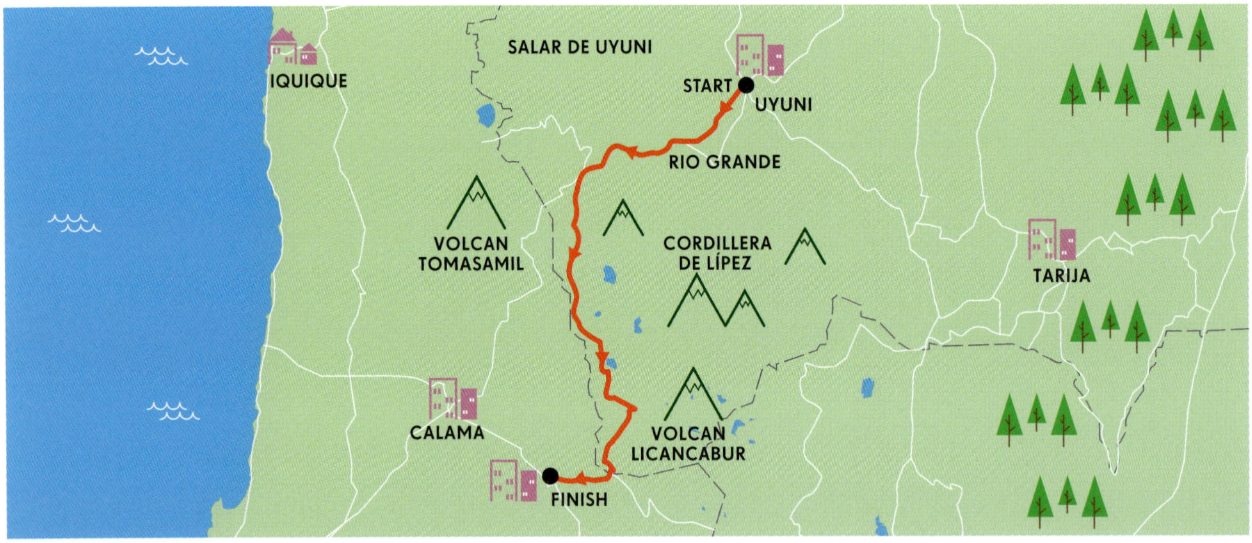

"I'm up early the next morning to photograph the flamingos as the early-morning light touches the water"

Picking its way across such landscape, the Lagunas Route is a popular and relatively accessible way to explore the region, crossing the dry but colourful Cordillera de Lípez mountains, between Uyuni and San Pedro de Atacama in Chile. As a standalone ride, this remote seven-day trip is certainly a once-in-a-lifetime cycling experience, but it's also popular for 4WD tours. While it has a reputation for strong winds and rough roads, the memories of countless pink flamingos strutting in the lakes, wind-eroded rock formations, steaming geysers and the 'Martian' volcanic desert are sure to outlast the discomforts of corrugated tracks and dusty campsites.

In Uyuni, the wind bounces a tumbleweed down the street, along with a waft of barbeque chicken, cooked at a street stall by women in big skirts and bowler hats. In town we buy a week's worth of food for the route, including hard-to-find staples such as instant potato and milk powder. We'll be able to buy basic snack foods and perhaps a meal or two at a couple of villages and hostels en route but, after the first two days, settlements will be scarce.

Remnants of Bolivia's former rail network are a theme for the first couple of hundred kilometres. Just outside Uyuni lies the eerily captivating Cementerio de Trenes. A train 'graveyard', it contains the hulking iron carcasses of 19th-century steam engines, tainted with rust but polished by sand-laden winds and the hands of many tourists. On the second day we pass through San Juan, a former *estacion* that's now a living museum, with its silent tracks and century-old rail infrastructure. At Chiguana, we camp at an abandoned railway station, pitching our tent in one of the derelict rooms to escape the wind. Outside, across the immense desert basin, the setting sun silhouettes a conical volcano and casts a firestorm of orange into the clouds as we eat dinner.

The first real climb comes the following morning, as we cross the shoulder of Volcán Tomasamil on sandy tracks. It's the first high pass of several between 13,000ft and 16,400ft (4000–5000m). Despite having three-inch tyres, we have to hop off and push for a while, as the wind picks up. With only patchy, low-lying scrub and tussock growing on the puna, there's little to slow the westerly. The descent takes us to the first of many lakes. During the wet season these saline lakes are home to large flocks of flamingos, who migrate here to feed on plant and animal plankton, and also to breed.

At the next lake, Laguna Hedionda, there's an isolated hotel used by tour groups. We sleep in a basic outbuilding bunkroom

PINK FLAMINGOS

During the central Andean wet season, hundreds of lakes become a high-altitude breeding ground for migrating flamingos. These lean-legged, handsomely beaked birds are famous for their lurid pink plumage. In the monotone environment of the desert, it's the opposite of camouflage. Blame lies with their diet of carotenoid-rich algae and brine shrimp, the pigments of which colour the flamingos' feathers – proving that you really are what you eat.

Clockwise from top: islands in the salars are populated by giant cacti; wrap up warm for camping; rock sculpted by the wind. Previous spread: the salty surface of the salars is quite firm; flamingos feeding

Mark Watson

and I'm up early the next morning to photograph the flamingos as the early-morning light touches the water. It's a spectacle like I have never seen, as hundreds of the striking, slender-legged birds feed and preen and court, the lake's surface mirroring the reds and yellows of the volcanic landscape.

Our days follow a pattern of passes, lagunas and sandy 4WD tracks. But as we ride deeper into this extraordinary land the sights become increasingly spectacular, like nowhere else I've seen on earth. With soft tyres to absorb the corrugations, we sometimes ride under the watchful eye of small herds of caramel-fleeced *vicuña*, a wild relative of the llama and the animal from which alpaca were domesticated. Scurrying *viscacha*, a wild rodent, are also easy to spot in the otherwise motionless landscape, and we catch sight of an Andean fox too. We make camp late in the day, sheltered within a labyrinth of sandstone outcrops in the Siloli Desert. Here, an oft-photographed boulder is the Árbol de Piedra (Stone Tree), a monolithic 'ventifact' that's almost holographic in the way the hard shadows of evening reveal different faces and expressions as I walk around its narrow base.

The most impressive of the lakes we pass is Laguna Colorada; popular for the deep red of its waters, which draw hundreds of flamingos too. We wash off the desert dust at the Chalviri thermal pools and stay at the nearby hostel. Guarding our exit from the high puna are two towering cones, those of Volcanes Licancabur (19,409ft/5916m) and Juriques (18,714ft/5704m), which each have a footing in both Bolivia and Chile. Beneath their soaring slopes we pass Lagunas Blanca and Verde, before reaching the border and a welcome 7545ft (2300m) descent to the richer air and plentiful food of San Pedro de Atacama. **MW**

Mark Watson

TOOLKIT

Start // Uyuni, Bolivia
Finish // San Pedro de Atacama, Chile
Distance // 287 miles (462km)
Getting there // Cycle from La Paz via Oruru, to the Salars de Coipasa, or de Uyuni, or directly to Uyuni for the classic Lagunas Route. For a more adventurous introduction to the puna, cycle to Coipasa via Volcán Sajama and the Ruta de las Vicuñas, then onto the *salars*. There are regular buses and flights from La Paz to Uyuni.
When to go // Winter to spring (May to November) is the best time, but from May to August temps can get as low as -15°C (5°F). Spring is warmer but can also be stormier. Summer rains make the *salars* impassable.
What to wear // This is an exposed, high-altitude route, requiring warm and waterproof clothing, such as you'd carry for alpine hiking.
What to pack // A three- or four-season tent and sleeping bag rated to -10°C (14°F).
More info // www.itsdownhillfromhere.com/2016/11/21/riding-the-lagunas-in-south-west-bolivia-a-practical-guide-for-cyclists/
Things to know // This route begins at 11,811ft (3600m) and crosses five major passes over 14,763ft (4500m) in height. Acclimatisation is essential before setting out.

Opposite: vicuñas on Bolivia's salt flats; the vast Puna landscape of the Andes

MORE LIKE THIS
RIDES IN THE CENTRAL ANDEAN DRY PUNA

RUTA DE LAS VICUÑAS

This picturesque five-day ride is the ultimate precursor to the Lagunas Route, offering a taste of the Dry Puna's challenges and scenery, but with easier riding, fewer passes and a lower average altitude. Hugging the Chile-Bolivia border, it follows mostly good-quality dirt and paved roads through two national parks, with lots of opportunity for sighting wildlife, including the namesake *vicuña*, one of the wild camelids of South America. This route has an evident human history too, imparted by crumbling hamlets and characterful adobe Jesuit Mission churches – often in the middle of nowhere. The region's topography and geology is fascinating too; dramatically shaped by tectonic activity that has created a land of steaming volcanoes, hot pools, cliffs, canyons and salt flats over millions of years.
Start // Putre, Bolivia
Finish // Uyuni, Bolivia
Distance // 358 miles (576km)
Info // www.bikepacking.com/routes/ruta-de-las-vicunas-northern-chile

RUTA DE LOS SEIS MILES

A mind-bending, physically challenging journey through a desert corridor of remote, high-altitude volcanoes (19,685ft/6000m), Ruta de los Seis Miles has a reputation as one of the hardest documented bikepacking routes in the world. It earns this due to its numerous high-pass crossings (up to 16,400ft/5000m) on often sandy, unformed vehicle tracks. Coupled with the need to carry over two weeks' worth of food (for the Norte section), and sometimes two to three days' water at a time, this is a route to bring your best legs and lungs. Being comfortably acclimatised to 14,750ft (4495m) is a prerequisite (Lagunas Route is the ideal training ride), along with a plus-tyred bike, wilderness experience and self-reliance. Those who do commit to this month-long crossing of the puna will be rewarded by the experience of independently traversing one of the most amazing places on Earth.
Start // San Pedro de Atacama, Chile
Finish // Guandacol, Argentina
Distance // 808 miles (1300km)
Info // www.bikepacking.com/routes/ruta-seis-miles-norte

PASO PIRCAS NEGRAS

At the southern end of the Andean Dry Puna, twin passes Pircas Negras and Agua Negra cross the Andes over the continental divide that separates Chile and Argentina. The northern of the two, Pircas Negras, provides some of the experience and scenery of the high and dry Andes, without the commitment of several days at high altitude. Cycled in either direction, a long uphill approach leads to a 58-mile (93km) stretch where the riding doesn't drop below 13,000ft (3962m), meaning only one or two nights need be spent sleeping at that elevation. This is the section with the most vividly coloured volcanic landscape, so it's worth taking your time. There are a couple of historic 19th-century stone huts to shelter in and the riding is on good-quality paved and gravel roads.
Start // Copiapó, Chile
Finish // Villa Union, Argentina
Distance // 461km (287 miles)
Info // www.highlux.co.nz/category/argentina

Federico Lupis/Alamy; Travel Beat Photography/Shutterstock

THE MONUMENTAL LOOP

New Mexico's Monumental Loop blends dreamy desertscapes with historical sites ranging from early humans to the space race. No wonder it sparked a bikepacking boom.

I prefer to research, plan and scout my own bikepacking routes. I enjoy the process of finding interesting trails or landmarks on a map, zooming out and trying to link everything together into a cohesive journey. The Monumental Loop isn't a route of my own creation, however, but rather the brainchild of Matt Mason, of bikepacking.com. And, I'm happy to admit, it's also one of the most spectacular, well-designed routes I've ever had the pleasure of riding.

The route was originally intended as a tour of Organ Mountains-Desert Peaks National Monument, the 'monument' in question comprising four mountain ranges in the Chihuahuan Desert and which lie within the national park's 776 sq mi (2009 sq km): the Organ; the Doña Ana Mountains; Sierra de las Uvas; and the Robledo Mountains.

As is often the case, it was my good friend Joe Cruz who pitched the idea to head down to New Mexico with a small group, to ride the Monumental Loop. The route was new to us but, having already heard many good things, it didn't take much for Joe to convince us. My partner Emily and I flew to El Paso, in Texas, hitched a ride to Las Cruces and, a few days later, met up with Joe and his friend, Willie, to start our ride.

The original route has undergone a few updates in recent years – a consequence of hard-to-follow, poorly maintained trails – and this has resulted in a greatly improved rider experience. We followed this 250-mile (402km) 'Monumental Loop 2.0', which runs in a figure of eight and still takes in all four of the Monument's ranges. With Las Cruces smack in the middle, it's a distance you can cover in about six days.

Riders usually start by heading north, toward the Doña Ana range and Sierra de las Uvas. On our first day, riding along the Rio Grande beside pecan orchards, a woman yelled out: 'The Loop!' Spotting the Monumental Loop logo on her t-shirt, I responded with an enthusiastic whoop. The original route sparked a bikepacking boom in and around Las Cruces, was subsequently embraced by locals and now provides the community with low-impact, recreational tourism. It also means you'll find tacos for sale in small towns all along the Rio Grande, as well as several wineries.

We navigated dirt roads and small sections of singletrack, towards the village of Hatch, famously known as the 'Chile

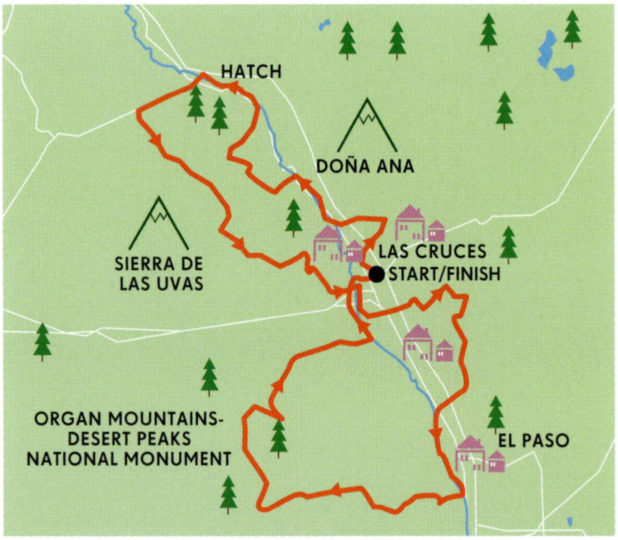

Miles Arbour

Capital of the World,' due to the region's industrial-scale production of chile peppers. After a (spicy) bite to eat, we decided to camp just outside of town – in just the sort of spot Matt had instructed us not to.

It was January, and although I've ridden in winter-desert conditions numerous times, nothing prepared me for the massive temperature swing that night. Seasonal averages here range from daytime highs of 15°C to night-time lows of -4°C. Like polar explorers of old, our group of four huddled inside my two-person tent before Joe and Willie made the brave decision to crawl into their bivvy bags in the freezing wind outside.

It's worth noting that, despite adjacent tourist attractions, Monumental Loop is hardly a Sunday-afternoon spin. Despite being a non-technical ride, the Loop throws some curveballs which might catch off guard those who are unprepared or unfamiliar with desert bikepacking. As well as dramatic temperatures, there aren't many water sources along the route, which means you're carrying several litres between resupply points. Added to which, everything is either pointy or prickly, and eager to tear a hole in your tyre or sleep gear.

What really stood out for me was the variety of terrain. One minute you're riding alongside the Rio Grande, gazing up at the Organ Mountains; the next, you're navigating sandy tracks tucked between steep canyon walls. It's impossible to get bored or feel beaten down because, as soon as it gets hard (and it

Miles Arbour

THE ROCK ART OF NEW MEXICO

A short ride northwest of Las Cruces in the Organ Mountains-Desert Peaks National Monument, lie petroglyphs (rock art) dating from 900 to 1400 CE. They often depict humans, animals and plants. The region's most celebrated rock art is at Three Rivers, a 50-acre site in the northern Chihuahuan Desert that is home to 21,000 such glyphs, believed to be the work of the Jornada Mogollon, a prehistoric indigenous culture.

Left to right: the Sierra de las Uvas Wilderness; heading north of Las Cruces; welcome to the chile capital of the world. Previous spread: overlooking Kilbourne Hole, northeast of El Paso, Texas

Miles Arbour

does, frequently), the terrain changes and your spirits are lifted. Giving ourselves just under six days for the Loop felt reasonable, but we wished we'd had more time for side-missions, to check out optional points of interest just off the main drag.

What the Monumental Loop does well is blending diverse desert landscapes, by turns serene and gruelling, with intriguing historical timelines. Where, for example, would you find so close together NASA training-sites (for the Apollo missions), the spot where frontier-lawman Pat Garrett met his end, and the very rocks where woolly mammoths once came to scratch their prehistoric itches? And that's before you even get to the myriad petroglyphs whose origins remain steeped in mystery (see panel).

If you want to do yourself a true favour, spend a night in Las Cruces, around the halfway point; if not for me, do it for the food. A few of our favourites included Bosa Donuts & Burritos, Nopalito Restaurant (both Las Cruces) and, in Mesilla, Chala's Wood Fire Grill. A highlight, on our final approach to Las Cruces, was grabbing dinner at Public House 28 Brewery and then camping at Sombra Antigua Vineyard and Winery.

We ended up sharing the tasting room with a couple who live close by, but who told us that when they make their regular visit to the winery on Valentine's Day, they camp at the venue so as to avoid the drive home after a drink. As a checklist for this epic ride, it seemed a fitting summary of what this ride has evolved to become: scenery, history, winery. **MA**

TOOLKIT

Start/finish // Las Cruces
Distance // 250 miles (402km)
Getting there // Fly to El Paso from US hubs; a commuter bus links El Paso to Las Cruces, dropping riders at the university, which is on the route.
When to go // October to April.
What to wear // T-shirt and shorts during the day but packable warm clothes for nights. A windproof is useful.
What to pack // A sleeping bag rated to below freezing is vital. Tubeless tyres and repair kits are also critical. Large-volume tyres, too: this off-road route features deep sand and rocky descents.
Where to stay // Dispersed camping on public land sites within the Monument may require permits.
What to eat // There's more to life that tacos; in Las Cruces, so much more
More info // The official route guide, the route, more information, and a video overview are at www.bikepacking.com/routes/monumental-loop

Clockwise from top left: wildflowers at Madera Canyon; an elegant trogon in Madera Canyon; riding on the Fool's Loop route

MORE LIKE THIS
DESERT RIDES IN THE SOUTHERN US

FOOL'S LOOP

The southwestern United States has some of the best winter bikepacking around, so it's no surprise I've escaped my native Canada most years to enjoy the sun and fantastic riding. I've had the pleasure of creating several bikepacking routes around this migratory concept, and they remain some of my favourite rides. At 277 miles (446km), the Fool's Loop, located near Phoenix, is a challenging yet rewarding week-long route that follows gravel roads, rough doubletrack and desert singletrack. It starts (and ends) deep in the city, winding its way north before eventually linking with Brown's Ranch Trailhead, as well as a section of the newly developed Maricopa Trail. The eastern edge of the Fool's Loop travels through the beautiful Tonto National Forest and eventually joins up with the Black Canyon Trail before meandering back into central Phoenix.
Start/finish // Phoenix
Distance // 277 miles (446km)

QUEEN'S RANSOM

The Queen's Ransom, created by John Schilling, is another masterpiece that is a prime example of an exceptionally well-thought-out bikepacking trip. The 227-mile (365km) route around Phoenix's greater East Valley weaves together many of the area's popular singletrack trail systems, regional parks and the Arizona National Scenic Trail. Here, the Sonoran Desert guarantees stunning topography, rolling dirt roads and some challenging terrain. While there are close to 100 relatively flat miles on the Queen's Ransom, in no other sense is it an easy ride. That's because the other 127 or so miles are demanding, rugged and require not just fitness but your full attention (and all of the time). Gaps between resupply can be lengthy on sections of the route, and riders may need more water than usual due to the dry climate. If you're looking for an enriching desert run, however, the Queen's Ransom is hard to beat. A mountain bike – not gravel –is a must.
Start/finish // Phoenix
Distance // 227 miles (365km)

MADREAN RUGGED RAMBLE

A 260-mile (418km) loop showcasing some of the best the region has to offer, this route heads out of Tucson bound for Saguaro National Park. Here you'll pick up the Arizona Trail, which brings some genuinely technical sections before delivering you to the grasslands around Sonoita and on to the dirt roads near the town of Patagonia, AZ, that have earned the region its reputation for exceptional gravel. Skirting the US-Mexico border, the route next heads to the Santa Rita mountains, tacking around them to the Salero Canyon, with views of the Elephant Head butte. Madera Canyon brings long sections of singletrack, as you pick your way through stands of cacti. If the approach back into Tucson pales in terms of scenery, there's some consolation to be found in the city's excellent bike paths. Celebrate your 'homecoming' with dinner and drinks on Tucson's 4th Ave, renowned for its Mexican restaurants and vibrant nightlife.
Start/finish // Tucson
Distance // 260 miles (418km)

Sterling Lorence Photo/Getty Images; Manuela Durson/Shutterstock; Philip O. Lowe/Shutterstock

THE NATCHEZ TRACE PARKWAY

The Natchez Trace coasts through three southern states of America, with thousands of years of history beneath your wheels and the sounds of Elvis in your ears.

At the northern terminus of the Natchez Trace Parkway, a milepost sticks up like a thumb on the side of the road. For many bikers, the brown sign represents the final lap, an exclamation point punctuating a two-wheeled odyssey that started two states away in Mississippi. For southbound cyclists like me, however, the marker is just the beginning. 'Mile one,' I exclaim ceremoniously, translating the sign's three digits.

Over 10 days, I will pedal 444 miles (714km) from Nashville to Natchez, with a small wedge of Alabama in between. During my journey on the National Park Service road, I will roll through thousands of years of history, and not necessarily in order. I will follow in the footsteps of prehistoric giant sloths and Chickasaw tribes, Kaintucks (Ohio River farmers and boaters) and Elvis, Civil War soldiers and Oprah.

During hours-long rides, I will share the two-lane paved road with a handful of cars and motorcycles (the maximum speed limit of 50mph deters rushed drivers), kindred spirits in padded shorts and helmets (peak season is autumn) and countless critters, including armadillos both dead and alive. And in and out of my saddle, I will experience southern traditions that touch all aspects of life, from grits to music to football.

The New Trace, a straight arrow that dates from 1936 and roughly parallels the original foot trail, is not as arduous as the Old Trace, a meandering dirt path studded with rocks and roots. Nor is it as perilous: the poisonous snakes, tribal attacks and bandits appear only in yellowed accounts.

But the communities are still dispersed like distant beacons. I have to watch the clock and my pace if I want to arrive at my

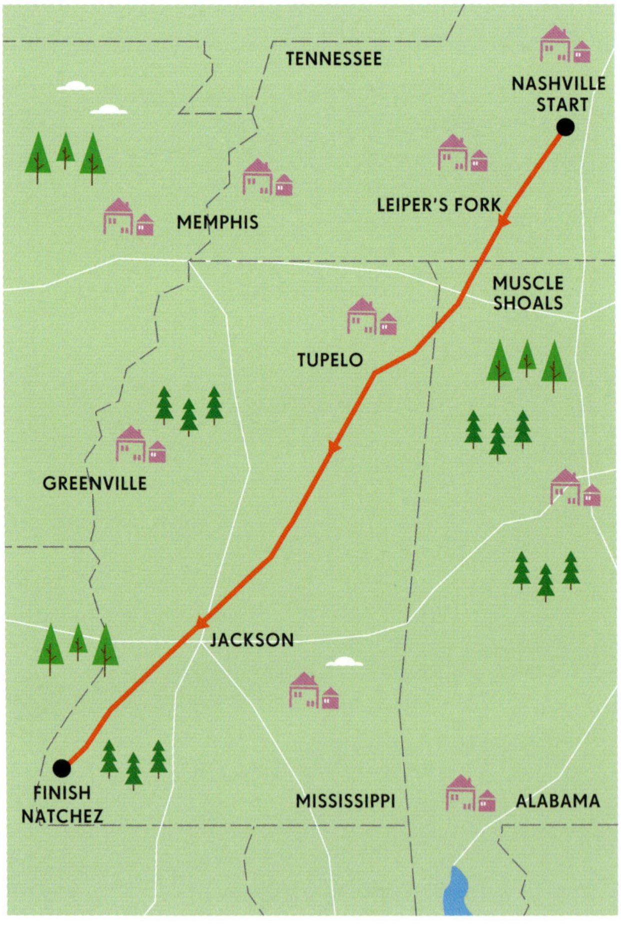

Dee Browning/Shutterstock; fotophoto/Shutterstock

SECOND FIDDLE
Layla's
JACKS
BAR-B-QUE
STAGE

lodging before nightfall – or, in the case of Leiper's Fork, to catch open-mic night at Puckett's Grocery & Restaurant.

The 19th-century village, about 15 miles (24km) from the Trace entrance in Tennessee, is a darling among Nashville stars (the Judds, Carrie Underwood) and troubadour musicians seeking an impromptu jam (Aerosmith bandmates). When I enter Puckett's, two young guitarists are electrifying the crowd with a Jimi Hendrix cover. I'm introduced to the unofficial mayor of Leiper's Fork, a towering gray-haired man in a baseball cap, named Goose.

'This is one of the prettiest parts of the country, especially on the Trace,' Goose yells into my ear, mentioning the maple and oak trees lining the parkway. He then directs my gaze to the stage, pointing to the keyboardist, who plays with Neil Sedaka, and the guitarist, who tours with Ted Nugent. He widens his sweep to point out Naomi Judd's husband and a CIA agent who I am supposed to forget instantly.

I don't have much time to ease into the Trace. The longest distance – 72 miles (116km) – falls on the second day. The Tennessee portion is the hilliest, slowing my speed and stretching my energy reserves. Informational placards and historic sites further impede my progress. At the Meriwether Lewis National Monument, I meet a New Orleans–bound skateboarder tending to his injuries after a crash and the Nashville couple who have been cheering me on with fist pumps through their sunroof. We discuss the rumor that Lewis, the famed explorer, died of syphilis. But the National Park refuses to gossip. An interpretive sign by a stone memorial elusively explains that his life 'came tragically and mysteriously to a close'.

"At FAME Recording Studios, an employee invites me inside Studio A, where Aretha Franklin cut two hits"

In Florence, at Milepost 338, a group of motorcyclists huddle around Tom Hendrix to hear the emotional tale of his great-great-grandmother. As a Yuchi girl, he explains, she was forced to leave her tribal land in Alabama for Indian Territory in present-day Oklahoma. She was restless, however, and reversed course. She spent five years searching for her way back home.

In the 1980s, Tom started to collect millions of pounds of rocks and to build the 1.5-mile (2.5km) Te-lah-nay's Wall to honor her life and spirit. The eastern portion runs in a direct line and represents the Trail of Tears; the western section sprawls in many directions, symbolising her meandering return route.

Gordon Ball LRPS/Shutterstock; House Of Fame LLC/Getty Images; The Washington Post/Getty Images

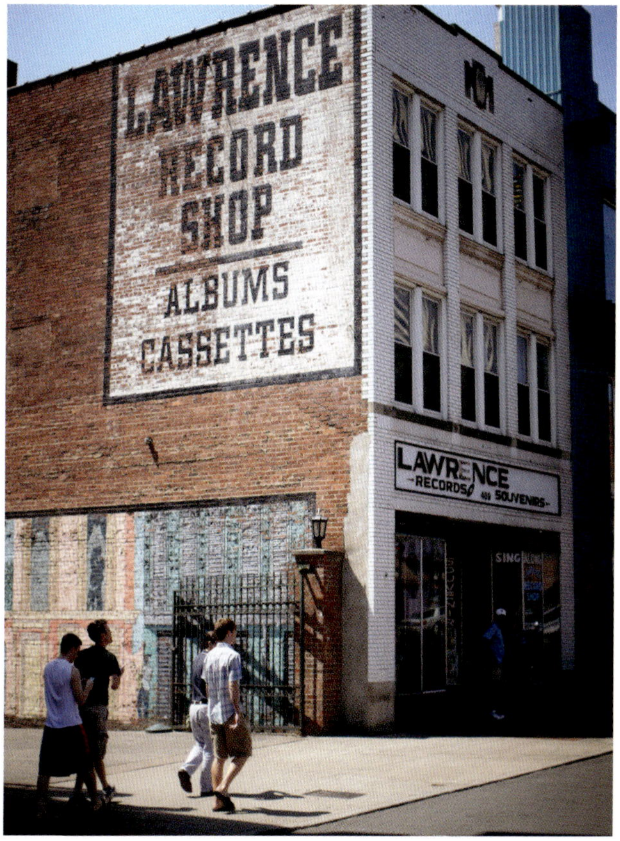

THE HOME OF ELVIS

The birthplace of Elvis is the B-side of Graceland. In Tupelo you can visit the 15-acre park complex that houses both his humble childhood home and a museum of memorabilia. There's also the legendary Tupelo Hardware Company, which still sells tools and instruments. Inside the store, stand on a black X that marks the spot where the future rock 'n' roll star picked out his first guitar.

Left to right: Alicia Keys at FAME Studios; the birthplace of Elvis Presley; Leiper's Fork; Lawrence Record Shop in Nashville. Previous spread: nightlife in Nashville; the Natchez Trace Parkway Bridge in Tennessee

Muscle Shoals, about 20 miles (32km) off the Trace in Alabama, is where some of the biggest names up and down the radio dial have recorded, such as Otis Redding, Etta James, Paul Simon, Bob Dylan, the Rolling Stones and Band of Horses. At Muscle Shoals Sound Studio, a museum guide encourages me to shake a pair of maracas in the booth where Mick Jagger and Keith Richards belted out three songs on *Sticky Fingers*. A German tourist ducks into a sacred but still-operating space: the bathroom where Richards wrote 'Wild Horses'.

At FAME Recording Studios, an employee invites me inside Studio A, where Aretha Franklin cut two hits and Alicia Keys played the piano for the 2013 documentary film, *Muscle Shoals*. In Studio B, he tells me that Duane Allman once slept and performed here. For the next 60-odd miles (100km) to Tupelo, I have southern rock stuck in my head.

For 361 miles (580km), I have biked solo. But one morning, I become a duo. A French-Canadian in striped long underwear sidles up next to me and strikes up a conversation. We become a trio when a former turkey farmer from North Carolina joins us.

We count down the final distance together, with the French-Canadian throwing up his arm at significant intervals. For the 3-mile (5km) mark, I start to feel a mix of elation and deflation. At the last mile of Natchez, I pedal slower, savouring it as much as I did the first mile in Nashville. **AS**

TOOLKIT

Start // Nashville, Tennessee
Finish // Natchez, Mississippi
Distance // 444 miles (715km)
Getting there // Natchez is not that close to airports. Alexandria (Louisiana), is 70 miles (113km) away; Baton Rouge (Louisiana) is 90 miles (145km). Catch a Greyhound bus to the start of your ride or take an airport shuttle. Nearby bike shops can box and ship your wheels.
Where to stay // For overnight options, cyclists can pitch a tent at more than a dozen campgrounds, including several bicycle-only sites, or pedal into Collinwood, Tennessee; Florence, Alabama; and Houston and Kosciusko in Mississippi.
Where to eat // The Trace does not provide any food concessions beyond the rare vending machine at a rest stop. Pack meals in panniers.
More info // www.natcheztracetravel.com

Myles New for Lonely Planet

Opposite: Linn Cove Viaduct on the Blue Ridge Parkway in North Carolina

MORE LIKE THIS ALL-AMERICAN RIDES

KATY TRAIL, MISSOURI

Ride the country's longest rail trail across the Midwest state of Missouri to discover quaint country towns, the thriving city of St Louis, and echoes of the westward movement of settlers that shaped America. When the Missouri–Kansas–Texas (MKT) Railroad gradually closed in the 1980s, one section of the line – from St Charles near St Louis to Sedalia in eastern Missouri – was marked for conversion into a rail trail. Construction started in 1987 and the final sections were completed in the 1990s. The result is arguably the finest rail trail in the US, running along the state's eponymous river. There are no fewer than 26 trailheads along the route that provide restrooms and sometimes water fountains. Towns arrive at frequent intervals, including state capital Jefferson City. The Katy Trail can be ridden in either direction. Much of the route is on the St Louis to Kansas City Amtrak line, so you can start from St Louis, take the train to Sedalia (near Clinton) and ride back.

Start // Machens
Finish // Clinton
Distance // 238 miles (383km)

BLUE RIDGE PARKWAY, VIRGINIA TO NORTH CAROLINA

The iconic Blue Ridge Parkway rises and falls like a roller-coaster track running from Virginia's Shenandoah National Park to North Carolina's Great Smoky Mountains National Park. Most bikers budget about 10 days to complete the 469-mile (755km) route, which crosses four national forests and features 176 bridges, more than two dozen tunnels and hundreds of historic sites. Riders will experience the America that inspires patriotic songs: uninterrupted forests, burbling rivers, splashy waterfalls, vibrant wildflowers or foliage (depending on the season) and mountains haloed in clouds. Roadside diversions abound, such as the Blue Ridge Music Center, Julian Price Memorial Park and Craggy Gardens. Time your visit to Waterrock Knob to coincide with the sun's aerial spectacle.

Start // Shenandoah National Park near Waynesboro, Virginia
Finish // Great Smoky Mountains National Park near Cherokee, North Carolina
Distance // 469 miles (755km)

GREAT ALLEGHENY PASSAGE (GAP), MARYLAND TO PENNSYLVANIA

The chirps of bike bells have replaced the toots of train whistles that once rang through the corridors of the Great Allegheny Passage (GAP). The 150-mile (241km) biking and hiking trail (no cars allowed) sprang from mostly abandoned railbeds laid between Cumberland, Maryland, and Pittsburgh, Pennsylvania. The trail is flat and leisurely, and coasts by some remarkable landmarks. On the 13-mile (21km) Frostburg–Meyersdale leg, for example, the wow list includes the Mason–Dixon Line into Pennsylvania; the 3295ft-long (1005m) Big Savage Tunnel, which was named after the stranded 18th-century surveyor who had offered himself up as food to save his men; the Eastern Continental Divide, the trail's highest point at 2390ft (728m); and the curved Keystone Viaduct. Charming towns such as Confluence, on the Youghiogheny River, and Ohiopyle, a hyperactive hub of outdoor activities, entice bikers to hop off and stay awhile.

Start // Cumberland, Maryland
Finish // Pittsburgh, Pennsylvania
Distance // 150 miles (241km)

OH BOYACÁ!

Exploring Colombia's mountainous Santander and Boyacá departments on winding dirt roads reveals a feast of the country's uniquely rich biodiversity, lively culture and picturesque towns.

Our initiation into Colombian cycling taught us a number of lessons. Firstly, you must earn your empanadas here. I had, foolishly it transpired, imagined that in these northernmost reaches of the Andes, the riding might be less demanding than in the 'proper' mountains further down the continent. While it's true that the altitude and cold are less extreme here, the mountains are just as crumpled and steep – to assume otherwise is akin to thinking a ride from north to south will be mostly downhill. Secondly, if you put in the work you'll be rewarded with a diversity of microclimates like few places on Earth, as cactus-filled canyons, glacial valleys and lush rainforests unfold in rapid succession. And, the third lesson, Colombianos really do put cheese on anything.

Since its development in 2015, the Oh Boyacá! route has become a staple chapter of the great South American traverse, though for us it was the crux of a trip focused very

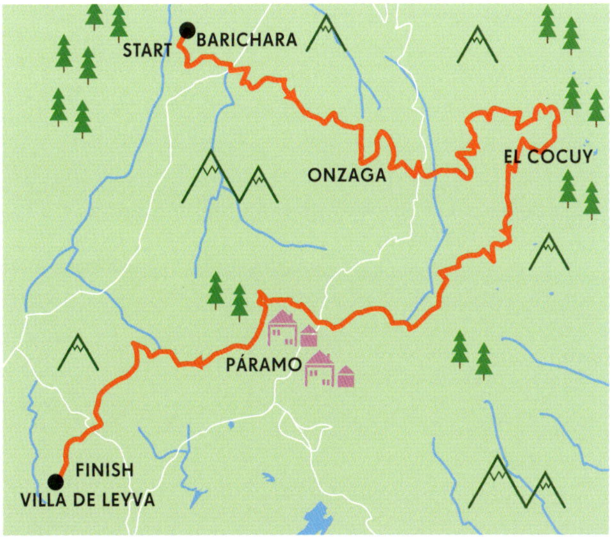

Eileen Schwab; art by Marco Aurelio (@anniosart)

much on Colombia. Along twisting, mountainous dirt roads, Oh Boyacá! weaves together a vivid collection of the region's natural and cultural treasures, bookended by two of Colombia's most beautiful heritage towns. In the minds of many, my own included, this country's dark history and subsequent reputation still linger, yet time spent here rewrites such negative impressions, into joyful, open-hearted ones, in a country with a capacity for reinvention.

At the start of the route, buzzing little Barichara provides a relaxed welcome with its hilly, cobblestone streets, whitewashed facades, shops and cafes. We take a morning stroll before our planned departure and learn that the bustle of activity that's sprung up in the main plaza is for the Vuelta a Colombia Femenina, Colombia's version of the Tour de France Femmes. The day's stage is a time-trial from San Gil, ending on a climb to the main square. We delay our departure to join the boisterous cheering as the riders sprint to the finish line, relishing this impromptu immersion into the local riding culture. This passion for cycling is something we'll see more of as we pedal south. Sundays are especially fun to ride, as Lycra-clad locals are out in groups and we're often greeted enthusiastically.

After our late start and via some bucolic backroads, we make it only to San Gil for the night, an adventure hub that feels loud, even rowdy. From here, we delve into the layered green hills, jumping between pavement, gravel and dirt tracks and, after another few villages, we end up in sleepy Onzaga, at a delightful guesthouse. It's soon apparent how markedly different the personalities of each place can be, with rough, functional mining towns only a few miles from those more lovingly maintained and adorned with colourful murals. Altitude plays a part too, influencing whether life spills into the streets or stays indoors; the different clothing, food and even the hours people keep, in order to make the most of the coolest, or warmest, hours of the day.

Wherever we are, a reliable constant is coffee, or *tinto*, around the central plaza. Sipping on these small cups of strong, sweetened black coffee becomes a welcome ritual to start our days, watching life go by and locals gather to gossip on street corners. Next comes the enjoyable pastime of sniffing out and sampling the local food, though it can be a hit-and-miss endeavour, with the freshness of snacks sitting in glass cabinets hugely variable. Colombia is a dairy-farming country so cheese features heavily, in ways both traditional and conventional.

Thus, as a cheese lover, I'm willing to try the local specialties, and become quite fond of *bocadillo con queso*, a favourite sweet-and-savoury combo of cheese and *bocadillo de guayaba* (a firm block of guava paste), that's eaten in slabs, one on top of the other. I can even get on board with *salpicon con queso*, a fruit-salad drink topped with ice cream, condensed milk and

PÁRAMO AND FRAILEJONES

Páramo are unique, high-altitude tropical mountain ecosystems primarily found in Colombia and northern Ecuador. The Oh Boyacá! route offers a rare opportunity to visit several *páramo* areas where not just a few, but thousands of trademark frailejon plants blanket the mountains. These towering shrubs grow only a few centimetres each year (and can subsequently live for hundreds), capturing moisture from the air and releasing it through their roots into the soil.

Clockwise from top: frailejon plants; exotic moth orchids near Villa de Leyva; a bocadillo snack of guava paste; coffee at Casa Lacambra guesthouse in Onzaga; Previous spread: the mountain town of Soatá; Guacamayas, famed for its street art

Eileen Schwab

grated cheese. I do, however, draw the line at thick slices of cheese in my hot chocolate.

The highlight of Oh Boyacá! comes near the halfway mark, a loop near the Sierra Nevada del Cocuy, skirting the magnificent mountains and jagged slabs of rock within the national park. Simply riding this loop is stunning, but we can't pass up the opportunity to press deeper into the mountains, despite some logistical hurdles of permits and arranging a compulsory guide.

Fortunately, the location to arrange all this is the charming town of El Cocuy, where a distinctive mint-green colour palette accents every building, so a rest day is more than welcome. We're dealt some fickle weather, which comes as standard in Colombia, so our views of the mountain peaks are often limited. Still, the distinctive *páramo* landscapes are enchanting, studded with thousands of otherworldly shrubs known as *frailejon*.

The *páramo* landscape that forms the area's signature is, along the route, joined by numerous others, a staggering array of frequently altering vistas and microclimates; verdant jungles and arid canyons, glacial valleys or vibrant patchworks of farmland atop layers of striped and folded rock. And, interspersed between them, the countless villages offering shared moments of daily life.

If such abundance is a bikepacker's dream, so too is what awaits us in lovely Villa de Leyva where the Oh Boyacá! ends and the next, more improvised part of our ride will begin. For now, it's an ideal spot to while away a few days, people-watching on the fringes of the impressively vast Plaza Mayor, or else indulging in calorie-loading as we ready our weary legs to take to the hills once again. **ES**

"Sipping on these small cups of strong, sweetened black coffee becomes a welcome ritual to start our days"

TOOLKIT

Start // Barichara
Finish // Villa de Leyva
Distance // 378 miles (608km)
Getting there // Buses from Bogotá service San Gil near Barichara and Villa de Levya. They're comfortable, affordable and will accommodate bikes.
When to go // The driest months, in what is a notoriously rainy place, are from December to March, with a shorter, second dry season from July to August.
What to pack // Not too much! Be prepared for rain and a wide range of temperatures, but the substantial amount of climbing means packing light is preferable. With some planning, it's possible to ride town-to-town, without camping or cooking equipment.
Where to eat // The *almuerzo ejectivo* or *menú del día* is an affordable and hearty lunch deal offered almost everywhere.
More info // www.bikepacking.com/routes/oh-boyaca-colombia

Eileen Schwab; Mauricio Acosta Rojas/Shutterstock

Opposite: Colombia's Cocora Valley, near Las Nevados

MORE LIKE THIS
ANDEAN ADVENTURES

AROUND LOS NEVADOS

In Colombia's Cordillera Central, a route linking Los Nevados National Park and the Zona Cafetera shows off a staggering range of climates, from high-altitude volcanic landscapes to palms swaying in the warm breeze. The centrepiece of Los Nevados is the 17,457ft (5321m) Nevado del Ruiz, one of the most active volcanoes in the Americas. In 1985, a significant eruption buried the town of Armero on its eastern side. It's an eerie place to visit, and also where the hefty 48-mile (78km) climb to Alto del Sifón begins, gaining a lofty 12,894ft (3930m). Dropping down to Villamaria, back roads connect to Santa Rosa de Cabal then Salento, the heart of the temperate coffee-growing region. Colourful, whimsical Salento is the base for the Cocora Valley, famed for its Quindío wax palms, an iconic national treasure. From Salento, riding through the Carbonera Valley reveals even more impressive palm groves en route to Toche and Ibagué.

Start // Armero
Finish // Ibagué
Distance // 230 miles (370km)

AUSANGATE

Andean adventures don't come much more epic than Ausangate, a jewel in the Peruvian Andes. Typically a trekking route, it features its share of hike-a-bike, and at high altitude no less, but the scenery is spectacular. Making a loop from Pitumarca, you'll have an entrée of roads before the main course of the trail itself, where you'll ride deep in the mountains, rolling along at the foot of glaciers, hopping across mountain streams, sidling along turquoise lakes, ripping down some sublime singletrack and ending days in the most jaw-dropping camp spots. Proper acclimatisation and gear is essential; with the altitude reaching 16,400ft (5000m), mountain-biking skills and bike-maintenance knowledge are also needed to do this safely. For an unforgettable challenge, Ausangate is bucket-list stuff.

Start/finish // Pitumarca
Distance: // 78 miles (126km)

TRANS ECUADOR MOUNTAIN BIKE ROUTE (TEMBR)

The TEMBR is a tough dirt-road adventure running the length of the country, from its Colombian to its Peruvian borders. It navigates remote backcountry along a volcanic corridor, while weaving some of the country's classic sights into the itinerary. Three mighty volcanoes are highlights (Cotopaxi, Quilotoa and Chimborazo). You'll also meander through páramo ecosystems, Incan ruins and bustling indigenous markets; plus, there's the alluring colonial city of Cuenca. As you might expect in the Andes, the climbing is arduous, the cobblestones are bone-rattling (bring a mountain bike), the altitude yo-yos wildly and even in the 'dry' season you'll likely encounter your fair share of rain and freezing temperatures. Bring a resilient attitude, an adventurous spirit and immerse yourself in the rugged beauty of the Ecuadorian Andes.

Start // Tulcan
Finish // Vilcabamba
Distance // 858 miles (1381km)

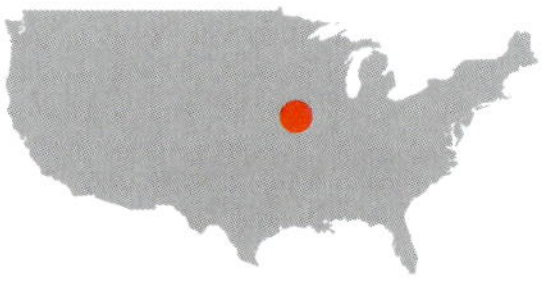

THE REGISTER'S ANNUAL GREAT BICYCLE RIDE ACROSS IOWA

Nestled in the belly of the Midwest is an organised ride so hometowny, welcoming and wonderful that you'll swear you've been there before.

This seven-day, 450-mile (725km) ride has been held every summer since 1973, when two editors from *The Des Moines Register* newspaper decided to ride across the state for a story and invited the public to join them. It has since grown from 500 participants into the oldest and largest organised ride in the world, typically fielding more than 20,000 riders each year. It's become one of the most storied rides in the country, known as a giant, week-long party. This ride crosses Iowa, starting at the western border of the state, where most riders dip a wheel in the Missouri River, and finishes up on the eastern side, with another rubber baptism in the Iowa River. Though the exact route varies from year to year, the authentic immersion in Midwest culture and hospitality is never underserved. We rode beside bicycle riders from all tribes, including grannies on their beach cruisers, tandems, a triple tandem and a guy blasting country music from huge speakers strapped to a rack. We saw someone dressed in a full Spiderman suit, a man riding in flip-flops and overalls, a pair of unicycles, and families on e-cargo bikes towing little kids and dogs.

At the first town we came to along the route on Sunday morning, the streets were so thick with people and bikes we had to dismount and walk, and somehow I got separated from the

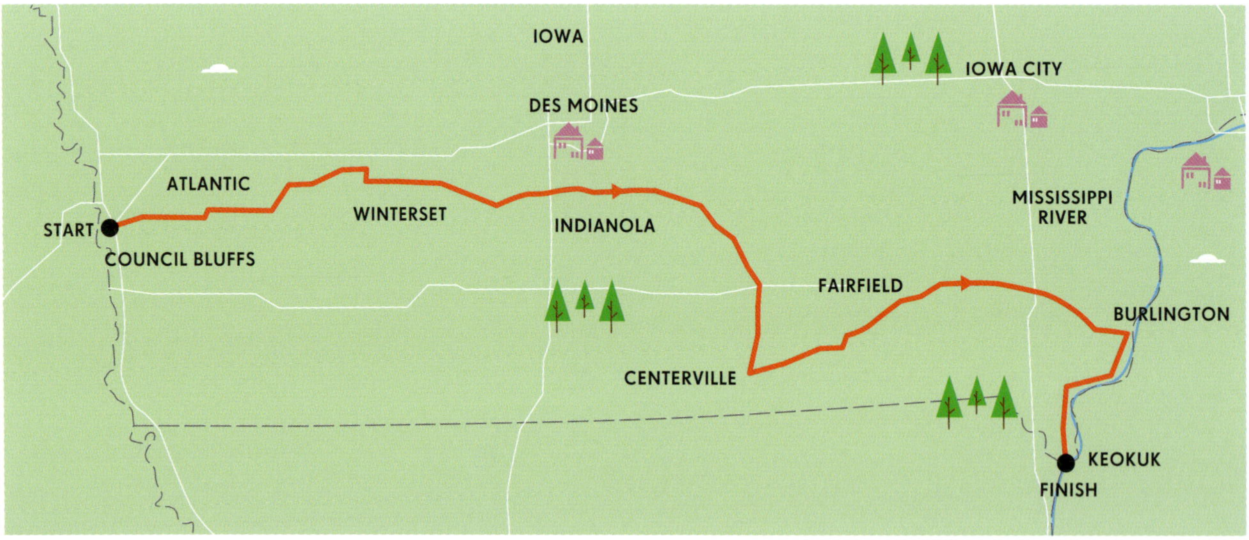

N CANDY KITCHEN
Nopoulos Family
SINCE 1910
Lunch
Soda
OPEN

group between the grilled cheese food truck and the temporary tattoo booth. (I selected one that was an ear of corn.) There was music coming from a few blocks up ahead. I realised, as we got closer, that it was a stage offering karaoke. A beer-bellied man with an impressive voice was singing 'Ring of Fire'. We stopped to refill our bottles at the makeshift water fountain at the fire station.

About an hour down the road, we passed a sign that read 'Free Margaritas'. We screeched to a halt, pulling into a gravel parking lot. The sign was in front of a restaurant overlooking a sparkling blue lake with a cement boat launch and a string of pontoon boats tied together a few metres offshore. I skittered down to the edge and clicked off my shoes, peeled off my socks and dangled my feet in the water. It was only mid-morning, but it was hot; other riders were jumping right into the cool water. Tempting as it was, we reminded each other how awful it would be to ride the next 40 miles (64km) with a soggy chamois. As we sat there on a cluster of large rocks with our feet in the water, a man from the pontoon chain waded over with a cooler in one hand.

'You guys like beer?' he asked us. We nodded gratefully, and he handed us slightly cool cans of Bud Light.

'How far you going today?' We told him we'd come 15 miles already and had about 45 to our next stopping town.

'Whoo-wee!' He offered us some protein bars from his cooler, too. We sat and shot the breeze with him while people on the pontoon boats laughed and whooped. With a long way still to go, we thanked the man and got back on our bikes.

Suffering from serious FOMO from skipping a jump in the lake, we left the house the next day with swimsuits wadded up in our jersey pockets. We promised ourselves that any sign of a lake and we would pull over and take a dip – it would feel so wonderful in the middle of a long day in the Iowa sun.

About mid-afternoon, we found what we were looking for in the form of fire hose races. The fire station had strung up a buoy on a wire about 15ft (5m) in the air, and two people with hoses were using the strong stream to push the buoy to their opponent's side. We pulled over in a convenience store car park and took turns slipping on our swimsuits in a portable toilet, then crossed the road to the park. The wet cement was warm under my bare feet, but the spray from the hoses was refreshingly chilly. Kitted-up onlookers laughed as we battled the buoy back and forth across the basketball court. While I watched two of my friends play, I realised the fireman had a lever to control how much water went into each of the hoses, and were snickering to themselves as they channelled it all into one hose and my friend Vance got completely soaked by his wife Courtney. We rode the rest of the way with damp hair and giant grins.

Saxton Studio/Shutterstock; Wirestock Creators/Shutterstock

IOWAN CORN

Every day along the route, the Iowa Corn Growers Association sets up a free corn stand (donations accepted). After riding through miles and miles of cornfields, you'll probably want to stop to eat some. 'Butter?' the volunteer asked. I nodded, and he dipped the yellow cob into a pot of melted butter and passed the glistening hunk of steaming starch into my hands. Holding it firmly by the husk, I sunk my teeth into the delicious, salty gold. It was glorious.

Left to right: Iowa's fields; Dubuque; bicycles and big tractors; Des Moines. Previous spread: refuelling at a candy store; rural riding

We stopped at a family-owned slow-roasted pork-chop stand, and later at a table where women from the local church were selling homemade pie: strawberry, apple, banana cream and pecan. Families brought out their animals: in a few towns there were piglets available for photo opps, and you can even kiss one if that suits you (pigs are loud squealers – it did not suit me). I was sitting on the cool grass under an oak grove in front of a farmhouse, enjoying my pork chop, when a kitten wandered over to my feet. Even the animals were excited to greet us as we buzzed across the state.

Overnight, local families hosted us. They opened up their homes (and their fridges!) to a group of sweaty riders, eager to get to know all about us and where we came from. We spent nights on strangers' air-conditioned living room floors, our bellies full of well-earned beer and dinner.

The Midwestern route traces rolling farmland, past sparkling lakes and through acres of cornfields. The views that you don't forget, though, come at the end of the day: sitting around in a circle of camping chairs in a new friend's front yard, the ring of sunburned faces feeling like family. As the campfire died down, we slowly retreated to our campers and air mattresses, eager to sleep hard and find some more adventures tomorrow. **RM**

TOOLKIT

Start // Western border of Iowa (the start city and route are determined each year)
Finish // Eastern border of Iowa
Distance // Roughly 435 miles (700km)
Getting there // Fly into Des Moines or Omaha (depending on which is closer to the starting city) and hop on a bus chartered by the start city to the beginning of the ride.
When to ride // Mid-July. It's hot and sunny, but pack for a few summer showers, just in case.
Where to stay // Host housing is available, as is camping, or ride-supported camping.
What to take // A support driver: if your group takes turns driving, it's feasible to bring a camper or van with everyone's gear and luggage rather than carrying it all.
Tip // You don't have to commit to the whole week! Riding a few days will give you the Midwestern experience.

Opposite: riding towards Maroon Bells in Colorado

MORE LIKE THIS ORGANISED MULTIDAY ROAD RIDES IN THE USA

EMPIRE STATE RIDE, NEW YORK

The state of New York's headline acts take centre stage on this annual, seven-day cycle ride across the Empire state. Typically covering more than 500 miles (805km), the route varies from year to year but the destination is always unforgettable: the Niagara Falls. You'll be setting off from the borough of Staten Island and resting each night at a shared campground with your own tent, mattress and meals. Stops range from the state capital of Albany to the historic village of Weedsport, near the Erie Canal. Organisers offer a hilly route or an easier option for more relaxed riders (plus mechanical support, a medical team and more). But everyone is pedalling for the same purpose: to raise funds for cancer research.
Start // Staten Island
Finish // Niagara Falls
Distance // 500 miles (805km) over seven days

BICYCLE RIDE ACROSS GEORGIA

Inspired by RAGBRAI, Liberty County resident and local newspaper columnist Dot Moss founded and planned Georgia's first Annual State Bicycling Event in 1980. She started the inaugural ride in Savannah with 120 fellow cyclists and finished 300 miles (484km) later in Columbus, on the western border of the state, with just 60 riders. Now renamed BRAG, today up to 3000 cyclists pedal across the Peach State, covering about 55 miles (88km) daily for a week. The route varies each year but always sets off in the early summer and takes in quiet rural roads and welcoming small towns, with everything from massages and meals to mechanical support provided. Accommodation options include indoor and outdoor camping or hotels.
Start/finish // Route varies
Distance // 300 miles (484km) approximately over six days of cycling

COLORADO'S RIDE BICYCLE TOUR

This mountainous adventure offers some serious climbing – up to 6000ft (1828m) of elevation gain per day. Pedal through green meadows and over snowy peaks as you make your way through the Rocky Mountains of northwestern Colorado. Aid stations are available along the route in scenic locations, with free support as well as food vendors. A notable element that makes this ride especially challenging is the altitude. The ride takes place between 6000 and 12,000ft above sea level. Lower oxygen levels in the air can be managed by maintaining a slower, steady pace and staying hydrated. Ride organisers provide week-long parking and luggage shuttling, as well as free camping space and discounted hotel booking in adorable mountain towns.
Start/Finish // Route varies (decided in late winter each year)
Distance // 400–450 miles (650–725km) over six days

PERU'S GREAT DIVIDE

This pass-hopping, dirt-road journey along the roof of Peru encounters Andean communities as vibrant as the minerals and lakes that colour this spectacular mountain landscape.

I've been glancing across the valley as we ride, watching darkening thunderstorm clouds as they obscure our view of the highest peaks. As our road saunters up the last of the long switchbacks to the 14,700ft (4500m) pass, a slash of lightning splits the sky and sheets of hail fall in the distance.

Since our early start from last night's peaceful camp, it's been a typical day on the Great Divide. We've climbed gradually for 19 miles (30km) on a narrow dirt road, snaking upwards through craggy mountains; past soaring rock buttresses, boulder fields, lakes and rock mounds left by glaciers long gone. It's only typical in the sense that we've come to expect such spectacular scenery daily on this traverse of the continental divide.

A peppering of hail is followed by a flurry of wet snow which splatters on my arms as we crest a short climb and notice two *chozas*, the simple stone-and-tussock thatch dwellings of *campesinos* (peasant farmers). Hearing us, a lone woman scrambles out of the low door of one of the huts. She's dressed in a brightly coloured wide skirt, blouse, a couple of cardigans and leg warmers, with an alpaca shawl on her shoulders. It's the distinctive style of the Quechua, the predominant indigenous group of the Peruvian Andes. Like everyone we've met on this route she's friendly. We chat in Spanish and she points to a site on the open pampa for us to camp and shows us where to find water.

She's lived here mostly alone, she says, minding the animals for two years, while her husband studies in the city. Her *choza* is bigger than it looks, dug down into the ground for insulation, but there's just the bare necessities inside – a pile of blankets, and a soot-blackened pot and utensils alongside a small fire. The dried alpaca meat, maize and stack of potatoes are familiar sights now. In return for her help, we offer the woman a mandarin and chocolate bar, which she accepts with a smile.

Predictably, morning dawns clear and cold, with a cap of ice in my water bottle and a dusting of snow. We pack the tent with cold fingers, but after an hour of riding we're down to t-shirts,

Mark Watson

warmed by the harsh sunlight. Such are the temperature contrasts of this high-altitude route.

We kicked off our ride from Huaraz. In the shadow of the icy peaks of the Cordillera Blanca, this small city is the hub for trekking, climbing and bikepacking in the *cordillera*. Peru's destructive 1970 earthquake levelled the original city, but what it lacks in colonial character it makes up for with a lively tourism scene, which blends seamlessly with rural life. You can sip a perfect latté, yet at the same time see traditionally dressed women selling donkey feed or homemade *queso* (cheese). For most, one of the highlights of cycling in the Peruvian Andes is the highly visible culture of the indigenous mountain people. These descendants of the Inca recognise and celebrate their culture through traditional ways of living and farming, as well as distinctive, colourful dress and lively festivals.

There are many passes between 13,000ft and 16,400ft (4000–5000m) on Peru's Great Divide, so each day has involved tackling at least one or two of these hard-won heights. But though we ceaselessly spin the pedals and our lungs work hard, we're absorbed by the variety of riding through these colourful, mineral-rich mountains. It was the hunt for minerals that originally led mining prospectors to carve many of these roads through the pampa, but these days they're hardly busy. This is a route with few people and even less traffic.

Yesterday, a couple of farmers on motorbikes waved as they zoomed past, bouncing in the potholes with their fresh supplies, but sometimes we'll ride all day without seeing a vehicle. It's mostly small herds of alpaca and llama that keep us company,

POWER OF THE POTATO

One of the more humble Peruvian marvels is the potato. Of more than 3000 varieties domesticated here, one you're likely to encounter is the *chuño*, which is naturally freeze-dried by the Quechua people. Over a few days, the potatoes are exposed to sub-zero nights, followed by intense sunlight, then trampled before a final sun-drying. Once dehydrated, these small, waxy and nutritious potatoes are a winter staple and can be preserved for many years.

Clockwise from top: a festival in Oyon; a high point; find a sheltered camping spot; a breakfast of bread rolls and fried eggs

Mark Watson

turning their heads in curiosity as we ride by. While alpacas have a comical fluffiness, llamas are more graceful and athletic, an elegance often enhanced by colourful decorations on the animals' ears to identify ownership. They were a sacred animal to the Inca, one that could haul loads as well as provide fleeces and meat. Sometimes we spot viscacha too, rabbit-size rodents which scurry about rock formations alongside the road.

Towards midday we roll into a village of mud-brick buildings and unpaved streets. The women wear garlands of flowers in their hats, and two men are loading sacks of dung, for the fire, onto a mule. They point to a *comedor*, where we hope we'll find a *menu del dia almuerzo* – a basic but affordable set-menu lunch of typical rural food, including soup, hearty stew, bread and coffee.

As remote as this ride feels at times, with basic resupplies every two to three days, most days there is at least the chance of *pan y huevos* (bread roll with fried egg), in one of the many *pueblecitos* (small villages) that punctuate the route. Sometimes we'll opt for a local meal at night and a room in a cheap lodging, or *hospedaje*, but as interesting as it is staying in the villages, it's the quality of the camping on the Great Divide that sets it apart from many other bikepacking routes: the lack of fencing, combined with abundant groundwater and natural landscapes makes camping reliable; and it's rare that you'll be disturbed in this peaceful land that the locals call El Silencio – The Silence. **MW**

Mark Watson

Previous page: bikepacking alongside the Cordillera Paricaca; the village of Tanta

TOOLKIT

Start // Huaraz
Finish // Abancay (the route can be cycled in either direction but north to south is the most common).
Distance // 997 miles (1605km)
Getting there // Reach Huaraz by bus or air from Lima.
When to go // Dry season (April/May to September) runs through winter, offering generally stable weather with clear skies and light winds, but freezing night-time temperatures. Thunderstorms can occur any time of year. Expect upwards of 5000ft (1500m) of elevation gain per day and allow time for acclimatisation.
What to wear // This is an exposed, high-altitude route, requiring warm and waterproof clothing, such as you'd carry for alpine hiking.
What to pack // A three- or four-season tent and sleeping bag rated to -8°C (17.6°F).
More info // bikepacking.com/routes/peru-great-divide

Opposite: floating accommodation on Lake Titicaca on the Camino del Puma

MORE LIKE THIS
ANDEAN ADVENTURES

CONES AND CANYONS

For a continuous traverse of the western Andes, the diverse Cones and Canyons links seamlessly with Peru Great Divide, for a bikepacking through-ride of more than 1429 miles (2300km). For the first few days, Cones and Canyons unfolds in a similar vein to its sister route, before descending into the cactus-studded Cotahuasi Canyon. With a cavernous depth of 11,003ft (3354m) at its lowest point – between the Coropuna and Surimana massifs – the world's deepest canyon also signals entry into the Central Volcanic Zone of the Andes; an *altiplano* region extending through Bolivia into Chile and Argentina, where conical volcanoes are a regular feature on the horizon. The beautiful colonial city of Arequipa is a pleasant location to start or finish this route, as well as being a base for ascents of the beautiful Volcan Misti at 19,127ft (5830m), or the 19,931ft (6074m) Volcan Chachani.
Start // Hwy 30A (Peru Great Divide)
Finish // Arequipa
Distance // 488 miles (785km)

CAMINO DEL PUMA

Named for the puma's importance in the mythology of the Andes, Camino del Puma continues the volcanic theme of Cones and Canyons towards Lake Titicaca, South America's largest lake. This roaming *altiplano* route can be cycled as a loop, starting and finishing in Arequipa or, conveniently, either the northern or southern legs can be followed to extend (or connect with) Cones and Canyons. Southbound, the route climbs back to the *altiplano* before passing Peru's most active cone, Volcan Ubinas (18,609ft/5672m), then descending to the colossal inland basin of Lake Titicaca. Vestiges of former South American civilizations can be seen nearby, in the form of distinctive funerary towers and the arches and monoliths of the Tiwanaku archaeological site. The southern leg has a profound contrast in elevation, as it leaves the puna-like high-altitude landscape of volcanoes and desert for the depths of the Rio Tambo canyon.
Start/finish // Arequipa
Distance // 780 miles (1255km)

MAMA COCA

For bikepackers in search of adventurous singletrack in the Bolivian Andes, Mama Coca traverses the eastern *cordilleras* via a network of dirt roads, doubletrack and shepherds' pathways. This route leads you close to some of Bolivia's highest mountains. It hops passes between two ranges, the Cordillera Real and Cordillera Quimsa Cruz, before it sidles the vast post-glacial landscape of the ranges' fringe, past azure lakes and occasional settlements. It's a route with limited resupply and sections of untracked riding and hike-a-bike, mostly at elevations above 13,123ft (4000m). Those prepared to travel light on a hardtail, or with big tyres (2.35 inch-plus), will discover a singular mountain riding experience.
Start // Tablachaca
Finish // Sorata
Distance // 286 miles (460km)

Philip Lee Harvey for Lonely Planet

THE PACIFIC COAST

With the shimmering Pacific horizon to your right and an endless ribbon of blacktop ahead, this ride traces the dramatic western edge of North America.

For cyclists who live to ride, this is a once-in-a-lifetime trip, the kind of experience that's a culmination of years of daydreaming and months of planning. I'd wanted to ride an extended stretch of the Pacific Coast Hwy for years, but the challenge is no joke: the jagged western edge of the continent has plenty of long, tough climbs and lonely stretches of blacktop that demand tenacity and self-sufficiency. But the rewards make it one of my favourite rides. Sunsets inflame the horizon, dizzying cliffs drop into the crashing surf, and redwood giants tower above. Over the years, I've ridden plenty of beautiful miles on Hwy 1, but none more exciting than the stretch between Seattle and San Francisco – an epic 980 miles (1577km) with incredible sights, great camping and plenty of diversions.

Scores of cyclists make the southbound trip on the Pacific Coast Hwy every year – mostly in the summer. I took the trip solo, but the camaraderie of the riders who gather around nightly fires at the hiker-biker campsites balanced a month of solitary days in the saddle. I met John and Margaret, a pair of sweetly sardonic teachers sporting classic '80s touring rigs, gadget-obsessed twin sisters from Victoria, BC, on their way to Los Angeles, and a handful of grizzled vagabonds attempting solo trips to Mexico and beyond. And everyone had a story – about troubleshooting a mechanical nightmare in the rain, or a truck-driving redneck with an axe to grind, or climbs that seemed never-ending.

Although I was determined to camp – there are campgrounds every 50 miles (80km) along the route with sites designated for cyclists – there are also lots of opportunities for so-called 'credit-card' touring, for riders who travel light and prefer a soft bed.

Michael Overstreet/Getty Images

The complete trip between Seattle and San Francisco can be done in 15 days (for a powerhouse cyclist with very little gear), but I took twice as long with a fully loaded touring bike. Although I met plenty of riders ticking away miles on a tight schedule, I knew quickly that this wasn't my style. The flexibility of my itinerary enabled some of the trip's rewarding memories: pints of world-class beer at the Six Rivers Brewery, naps under swaying redwood trees, and cliff-top whale-watching. In other words, little pieces of heaven.

Before leaving Seattle, I spent an extra day or two fuelling up on the city's excellent food scene. Exploring the narrow alleys and bustling stalls of Pike Place Market, I got some fancy campfire supplies for the days ahead, and dug into the city's best: steaming bowls of ramen and fresh-that-day crab.

My detours began as soon as the trip did, as I tacked on some days to cruise around the Olympic Peninsula. With misty rides on near-empty roads, the trip began with a surreal tranquility. It didn't take long to get what I came for: brackish ocean breeze and mind-blowing vistas as I cruised along spine-tingling cliffs, shovelling down snacks at quirky little roadside bodegas.

It took a long three days to get around the whole thing, but it was worth every minute: views of the Strait of Juan de Fuca, quiet farms, remote beaches and ancient forests. The camping was a superlative highlight.

Some of the best Pacific Coast lies in the coastal campgrounds of Oregon, which make up the bulk of the trip. I loved Fort Stevens State Park, a 4200-acre (1700ha) park with incredible biodiversity – displaying everything from gusty sand dunes to freshwater wetlands – and a number of historic military sites dating from the WWII fortification of the coast. Many of the coastal Oregon parks further south made me consider lingering

CONTINUING ON...

Although the ride from Seattle to San Francisco is a favourite section of the Pacific Coast, because of the quality of the scenery, the relatively quiet roads and the superlative options for camping, a cyclist with enough time and energy can keep pedalling for weeks along the Pacific. The stretch from San Francisco to Los Angeles is also a scenic stunner, though narrow shoulders and heavier traffic make it more of a challenge.

Clockwise from top: Cannon beach in Oregon; Hwy 101 from Cape Sebastian; plenty of eating options in Point Reyes Station, California; the Golden Gate Bridge. Previous spread: riding the redwood-lined Avenue of the Giants in California

Matt Munro for Lonely Planet; bluestork/Shutterstock

longer than planned, like Cape Lookout State Park, where the beachside hiker-biker sites are blissfully remote from the RV sites.

Although the camping in Oregon was the best on the trip, I discovered the most staggering vistas south of the California border. The ride here is a constant parade of awe-inspiring natural beauty, particularly when you reach the Avenue of the Giants, a paved byway surrounded on all sides by towering old-growth redwood trees. (If you're into mid-century kitsch, there are even several that you can ride through, near Leggett.)

Cycling along the edge of the so-called Lost Coast, I paused for a breather and saw the white flumes of whales, on their migration to Mexico. As I pedalled further south, I slowed for the seaside holiday towns lining the coast of Northern California. In one of them, Mendocino, there's a tidy grid of cute shops and four-star restaurants next to gorgeous headlands. I also paused for fresh seafood in Point Arena – which has an amazing bakery and a historic theatre.

By the time San Francisco drew close, I was in great shape for the most challenging section of the ride, Sonoma County. Thankfully, this also has the best views, with rock formations in the waters that rival the dramatic power of the famed Big Sur coastline south of San Francisco. Here, Hwy 1 offers paved rollers along the cliffs – three days in the rhythm of 20 minutes of lung-burning climbing followed by five minutes of glorious descending.

Reaching the coastal farms that supply San Francisco's foodie culture, I knew the end was near, and stopped into Point Reyes Station for locally made triple cream cheese at the Cowgirl Creamery. By the time I crossed the Golden Gate – 28 days and 980 miles (1577km) after my departure – this trip proved that the journey is the most magical part of travel. **NC**

"The ride is a constant parade of awe-inspiring natural beauty, particularly when you get to the Avenue of the Giants"

TOOLKIT

Start // Seattle
Finish // San Francisco
Distance // 980 miles (1577km)
Duration // Just over two weeks, though it's much more enjoyable with three weeks or more.
Getting there // If you fly in and out of Seattle, you can return with your bike via Amtrak at a modest additional fee, or ship your bike for a flat fee through REI (www.rei.com).
Where to stay // Hiker-biker campsites at the Oregon State Park System are exceptional value and they never turn away cyclists – even if the park is sold out.
What to read // *Bicycling the Pacific Coast* by Vicky Spring and Tom Kirkendall.
When to ride // You can do this trip any time of year, but summer and autumn are best.

Marisa Estivill/Shutterstock; Greg Vaughn/Alamy

Opposite: the Tahoe Flume Trail, part of the Tahoe Twirl; Old Bahia Honda Bridge on the Florida Keys Overseas Heritage Trail

MORE LIKE THIS
WATERSIDE RIDES

FLORIDA KEYS OVERSEAS HERITAGE TRAIL

Although still in development, the Florida Keys Overseas Heritage Trail (FKOHT) is shaping up to be as popular with locals as visitors. The completed trail will run for 106 miles (170km) from Key Largo to Key West and the 'overseas' part of the name is appropriate because it will cross 37 bridges – many formerly part of Henry Flagler's turn-of-the-century Florida East Coast Railway – as it follows the chain of islands that dangle from the tip of the mainland. At the time of writing, about 90 miles (145km) was ready, on a mixture of road and trail. Running alongside Hwy 1 for some of the time, the FKOHT is very much life in the slow lane, allowing you to notice Floridian details the drivers pass by, such as manta rays in the water, the Flagler-era work camp on Pigeon Key, and the No Name Pub on Big Pine Key. Tip: ride south with the wind at your back. You may prefer to rent a vehicle or take the Greyhound to travel in the other direction.
Start // Key Largo
Finish // Key West
Distance // 106 miles (170km)
Info // www.floridastateparks.org

THE TAHOE TWIRL, CALIFORNIA

Skip the crowds and circle Lake Tahoe by mountain bike through some of the most beautiful scenery in the Sierra Nevada. Rocky trails lead through pine forest and alpine meadows, with lots of camping options. The Tahoe Rim Trail (TRT) is one of the world's great hiking experiences, looping around this large, beautiful (and very busy) alpine lake through pine forests dotted with giant boulders. But on certain sections through designated wilderness areas, bicycles are banned – enter the Tahoe Twirl, an extended version of the TRT for mountain-bikers that skips the inaccessible parts and adds some sublime singletrack riding north of the lake. Although the Twirl doesn't stray far from settlements for sustenance, assistance and rest, it does rank as a route suitable only for fit and experienced bikepackers, on account of its huge elevation gain and the added hindrance of high altitude. Reno and Truckee are on Amtrak's California Zephyr train line; boxed bicycles can be checked in.
Start/finish // Anywhere along loop
Distance // 190 miles (305km)

DOWN EAST SUNRISE TRAIL, MAINE

This 87-mile (140km) section of the East Coast Greenway is all off-road – being part of the former Calais Branch rail line and now New England's longest rail trail – and is an accessible introduction to the east coast's scenic conservation areas. You might spot beaver or moose as you pedal past marshes and through forest with the Gulf of Maine a constant companion on one side, depending on whether you're heading north or south. Your other companions may be ATV drivers, horse-riders or hikers, since this is a multiuse trail (obeying the rules helps all the users get along). Typically, the Down East Sunrise Trail is divided into three stages: from the western terminus of Washington Junction to Cherryfield; from Cherryfield to Machias for the central section; and from Machias to Ayers Junction for the eastern trail.
Start/finish // Washington Junction/ Ayers Junction
Distance // 87 miles (140km)
Info // www.sunrisetrail.org

CANADA'S VIKING TRAIL

If Newfoundland's otherworldly landscapes are a chilly reminder of your insignificance, the charm of its people – plus a little riding – will soon warm you up again.

On Newfoundland's wild west coast, you can ride to a place where the Earth wears its insides outside. Roughly five million years ago, the ancient continents of Laurentia and Gondwana collided here and forced part of the Earth's upper mantle above the crust, exposing it to the sky. The Tablelands, the rare geological formation it created within Newfoundland's Gros Morne National Park, is one of the few places where you can see this phenomenon. A great way to do so is on the Viking Trail, a 310-mile (500km) cycling route that runs past it. Starting in Deer Lake, the trail's northern terminus is Saint Anthony, close to a former Viking settlement at L'Anse aux Meadows.

The island of Newfoundland is part of Newfoundland and Labrador, the province on Canada's east coast that is the traditional territory of the Mi'kmaq and Innu indigenous peoples. It was on the island's craggy and inhospitable shores that, around the year 1000, Leif Erikson landed to establish the only Viking settlement in America. Archaeologists have dated the settlement as closely as 1021. These Viking invaders were later followed by the British, in the late-15th century, the Portuguese and Basque (16th century), and the French (18th), all of whom were lured by the plentiful cod in North Atlantic waters.

The cod fisheries kept the province in food and trade for centuries after that, until the industry collapsed, more or less overnight, in 1992. In spite of ongoing economic challenges, the region's extreme conditions and geographic isolation continue to shape a unique culture, one of mutual support, disarming warmth – and salty humour.

From Deer Lake we took the ferry to Woody Point, hopping back on our bikes and on to Bonne Bay Rd, where I white-knuckled the descent towards a Mars-like landscape, the wind trying all the while to unseat me. Riding here seems to challenge both body and mind. On one side of the road is the Tablelands' barren, rust-coloured terrain, formed of igneous peridotite in which only the hardiest vegetation survives; on the other, a vibrant green landscape seemingly of somewhere else

Robert Harding Video /Shutterstock; EB Adventure Photography/Shutterstock

entirely. It's hard not to be awestruck and, in the face of such geological marvels, feel a little insignificant.

From the Tablelands we continued through Gros Morne, scrambling close to 3280ft (1000m) to take in views of the Long Range Mountains so perfect, they looked enhanced by AI. Back at sea level, we headed for Western Brook Pond, a fjord that was cut off from the sea by glacial activity and is now considered a 'fjord lake', the sort of spectacular natural feature which on the Viking Trail is commonplace.

On the west coast of Newfoundland, the prevailing wind blows from the southwest. If you catch it you'll fly; if you don't, you'll take a pummelling. For several days we rode, or tried to ride, into winds of 30mph (50kph), sometimes gusting to 44mph (70kph). It's part of the route that hones your sense of determination. The further north we got, the shorter the trees and smaller the villages became, yet the daylight hours and the warmth and hospitality grew. More than a few residents stopped to enquire why, in the name of God, we were biking up such windy roads – cyclists here need to be hardy, first and last.

Just ask Kevin Flynn, a former president of Bicycle Newfoundland and Labrador (BNL), a non-profit organisation that promotes cycling in the region. Of his numerous rides in this part of the world, Flynn particularly recalls cycling the Viking Trail in 2016, part of his ongoing mission to bike to all corners of the province.

'To be honest,' he tells me, 'we simply weren't prepared. Going down long, steep hills in Gros Morne National Park, we encountered such severe headwinds, that often we'd be travelling no faster than 7–9mph (12–15kph). I looked forward to pedalling up the hills just for a break.' In true Newfoundland

OVERNIGHT ON QUIRPON ISLAND

An unforgettable experience in this remote region is an overnight on Quirpon Island. To get there, hop a Zodiac from the town of Quirpon, then walk the boardwalk to Quirpon Island's northern shore, picking bakeapples and partridgeberries along the way. Home to a century-old lighthouse, the building has been restored into a 10-room bed and breakfast, from where you can see the lights of Labrador, as well as watch whales and, occasionally, passing icebergs.

Clockwise from top: a Viking interior at L'Anse aux Meadows; Western Brook Pond; Fox Point Lighthouse and a moose with calf near Saint Anthony, Newfoundland

Jukka Jantunen/Shutterstock; Patrick Jennings/Shutterstock

style, however, Flynn recalls how just a few hours later the wind changed direction. Then, perhaps like the Vikings before him, he found himself being blown along the coast.

We encountered similarly changeable conditions during our own ride north, not least on the 217-mile (350km) stretch from Western Brook Pond to Saint Anthony. At 37 miles (40km) out, it's the closest town to the site of Leif Erikson's one-time American outpost. More than once was I glad for my hat, gloves and raincoat, not to mention a hip-flask of whisky. Along the route, we passed abandoned houses and fishing stations, victims of the cod collapse and sad symbols of the livelihoods lost here. But we passed signs of resilience too: the dozens of fenced roadside gardens growing cabbage, carrots and onions. The basic ingredients, in fact, for Newfoundland's traditional Jiggs dinner, named for an Irish-American comic-strip character popular for the best part of 100 years.

In addition to the spruce and lupins that also proliferate here, such indications of renewal remind you of the value of endurance. As does the Viking village at L'Anse aux Meadows, although these days it is a 'recreated' Norse settlement made friendly for tourists. Ditching our bikes, we headed into the well-captioned monument to ponder just how Leif Erikson and his crew reached here more than a thousand years ago. To stand in the footsteps of Vikings at the end of our own windy, if two-wheeled, voyage seemed poignant. If this part of the world doesn't pique your interest in the vastness of the globe and humanity's desire to explore it, it's doubtful anywhere will. **CP**

gnagel/Getty Images; Curtis Watson/Shutterstock

Previous page: an aerial view of Saint Anthony; Bonne Bay Rd

TOOLKIT

Start/finish // Deer Lake
Distance // 310 miles (500km)
Getting there // Daily direct flights from Toronto, Halifax and St. John's to Deer Lake. There are also flights from Saint Anthony to Deer Lake.
When to go // June to August.
What to wear // Regular cycling gear is fine but be ready for changeable weather.
What to pack // Waterproof jacket and trousers, windbreaker, gloves, neck collar, hat.
Where to stay // Inns, such as Neddie's Harbour Inn and the Tides Inn, or simpler spots like Entente Cordiale in Portland Creek. There are also campsites.
Where to eat // The Cat Stop in Norris Point, or Seaside Restaurant in Trout River. Northern Delight has great fish and chips.
More info // Freewheeling Adventures offers tours.

Opposite: Reine village beneath the Lofoten Wall

MORE LIKE THIS
RUGGED COASTAL ROUTES

LOFOTEN, NORWAY

The Lofoten Islands is a 463 sq mi (1200 sq km) archipelago of glacial fjords, sharp peaks and secluded beaches nestled in the Norwegian Sea. Located on the 68th parallel (north), it's further north than Fairbanks in Alaska, but the Gulf Stream turns the islands lush in summer and in winter keeps temperatures at around 0°C (32°F). Arriving in Svolvær, take National Cycle Route 1 along the coast, southwest to Moskenes island. On the way, stop in at the quaint village of Henningsvær to check out the stockfish or *hjell* drying on racks, then nip in for some warming *bacalao* at the popular Klatrekaféen. In Reine village, scale the near-2000 'Sherpa' stairs for 360-degree views of the archipelago. It's a thriving four-season destination, but visit from late May to early July to ride beneath the midnight sun.
Start // Svolvær
Finish // Moskenes
Distance // 78 miles (125km)
Info // www.nordnorge.com

HAIDA GWAII, BRITISH COLUMBIA

Home of the indigenous Haida people for more than 10,000 years, Haida Gwaii is a remote archipelago that's a seven-hour ferry trip, or short flight, from Prince Rupert. At low tide, Agate Beach on Graham Island reveals long, hard-packed sand spits jutting into the north Pacific. Ride out to Rose Spit, birthplace of the Haida Nation, where humans were set free from captivity by a sacred raven. At Skidegate you can visit the Haida Heritage Centre to admire towering totem poles, and afterwards Jags coffee shop. Bike north to Tlell, Port Clements and Masset, stopping at Balance Rock, Jungle Beach and Pure Lake Park. You'll also see eagles, more Haida art and majestic old-growth forests. Haida Gwaii has become a bit of a hub for mountain bikers and gravel cyclists, so the more adventurous can hook up with those communities to explore the many logging roads that criss-cross the island.
Start // Skidegate
Finish // Masset
Distance // 62 miles (100km)
Info // www.bikepacking.com

WILD ATLANTIC WAY, IRELAND

The 1600-mile (2600km) Wild Atlantic Way takes cyclists along Ireland's western shore, starting in Muff. Looping north by way of Malin Head, and then south, there are numerous route options, broadly divided by county: Donegal; Sligo and Leitrim; Mayo; Galway; Clare and Limerick; Kerry; and Cork. Too many to number here, sights include coastal villages, natural arches and medieval architecture, as well as mountain passes, especially to the south near Kinsale, the trail's end. Well signposted and in places quite challenging, the Atlantic Way for cyclists mostly follows rural and secondary roads, through a wide variety of terrain. Highlights include MacGillycuddy's Reeks and the Iveragh Peninsula (Kerry), the climb of Caha Pass and Dromberg stone circle (Cork). You can also hop off to walk the Cliffs of Moher (Clare), where you might also spot seals and dolphins. Plus, more pub-hopping than is possible in a lifetime.
Start // Muff
Finish // Kinsale
Distance // 1600 miles (2600km)

MAINE'S EAST COAST GREENWAY

The ECG expertly guides riders through town and country, including one of the Eastern Seaboard's best off-road wilderness trails – and there are plans for more, reports Ethan Gelber.

The magic of long-distance cycle touring captured my imagination the summer after I turned 16. That was when my parents trusted me to take my first solo bike adventure – a month-long spin in New England. The final leg was a 150-mile (240km) pedal from Maine's southern tip to our Midcoast home near Belfast. All those years ago, I used Coastal Rte 1, already then a busy summer thoroughfare. As a practiced Maine hand, I knew to expect tough hills and town traffic, since Rte 1 paralleled the up-and-down coast and passed directly through maritime communities that were attracting more and more holidaymakers. But I loved the rolling landscapes, the sea-centred villages wrapped around their working wharves and the weatherworn old-timers who paused to ask, with genuine interest, where you were headed before spinning a yarn about how quickly Maine was changing.

Several decades later and a few years out of the saddle, I hatched the idea of a new biking beginning by revisiting my first epic ride in Maine and recapturing that sense of place and self-propelled travel magic. There would, however, be one big difference: instead of battling holiday congestion along Rte 1, I'd commit to a newer, bike-friendly boulevard – the East Coast Greenway (ECG).

I was thrilled right from the start, as the terrain of southern Maine immediately set the tone for the rest of the trip: a delightful mix of the usually unbusy, well-paved back roads in small urban concentrations like Biddeford and Saco, green-lawned suburban villages full of typical clapboard houses, and lengthy rural plunges along forests and fields dotted with working farms. These fit around two shaded and gently graded rail trails of hardpacked earth leading across woodlands and wetlands, such as Maine's largest saltwater marsh at Scarborough.

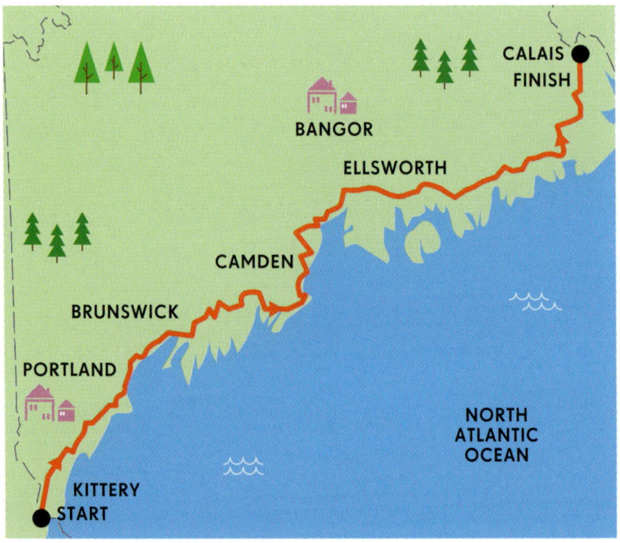

zimmytws/Shutterstock

To make the route even more enticing, the ECG in Maine is generously signposted; there's little need to consult maps at every turn. Leaving Kittery, the way markers are even paired with those of the Eastern Trail (ET) and US Bike Route 1 (USBR1). The ECG actually follows the ET, a 65-mile (105km) course with 22 off-road miles (35km), all the way to South Portland. (USBR1 is another in-the-works Florida-to-Maine cycle passage, albeit one that is entirely on-road; it regularly intersects the ECG.)

A lot of this I already knew. I'd been reading about the full ECG, a 3000-mile (4828km), multiuse trail system tracing the length of the Eastern Seaboard between Key West in Florida and Calais on the Canadian border in Maine. I was wowed by the resourceful nonprofit push of the East Coast Greenway Alliance to identify existing off-road paths – mostly municipal-, county- and state-owned rail trails – and stitch them together with two-wheel-tolerant, on-road routes selected for their traffic levels and speeds, shoulder widths and/or pavement quality, to complete the end-to-end connectivity.

This was on my mind as I slipped effortlessly into the city of Portland, Maine's largest. The ECG deliberately aims for major population centres, to connect people to them and vice versa. In fact, once in a metropolis, the routing adopts city cycling infrastructure, such as Portland's waterside Eastern Promenade, to cut through its busy, well-resourced and cultured core. This also helps with pacing. I planned for an average of about 60 miles a day, but with so many towns along the way, longer and shorter distances are easily possible.

"The ECG deliberately aims for major population centres, to connect people to them and vice versa"

Beyond Portland, I resumed riding on secondary suburban and rural roads, rising to hilltop pastures or timberland and dipping back down to cosy coastal inlets. Many of the byways were signed as local bike routes with large posted reminders to drivers that Maine law requires them to leave 3ft (1m) of space when passing cyclists. I rarely felt at risk.

In the pretty college town of Brunswick, I had to choose between the inland ECG 'spine' route or the coastal 'complementary' one. The inland incursion promised riverside rides, with traffic-free segments paralleling the Androscoggin and Kennebec rivers, not to mention the lure of cities like Lewiston, Augusta and Bangor. But I stayed true to my youthful itinerary and took the seaside swing.

Away from the 'spine' route, however, three things happened: the challenging hills of Midcoast Maine really kicked in, while

Sean Pavone/Shutterstock

A CAR-FREE ECG?

The ECG Alliance is building new off-road segments at an average cost of $1 million per mile. More than 940 miles are on protected paths today, but the goal is to make it all car-free, even as it traverses 450 communities in 15 states (plus Washington DC) and within 5 miles of 25 million people. Incredibly, the ECG is arguably the most ambitious infrastructure project in the US.

Left to right: the waterfront of Portland, Maine; taing a break in Portland. Previous spread: the harbour at Camden, Maine

the off-road respites and ECG signage disappeared, obliging greater reliance on the ECG Alliance's (excellent) web-based mapping tool, which can be adapted for use on mobile platforms. I ended up making frequent map-check stops, embracing the need to be sure of the way as a perfect excuse for pausing between climbs.

None of this dampened my enjoyment of rolling – panting and sweating! – through gorgeous green country and noteworthy towns: Bath and its memorable architecture; art-rich Rockland, home of the Farnsworth Art Museum; touristy Camden and its windjammer-filled harbour; and historic, maritime Belfast and Searsport.

The ECG's two routes merge at Bucksport, shortly after which, in Ellsworth, the 85-mile (137km) Down East Sunrise Trail begins. At present best suited to fat tyres and self-sufficient bikers, this off-road traverse of Downeast Maine's thick forests, salmon rivers and scenic national wildlife lands (keep an eye out for moose) is considered to be the most spectacular wilderness on the ECG.

In Calais, facing the Canadian border and the final yards of the ECG, it was the idea of new beginnings rather than endings that bubbled up in my mind. After about 350 miles (563km) in Maine, including more than 130 miles (209km) of protected greenway, I was ready to do as Forrest Gump had done: turn around and head for Florida. Only 3000 miles to go! **EG**

TOOLKIT

Start // Kittery, Maine

Finish // Calais, Maine

Distance // 367 miles (590km) on inland 'spine' route or 332 miles (534km) on coastal 'complementary' route

Getting there // Kittery is just across the Piscataqua River from Portsmouth, New Hampshire, which is accessible by car and coach from airport, train and bus terminals in Portland, Maine, and Boston, Massachusetts.

Where to stay/eat // Along the Maine ECG there is no shortage of markets, restaurants, campgrounds and hotels, though lodging should be booked ahead in high season.

When to ride // May through October is the best season for cycling. Summer months tend to be warmer and drier, while autumn is especially beautiful when the foliage changes colour.

More info // For maps, cue sheets and other ECG details, see www.greenway.org/states/maine

Opposite: the Cape Cod Rail Trail passing through Nickerson State Park

MORE LIKE THIS
COASTAL NEW ENGLAND RIDES

CADILLAC CHALLENGE LOOP, MAINE

Mt Desert Island is home to Acadia National Park, beloved for its gorgeous and dramatic nature: high and rocky Atlantic coast headlands and seven peaks above 1000ft (305m). This alone conveys what's in store for a lengthy ride around the island, complete with a circuit of the 27-mile (43km) Park Loop Rd and climb to breath-taking summit views from the 1530ft (466m) Cadillac Mountain – this is the first place in the US to spy the sunrise (in the fall and winter). For more than 35 years, the Cadillac Challenge Century, a free organized rain-or-shine ride held on the first Sunday in October, takes this all in, surrounded by the changing colors of fall foliage. Also, ask ahead if the park will have its mid-spring Bike in Acadia month that keeps roads closed to motorized vehicles.
Start/End // Bar Harbor
Distance // 100 miles (161km)
Info // www.cadillac challengecentury.com

CAPE COD RAIL TRAIL, MASSACHUSETTS

Cape Cod is that crooked curlicue of Massachusetts reaching east into the Atlantic Ocean. Largely low-lying and fringed by pristine sandy beaches, including the protected 40-mile-long (64km) stretch of Cape Cod National Seashore, it is a very popular summer holiday destination. And, to the great satisfaction of outdoor sports folk, the Cape Cod Rail Trail slices right through the middle of it on an old, converted railroad right of way. Designed as a multiuse path, with a well-graded and smooth surface, it is a favorite of walkers, runners, skaters and cyclists eager to burn some calories without getting scorched by vehicular traffic. Bike shops set right on the trail in Yarmouth, Dennis, Brewster, Orleans and Wellfleet promise service and rentals for all would-be two-wheelers without equipment.
Start // South Yarmouth
End // Wellfleet
Distance // 25 miles (40km)
Info // www.capecodbikeguide.com/railtrail.asp

WESTERLY TO WATCH HILL, RHODE ISLAND

Tucked into a coastal corner of New England, Rhode Island doesn't draw as much cycling attention as its larger neighbors, but it packs in plenty, especially for the smallest state in the US. One 50-mile (80km) route along rural roads well loved by the local Narragansett Bay Wheelmen club takes in the estates, estuaries and beaches of the southwest shores. Shortcuts along this loop can reduce the mileage a bit, but mean missing out on some of the most scenic and challenging parts, like the cove-line and oceanfront ride that includes views of Block Island Sound from the Watch Hill Coast Guard Station, or some lovely climbs in the hills overlooking the Pawcatuck River. For more details about this ride and others, visit the cycling club's website.
Start/End // Ashaway
Distance // 50 miles (80km)
Info // www.nbwclub.org

ASIA

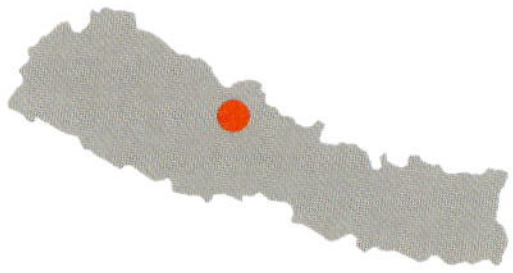

RIDING THE ANNAPURNA CIRCUIT

An arduous, high-altitude journey on Nepal's legendary Himalayan loop, from lowland jungle tracks to one of the world's highest passes, with killer views of 8000m (26,250ft) peaks.

The trail crunched beneath our feet as we pushed our bikes above 16,404ft (5000m), beneath purple dawn skies. It was at 6.30am when the stone hut appeared ahead, a beacon emerging in the light of a golden daybreak. As Annapurna's wonders began to reveal themselves fully, the prospect of a seat – not to be underestimated at this altitude – as well as a steaming flask of tea was in sight.

Following staccato sleep at Thorong Phedi base camp (14,764ft/4500m), we had risen in darkness, setting off with mild headaches, in a world limited to head-torch beams battered by frozen drizzle. There was solace in the packhorse-bell soundtrack, just as there was in the lights from others in our convoy on that first half-mile of sheer switchbacks.

By the time the sun made its warming appearance, we'd been on the move for a couple of hours but travelled barely two miles (3km). But, given our thin-air slowness since we'd started this Himalayan odyssey, we knew the day's three-mile (5km) 'queen stage' could not be done any faster. It would take us over Thorong La, a 17,769ft (5416m) pass and the highest part of our ride.

Regroup at aforementioned stone hut, then head up the last 500ft to the col together... That, at 4am, had been our decision over steaming porridge at the base-camp breakfast table. And now here we were, re-energised after our stop at Thorong High Camp teashop, and ready for a final push. A glance at the rocks weighing down the hut's sheet-roofing was a reminder of how adverse the conditions could get this high in the Himalayas.

Yet that morning, there was a calmness as we enjoyed our penultimate break before the pass. Every point on our journey thus far had been building to this moment, and the realisation we would soon be crossing one of the highest navigable passes in the world, the crescendo of the Annapurna Circuit.

We had arrived into a chaotic Kathmandu during Tihar – the five-day Hindu festival of lights celebrated in Nepal – and were soon accepting garlands of marigolds from strangers on the street. The golden flowers were everywhere, cherished as symbols of light, energy, creativity and enthusiasm. The celebrations made a perfect segue into our Nepalese journey, culturally and socially – we were frequently invited to dance.

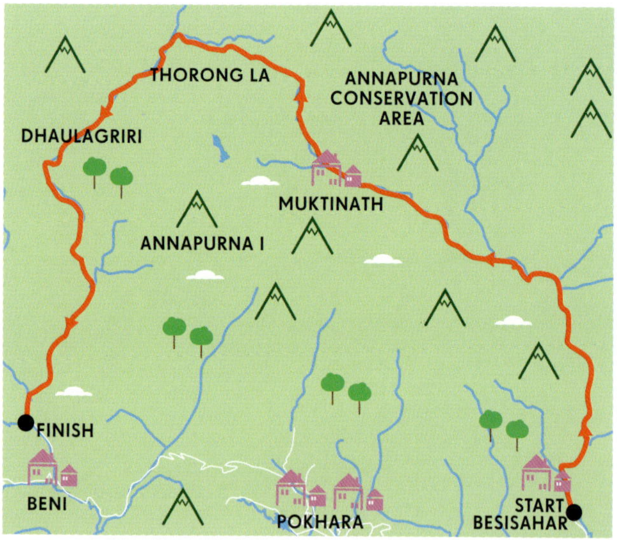

Stefan Amato; Moroz Nataliya/Shutterstock

Following a welcome ride in Kathmandu's surrounding hills, and with our ceremonial 'khata' scarves around our necks and bikes loaded onto pick-up trucks, we rolled out west. The 109-mile (175km) road-trip portion of our journey was slow going, but eventually brought us to the vibrant, paddy-terraced town of Besisahar, and the start of our ride on the Annapurna Circuit.

Established in the late 1970s to develop tourism in the region, the Circuit is a 137-mile (220km) route through the heart of the Nepali Himalaya. An inverted u-shape, it traditionally starts in Besisahar and ends in Nayapul, although modern hikers and bikers can opt for a number of variants. The route circumnavigates the mighty Annapurna I (26,545ft/8091m) and several of its smaller siblings, and also provides spectacular views of neighbouring 'eight-thousander' peaks, notably Dhaulagiri (26,795ft/8167m) and Manaslu (26,781ft/8163m).

The original route traced pilgrim paths connecting villages through two major valleys, Marsyangdi and Kali Gandaki, with the Circuit topping out at 17,769ft (5416m) at Thorong La. Crucially, the pass is the only route linking the holy town of Muktinath, roughly the Circuit's halfway point and of huge significance to both Hindus and Buddhists, with that of Manang and all destinations to south and east.

Whether hiking or biking, the altitude means it's sensible to start slowly. For the first few days, we rode from agricultural lowlands at 2297ft (700m), up through jungle gorges, to around 9843ft (3000m), from where the Annapurna region really unfolds.

ANNAPURNA – THE SILENT KILLER

Coming three years before Sir Edmund Hillary and Tenzing Norgay made the first ascent of Everest in 1953, Maurice Herzog's successful climb of Annapurna – with fellow Frenchman Louis Lachenal – was the first ascent of any the world's 14 peaks above 8000m (26,247ft). The last 'eight-thousander' to fall was Shishapangma, in 1964, yet Annapurna remains the most dangerous, with one death for every three climbers who make it to the top.

Clockwise from top: refuelling; central Kathmandu; the summit of Thorong La

Stefan Amato

We rode on, pushing higher, arriving in Manang on the evening of day three. Perched at 11,545ft (3519m), Manang is where the road ends, giving way to rougher tracks. It is also a rest-day town and a place to acclimatise to the thinning air. From a teahouse rooftop, we looked out on the valley below, dotted with monasteries. The treeline stopped at around 13,780ft (4200m), replaced by limestone shrubland. At around 15,748ft (4800m), the snowline started in earnest, continuing all the way to imposing seracs, an ethereal display of Himalayan splendour.

From Manang, we struck out for Thorong La by rising early, our days having already developed a rhythm. Dawn signalled adventure, packing bikes in the shadow of mighty Gangapurna before riding north, through Manang's old town, passing stupas whose prayer wheels we spun for good luck. The early start also ensured we avoided the notorious winds that blew up in the afternoon.

When we made it to the top of Thorong La, we took our time sipping tea, perhaps because it meant prolonging the inevitable. The 8530ft (2600m) descent was exhilarating, delivering us to yet more new worlds, of the Upper Mustang and Kali Gandaki Valley. But the paddy-field grass is always greener and it was only when we arrived back in 'civilization' that we realised what a privilege it had been to witness Annapurna's glories.

'Annapurna, to which we had gone empty-handed, was a treasure on which we should live the rest of our days.' Thus wrote Maurice Herzog, the French mountaineer who, in 1950, made the first ascent of Annapurna I. Leaving the Annapurna region on the boneshaking drive to Kathmandu, I couldn't put it better. **SA**

Stefan Amato

Previous spread: prayer wheels in Bhratang village; Thorong La

TOOLKIT

Start // Besisahar
Finish // Beni
Distance // 136 miles (220km)
Getting there // The main hub is Pokhara; fly from Kathmandu, or else road transfer.
When to go // Pre-monsoon (March to May), or post-monsoon (September-November); Tihar, the Hindu festival of lights, is a special time to be in Nepal.
What to wear // Kit for all seasons, plus riding shoes you can walk in comfortably over technical ground.
What to pack // Breathable layers and packable insulation, plus a snood for dusty trails. A water filter, too, and books and cards for evenings/downtime.
Where to stay // Teahouses and lodges.
Where to eat // Teahouses, often with impressively extensive menus; the regional staple is *dal bhat*.
More info // A full-suspension mountain bike is essential, as is technical riding experience is if you want to ride more and walk less.

Opposite: the Gata Loops on the Manali-Leh road

MORE LIKE THIS
RIDES FEATURING HIGH HIMALAYAN PASSES

UPPER MUSTANG, NEPAL

Starting out from Kagbeni at the head of the Kali Gandaki valley, accessing the extraordinary Upper Mustang region means journeying north, towards Tibet, into one of the most remote and isolated regions in the Himalaya. Situated in the rain-shadow of Dhaulagiri, the seventh-highest mountain in the world at 26,795ft (8167m), this area is special thanks to its arid desertscapes. This 44-mile (71km) route to the walled town of Lo Manthang includes Buddhist monasteries and mystical caves, along with prayer flags and gompas (monasteries) galore. Indeed, it's worth planning a trip to Upper Mustang to coincide with the Tiji festival, a 300-year-old Buddhist celebration which typically takes place in May. This being the Himalayas, there's also a handful of 13,000ft (4000m) passes that need crossing – note that permits are usually required to visit the Upper Mustang region.

Start // Kagbeni
Finish // Lo Manthang
Distance // 44 miles (71km)

SPITI AND KINNAUR VALLEYS, INDIA

Starting in Manali, this route through the remote Spiti and Kinnaur valleys makes for a memorable ride, south and east to Shimla, starting with the 14,931ft (4551m) Kunzum Pass. 'Spiti' translates as 'middle land', a reference to the valley's location between two mountain ranges, the Great Himalaya and the Zanskar. Villages dot the route, including that of Reckong Peo, popular with pilgrims given its views of Kailasa, the mountain said to be home to Shiva, for travelling cyclists, this also means homestays and increased resupply opportunities. Local Spiti people practice Tibetan Buddhism, so look out for Key Monastery, the largest in these parts. Alongside the main valley you'll find dirt and gravel roads, with lesser-ridden options on the other side of the Spiti River. To ride here you'll need the Inner Line Permit (ILP) required in certain parts of India.

Start // Manali
Finish // Shimla
Distance // 375 miles (604km)

MANALI-LEH, INDIA

Known as the 'land of high passes', this route to Ladakh averages a heady altitude of 13,123ft (4000m). Located in the borderlands of India, Pakistan and China, Ladakh's strategic importance continues to this day. Starting the ride in Manali 6726ft (2050m) allows for incremental acclimatisation as you climb a succession of increasingly high passes – Rohtang La (13,051ft/3978m), Baralacha La (15,912ft/4850m), Nakeela (15,548ft/4739m) and Lachlung La (16,598ft/5059m) – before descending into Leh. From here it's possible to ride on to Khardung La (17,582ft/5359m), the world's second-highest pass reachable by motor vehicles. Similar to the high passes of the European Alps, these routes are only rideable between May and September, due to snow. The building of tunnels will keep some roads open year-round, removing some of the traffic (and all the romance). Inner Line Permit (ILP) needed.

Start // Manali
Finish // Leh
Distance // 250 miles (402km)

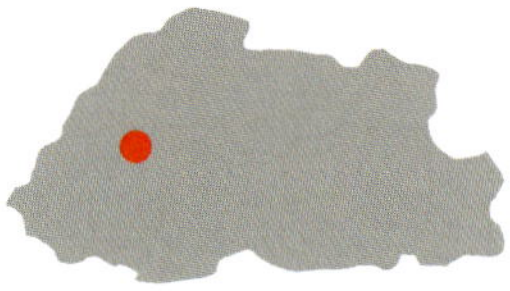

SPIRITUAL BIKING IN BHUTAN

From lung-busting climbs to 'impossible' cliffside monasteries and chilli-fuelled nights, the joy of mountain biking in Bhutan delivers adventure that lingers long after the final descent.

It was just before lunch when Mark cartwheeled over his bars. Dave followed him into a bush seconds later. By the end of that first trail in Bhutan, my ribs hurt; not so much from crashing but from laughing. None of us had known quite what we'd signed up for but when you find yourself skidding down high-altitude hiking paths disguised as singletrack, or tangling with giant rhododendrons while covered in dust, the only thing to do is to grin and keep riding.

That was my introduction to Bhutan; wild trails, thin air and pure joy. I've ridden bikes across Nepal and Tibet but Bhutan had sat at the top of my wish list for years. The thought of riding in a place so rich in spirituality exerted a pull I couldn't ignore. I'd brought with me a mixed bag, not just bike kit but nerves and excitement. Having jumped on this trip with six other riders who looked like they'd been born on bikes, my own training amounted to just a few rides at sea level. Now we were starting our days at 8200ft (2500m), my backpack crammed with snacks and cameras, my legs and lungs wondering what had hit them.

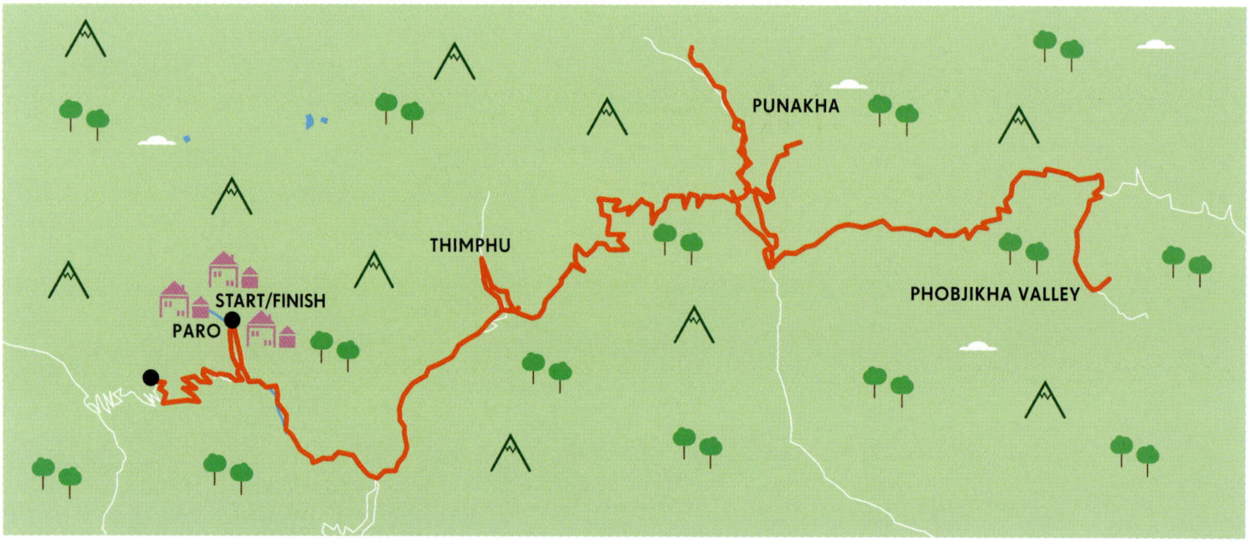

Kristina Vackova

"This time off the bike allowed us to absorb the country's rhythms, its rituals and landscapes"

Bhutan won me over instantly. Landing in Paro felt like slipping into another world. The tiny airport, its buildings more temples than terminal, sits deep within a narrow Himalayan valley. It's located at 7332ft (2235m) and surrounded by snowy peaks – only a handful of pilots are qualified to land here. When you're welcomed with ceremonial scarves as you step off the plane, you know the trip is going to be something special.

Our guide, Pelden Dorji, also greeted us with cold beers and a grin wide enough to cut through our jet lag. He's been showing riders the trails here for years, blending culture with adventure so seamlessly that you soon forget you're on a tour. Joining him was 'S.T.', with a quiet demeanour but built like a mountain goat (something that would come in handy).

Some trails in Bhutan are purpose-built for bikes, but many are pilgrim paths, forest shortcuts or goat tracks draped in prayer flags. Either way, they rode fast and loose, and meant we were only ever just in control. Dry leaves hid rocks and roots, sending us skidding and laughing so hard we could barely breathe. On one occasion, Mark even managed an uphill crash, tangling bars with Eilis before toppling headfirst onto a rock. Thankfully, the helmet gods smiled.

Evenings were for one thing only: chilli. In Bhutan, chilli is not so much a garnish as the main event. Dishes had us sweating, only for us be told, with a smile: 'Oh, this one's not spicy.' Beer never tasted so good. Each morning we went again, driving from valley to valley, selecting the best trails in each.

Even with so many to choose from, those around Punakha stood out. A scenic city of rice terraces and painted houses, it's also revered for its association with Drukpa Kunley, a maverick, 15th-century Buddhist monk known as the 'Divine Madman', whose legacy lives on in the giant phallic murals that decorate buildings here. A symbol of fertility, the first mural I saw covered an entire house, and pretty soon I was spotting the images everywhere.

The subsequent 'Madman Trail' lived up to its billing. We pushed our bikes up to 11,483ft (3500m), lungs burning, then dropped into another leaf-strewn chute that had us whooping with joy and clinging on for dear life. Mark, inevitably, provided comic relief by flipping into another bush. At the bottom, we lay in the dust, like kids after a playground brawl, high on oxygen-deprivation and adrenaline. Though the trails varied, S.T. was a constant. He made the climbs look flat, happily hauled extra backpacks, and still had the legs to push you uphill while pedalling his own bike.

Between rides, we explored more of Bhutan. We visited

STRAIGHT AND TRUE

Archery, or *dha*, was declared Bhutan's national sport only as recently as 1971. With its military origins, however, it dates back almost a millennium here, and today remains a centrepiece of the country's cultural identity. Matches take place using bamboo bows, with archers taking aim at targets set as far away as 475ft (145m). Opponents try to unsettle each other by chanting and dancing, while teammates break into song to celebrate a hit.

Clockwise from top: get ready for wobbly bridges; a local truck; rhododendron flowers. Previous spread: Punakha Dzong, one of Bhutan's most beautiful; steep switchbacks near Paro

Kristina Vackova

dzongs (fort-monasteries) where monks chanted hypnotically, watched archery matches (the sport here dates back to the 10th century; see panel), or else sat down to generous meals that seemed never-ending. This time off the bike allowed us to absorb the country's rhythms, its rituals and landscapes, and something of the spiritual presence that seemed to follow us from trail to trail. It turns out the King of Bhutan is a mountain biker. Rumour has it he's the only man in the country with an e-MTB. With royal approval, and trails that feel like they were dreamt up by mischievous spirits, it makes sense that mountain biking is growing here.

Our final challenge loomed, in the Paro valley: a climb to 13,123ft (4000m), followed by a 6561ft (2000m) descent to the famous Paro Taktsang Monastery, or Tiger's Nest. It's one of those places you've seen a thousand times in photos but visiting for real still takes your breath away. Perched on a cliff, clinging to the rocks, it looks almost architecturally impossible. We arrived sweaty and bruised, stuffing our shorts into knee pads to appear sufficiently respectful, and to meet the monastery's modest dress code.

The last descent was the stuff of legend. Steep hiking paths turned into singletrack plunges, rocks (and tourists) appearing from nowhere, my fellow riders yelling warnings and encouragement in equal measure. My legs were jelly, my head pounding, but I didn't want it to end.

Looking back, Bhutan gave me what I didn't know I was looking for. I'd expected stillness, maybe some spiritual enlightenment. Instead, I found it mid-trail; lungs burning, tyres skidding, mind stripped of everything except the turn in front of me. That, I realised, is its own kind of meditation. *Tashi delek*, and may your helmet be as lucky as Mark's. **KV**

Kristina Vackova

TOOLKIT

Start/finish // Paro
Distance // 12–22 miles (20-35km) per day
Getting there // Flights to Paro International, via a gateway hub such as Delhi or Kathmandu, or Bangkok or Singapore.
When to go // April–May or October–November, avoiding summer rains and winter cold.
What to wear // MTB trail gear is a necessity, including gloves, knee pads and elbows pads and, most definitely, a helmet.
What to pack // Wicking layers (you'll be working hard), plus plenty of lightweight insulation; it's the Himalayas after all. A dual-suspension enduro bike suited to long climbs, hike-a-bike sections, and steep descents. Bring essential spares, as parts are hard to source.
Where to stay // Accommodation is plentiful. Bhutan's 'high-value, low-volume' model includes tourist fees to fund healthcare, education, and conservation (and limit over-tourism). Arrive early enough to acclimatise to the high altitude, seek advice.
More info // www.mountainbikeworldwide.com

Opposite: rice paddies in Bhutan's Phobjikha Valley; Nagarkot in Nepal

MORE LIKE THIS
SACRED RIDES OF THE HIMALAYAS

BHUTAN XC

For those who'd rather cover ground than chase technical descents, Bhutan offers superb cross-country riding that blends endurance with culture. The journey begins in Thimphu, where trails like the K-C and Wangditse wind through pine forests and past landmarks. From there, rides link monasteries, valleys and villages. Dochu La Pass opens to panoramic Himalayan views before dropping into the rice terraces of Punakha, while suspension bridges, botanical gardens, and centuries-old temples punctuate the journey. Further east, Gangte/Phobjikha Valley delivers some of the country's most scenic riding, with trails tracing bamboo forests, marshlands and prayer-flagged ridgelines. Evenings bring chilli-fuelled meals, cold beers and warm hospitality in family-run heritage homes, or village guesthouses. It's a ride that rewards power in the legs and curiosity of mind, building distance while discovering Bhutan's traditions, and serene beauty.
Start // Thimpu
Finish/distance // various

NEPAL ENDURO

If you want supreme mountain biking with Himalayan drama, Nepal delivers riding on an epic scale. Just east of Kathmandu, Nagarkot's enduro trails wind through forested ridges and technical sections, home to the Asian Enduro Series and an Enduro World Series qualifier. Then head west to Pokhara and on into the Mustang Valley, where the Himalayas feel impossibly close. Switchbacks above 13,123ft (4000m) lead to vertical-kilometre descents across flowy singletrack, dirt roads and rugged forest paths. Here, trails weave between orchards, stone villages and some of the world's highest peaks; Annapurna and Dhaulagiri loom like giants. Sections are occasionally linked by suspension bridges swaying in the wind, offering their own kind of challenge for those not too comfortable with sheer drops to roaring water beneath. Get your breath back over *dal bhat*, apple pie and rooftop tea with locals. Big climbs, bigger views, and trails to match.
Start // Kathmandu
Finish/distance // various

EASTERN TIBET BACKCOUNTRY

Eastern Tibet delivers Himalayan epic-ness far from the crowds. Start in Kangding and climb through an alpine valley to the Panpan Pass at 13,778ft (4200m), before dropping through 11 miles (17km) of flowing singletrack back to your guesthouse. Tagong ridge follows, with long switchback climbs and ridgeline traverses framed by Yala Peak and neighbouring Gongga, then free-ride descents through alpine meadows. Yala, when you reach it, pushes you higher still, with several passes above 13,778ft (4200m), rewarded by fast, technical descents across grasslands and rocky trails. From Yulongxi valley, the Zemei Pass rises above 14,764ft (4500m), offering different views of Gongga, before a 19-mile (30km) descent off the Tibetan Plateau, crossing multiple climate zones. This is remote, less-visited riding with extended climbs, massive drops, and technical challenges at every turn. Off-grid guesthouses dot the route, offering a taste of traditional Tibetan and Chinese cuisine and a chance to pause in the quiet of the mountains. Challenging, scenic, unforgettable.
Start // Kangding
Finish/distance // various

Tomasz Wozniak/Shutterstock; Amazing Aerial/Alamy

ACROSS SOUTH KOREA

Purpose-built to welcome cyclists, South Korea's bike paths help riders indulge in a wealth of cuisine and history – with the spicy side-dish of the 'Korean Alps'.

PK289/Shutterstock

When was the last time you pedalled out of a major city and thought it easy and fun? My guess is never. Finding a decent escape route from a major metropolis is the cyclist's holy grail. Just thinking about the number of minutes and potholes it takes to get out of Toronto, the city of five million people where I live, is enough to make me consider cancelling my ride.

But in Seoul, a city with almost twice the population of my home town, cyclists can roll out easily, as I learned on the first day of a seven-day cycling trip across South Korea, from the capital to the southern port-city of Busan. On the first morning of our trip, we biked through the beautiful Yeouido Park – bypassing hundreds of cars in rush-hour traffic – via a network of connected bike paths along the Han River. With the sweet scent of white fringetrees in the air, and their seed-pods popping beneath our wheels, before we knew it we were clear of the city, with nary an irritated driver nor dead-end bike lane

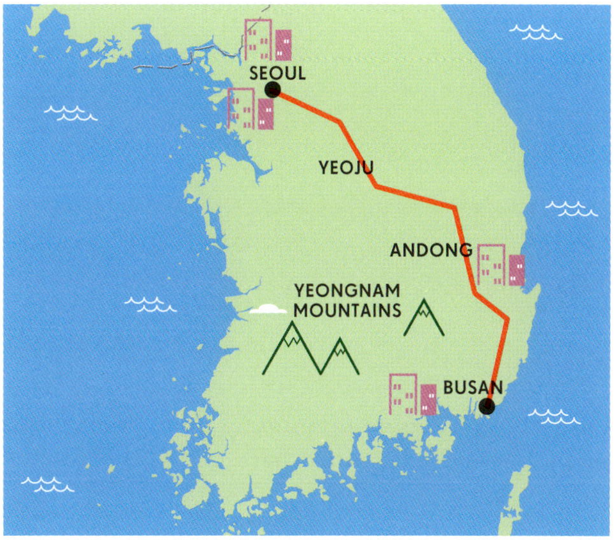

Left to right: Woljeonggyo Bridge in Gyeongju; Bulguksa Buddhist temple in Gyeongju; Cheomseongdae Observatory. Previous spread: Busan, the final destination of the trip

ANCIENT HISTORY

Even by South Korea's vaunted standards, Gyeongju is a city rich in history. Among its marvels are 23 'tumuli', vast burial mounds covering tombs from the 5th-century Silla dynasty, today located in Daereungwon Tumuli Park. Nearby is the Chemseongdae observatory, which dates to the 7th century and is considered the world's oldest astronomical institution. At night, the (modern) lights adorning another 7th-century treasure, the Woljeonggyo Bridge, illuminate peaceful Hyeongsan River.

to complain about. I enjoyed it so much I wanted to do it again.

As a cyclist, you're constantly reminded that you're a guest in a world made for cars. But cycling along the Han River Path, I had a different feeling – I felt welcome. The path is part of the 360-mile (580km) Four Rivers Trail, which criss-crosses South Korea. It was created in the late 2000s, as part of then-President Lee Myung-Bak's Four Rivers restoration project. Our 404-mile (650km) route, developed by TDA Global Cycling as part of their Journey to the East tour, includes much of the Trail, with the addition of some coastal sections, as well as climbs in the Yeongnam mountains, known locally as the 'Korean Alps'.

When people think of cycling in Asia, it's invariably Japan and Taiwan that spring to mind. Both countries have well-developed cycling cultures and the kinds of challenging topography that make heart-rates (and Strava scores) soar. If South Korea has flown under the radar, it shouldn't do for much longer.

Our first stop after Seoul was Yeoju, whose red-clay soil makes the rice taste better and the region's ceramics come out green. Yeoju's main claim to fame is that the aforementioned rice was served to monarchs throughout the Joseon dynasty, who ruled here from 1392 to 1910. (I'd be lying if I said my taste buds noted the superior 'earthiness' our guide described.) After Yeoju, we continued along the Namhan River to Suanbo, climbing up and over Ihwa Mountain Pass, at 17,68ft (539m) it's the highest point on the trail, and which offers stunning views of the surrounding mountains and towns.

In Suanbo, we were greeted by hot springs dating back

Daecheol/Shutterstock

30,000 years and, more recent, the plastic pheasant statues that welcome diners to the city's restaurants. I cycle to eat and South Korea did not disappoint. Dishes such as bulgogi and bibimbap have entered the world's culinary lexicon, but there are still countless regional specialties to discover, Suanbo's trademark pheasant among them.

From Suanbo, we took inland country roads, hitting 14% climbs and such long switchback descents I worried that I'd burn out my knees on the way up and my brake pads on the way down. 'Korea has so very many mountains,' explained Erica Kim, co-owner of Bike Makes Me Happy, one of Seoul's premium bike shops. 'In some areas you can ride 125 miles with more than 9850ft (3000m) of climbing.'

For a small country, South Korea goes big on variety, in its landscapes and local cuisines but also in terms of flora and fauna. 'Even cycling as little as 600 kilometres,' said Miles MacDonald of TDA Global Cycling, who scouted and mapped our route, 'you're passing through numerous distinct regions.'

At our next stop, Andong, we arrived famished and thus made a beeline for Andong Galbi Alley, a local foodie hotspot where a restaurant owner kindly schooled us in the authentic techniques of Korean barbecue, another global export. From here we visited Hahoe Folk Village, on the banks of the Nakdong River, a 'one-clan' community whose buildings and rituals have been preserved since the 15th century.

Next on our itinerary was Yeongdeok, a quirky seaside town where, in lieu of pheasants, the bridges and buildings are adorned with replicas of crabs, a not-so-subtle nod to the exceptional snow crab that proliferate here and are such a feature of local menus. It seemed wild to have biked more than 100km to dine on these crustaceans but, having ridden longer distances for lesser reasons, the crab were as good as their reputation suggested.

On a crab high, we travelled from Yeongdeok through the Korean Alps, no match for their European counterparts but challenging all the same. Bound for the charming city of Gyeongju, along the way we saw many now-familiar sights: seniors exercising at calisthenics machines; traditional *hanok* houses with their tiled roofs made from burned soil; rows of *onggi* pots used to ferment kimchi; and the many excellent cafes that seemed to pop up just about everywhere. South Korea has its coffee-culture dialled in to perfection, with no shortage of spots to enjoy a latte and a pastry along its bike paths. And, oh my, the public washrooms; often colour-coded (pink and blue) and invariably cleaner than my bathroom at home.

On our final day we cycled into Busan, arriving into South Korea's second-largest city via an elevated path over the Nakdong River. Below, its banks brimmed with markets and nightlife, with entry into the city as easy and convenient as our departure from Seoul. And which sent a clear message: 'Cyclists welcome'. **CP**

Julien Viry/Getty Images; Mirko Kuzmanovic/Getty images

TOOLKIT

Start // Seoul
Finish // Busan
Distance // 404 miles (650km)
Getting there // Korean Air flies to Seoul's Incheon International airport from major hubs.
When to go // May to mid-June, September to November.
What to wear // Typical cycling gear, waterproof and warm layers for rainy days and higher-altitude riding.
What to pack // A travel adapter – and an appetite.
Where to stay // In Yeoju, The Sun Valley Hotel; in Gyeongju, the Hwangnamgwan Hanok hotel.
Where to eat // In Seoul, *pyeonsu* dumplings or *kimchi-jjigae*; Suanbo's specialty is pheasant; in Andong, Jjimdak Alley for braised chicken, or Galbi Alley for the barbecue; Yeongdeok for crab. In Gyeongju, try *ssambap* (leaf wraps and rice). In Busan, street food at Changseon-dong.
More info // www.tdaglobalcycling.com

Opposite: taking a break on Eurovelo 1 near Porto; Porto's Dom Luís I bridge

MORE LIKE THIS CROSS-COUNTRY JAUNTS

BIKEPACK SCOTLAND, EAST TO WEST

In 2025, Bikepacking Scotland launched a 110-mile (177km) coast-to-coast route that starts in the medieval village of Culross, on the east coast. Heading west, it runs through Devilla Forest, Loch Lomond and The Trossachs National Park, and the Arrochar Alps, before ending in Kilcreggan. The route goes via some of the top-notch gravel sections Scotland has become known for, as well as lanes, forest tracks and loch-side trails. This mix of forested sections and Scotland's signature moody weather will doubtless beguile riders (and, occasionally, drench them). Ride the whole route and you'll be able to dip a toe in both the North Sea and the Atlantic Ocean. In between, you'll ride through farmland and river valleys, as well as towns. Visit historic landmarks like Alloa Tower, Dunblane Cathedral and Stirling Castle. The best time to ride is between April and October; hardier souls can plump for the 'year-round' option.
Start // Culross
Finish // Kilcreggan
Distance // 110 miles (177km)

PORTUGAL, NORTH TO SOUTH (EUROVELO1)

Cycle from Caminha, in the north, to Faro in the south, along 684 miles (1100km) of the coastal EuroVelo1. The route boasts endless ocean views and almost endless sunshine, around 300 days' worth a year. You'll pass through fishing villages, river valleys, and three UNESCO-designated cities: Porto, Coimbra, and Lisbon. The route uses cycle paths, country roads and urban streets. In the north, the terrain is hillier but don't worry, the Atlantic winds will be on hand to cool your brow. The central section is where things start to really heat up; but then you reach Lisbon, its vibrant culture, famous hills and stunning views, made all the more scenic by a cold beer. In the south, Alentejo and the Algarve, it gets hotter still, so avoid riding in the height of summer. Throughout the route, fuel your ride with *pasteis de nata*, piri-piri chicken, and *vinho verde*, although not necessarily in that order.
Start // Caminha
Finish // Faro
Distance // 684 miles (1100km)

VIETNAM, NORTH TO SOUTH

See much of Vietnam by riding 994 miles (1600km) south from Hanoi, to Ho Chi Minh City. Some cyclists tackle the journey via the coastal National Route 1A, riding through Huế, home to the UNESCO-listed Imperial City, Da Nang (spectacular beaches), Hoi An, Nha Trang, and the Central Highlands before arriving in Ho Chi Minh City. Others take the inland Ho Chi Minh Hwy, which runs to the west of National Route 1A but is more remote. No matter which route you choose, you'll experience the wealth of history and culture Vietnam has to offer, made all the easier by the country's ongoing investment in cycling infrastructure. In addition to reliable internet service and a favourable exchange rate for many currencies that keeps travel costs low, there's also the not insignificant draw of Vietnamese street food, which is among the finest on the planet.
Start // Hanoi
Finish // Ho Chi Minh City
Distance // 994 miles (1600km)

LANNA KINGDOM

Northern Thailand's first long-distance bikepacking route weaves through jungle trails, hill-tribe villages and cloud-draped mountains in the foothills of the Himalayas.

Sam Rice

My headlamp beam judders across potholes I can barely see. It's 4.45am and I'm riding blind up a mountain in Northern Thailand, chasing a red taillight that belongs to Nu. My hands ache from squeezing the bars too hard, knuckles white beneath gloves. Every shadow morphs into a cliff edge. Every pale patch of dirt threatens to send me sideways into the void. 'You alright back there?' Nu's voice cuts through the predawn darkness. 'Terrified, actually.'

He stops. Waits. His light swings back to illuminate the trail beside me, casting long shadows through the mist. 'Me too,' he says, 'but we're nearly there.' We pedal together, our lights overlapping on the rutted dirt, neither of us admitting that this climb to catch sunrise at Doi Dam might be the stupidest idea we've had all week. But when we crest the final rise and the view opens before us, I understand why Nu insisted.

Below, the valleys have disappeared, replaced by cloud. Not

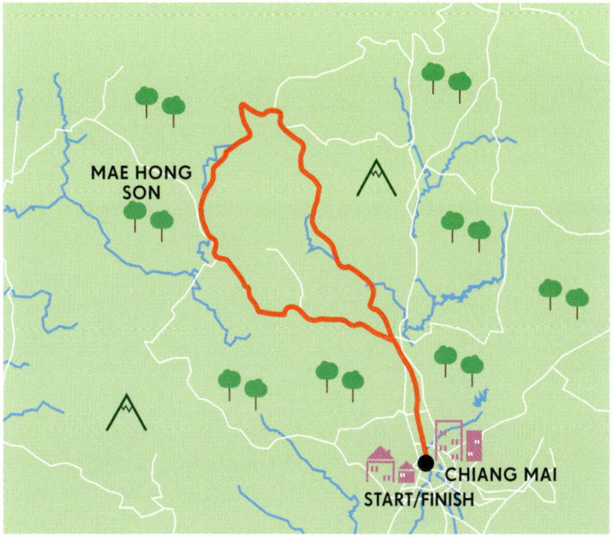

wisps or patches but an ocean, white and infinite, with mountain peaks spiking through. The sun breaks the horizon, turning everything copper, then gold, then blazing orange. The clouds don't stay still but surge and roll, breaking against ridgelines like waves. 'This is why we're building the route,' Nu says quietly, 'this is the Thailand I want people to experience by bike.'

We're standing at 5643ft (1720m), on our fifth day scouting what will become Thailand's first long-distance bikepacking loop. Nu Chaijinda owns Triple Cats Cycles, in Chiang Mai. He's spent years exploring these mountains, always believing they held world-class riding. When I'd visited his shop several years previously, passing through on a longer tour, he'd pulled out maps and started drawing lines with oil-stained fingers. 'Help me make this real,' he'd said. So here we are, testing whether 207 miles (333km) of dirt roads, jungle singletrack, and ancient elephant-migration trails can actually work as a cohesive route.

Thus far it's been brutal. We'd left Chiang Mai five mornings ago, rolling out before the city had wiped the sleep from its eyes. Tuk tuks coughed diesel into morning air. Monks walked barefoot through markets, their orange robes vivid against grey concrete. Within 12 miles (19km), pavement crumbled to dirt and the climbs started coming. Gradients that reared up at 25%, on loose gravel which offered no traction; the humidity had clung like wet wool, turning breathing into work. My romantic notions about Thai bikepacking evaporated somewhere around hour six of day one.

But then there were moments like Tung Hua. We'd arrived destroyed after a savage afternoon climb, legs twitching involuntarily, wondering if we'd made the route too hard. Ping, owner of Thung Yua Homestay and our evening's accommodation, met us at the gate, his weathered face split by a massive smile, a machete dangling from one hand. He sat us down beneath towering banana plants, fed us sliced mango and papaya so ripe the juice ran down our chins, then spent the evening cooking chicken inside bamboo tubes over crackling coals. As the fire popped and hissed, Ping explained how the different hill tribes ended up scattered through these mountains (see panel).

The food was extraordinary. Tamarind and ginger sharp on our tongues, the bamboo imparting a subtle sweetness to the chicken, chilli biting at the back of our throats. We ate until we couldn't move, while Ping's stories about his grandfather's journey here, from Myanmar, drifted on the evening air. Outside, the jungle breathed around us – the buzz and hum of countless insects, the distant croak of toads, the occasional call of a tokay gecko. That night, I understood what made this route special.

Day three brought us through Mueang Khong, a village so picturesque it didn't seem real. Wooden houses with steep roofs, shops serving sweet Thai iced-coffee, kids playing football in dusty streets, the rhythm of rural life unfolding at its own

HILL TRIBE HERITAGE

Dating back to at least the 13th century, the Lanna Kingdom, or Lan Na, was a region of ancient Thailand whose cultural development owed much to nearby India. In the intervening centuries, it has become a haven for the nation's hill tribes, among them the Karen, Hmong, Akha, and also the Lahu. Originally from China, Laos, and Myanmar (like Ping's grandfather), these communities now form an integral part of Thailand's national identity.

Clockwise from top: riding out of Mae Ya Noi; setting up camp at the top of Doi Dam; spring rolls and delicious Thai dishes. Previous spread: a homestay in Ban Thung Yua; crossing a stream on the way to Pai

Sam Rice

unhurried pace. We sat in plastic chairs, watching the world as Nu pointed out landmarks, told stories about friends who lived here, and explained the agricultural cycles governing village life.

The days blurred after that. More climbing than seemed reasonable. Rivers we had to ford, cold water rushing over our pedals and soaking our shoes. Sections so steep we pushed our bikes for hours, the sun beating down mercilessly. But also descents that made every painful metre worthwhile – flowing singletrack through jungle canopy, rooster-tails of dust behind our wheels, the pure childlike joy of momentum.

Day five's push to the ranger station at Doi Dam nearly finished me. Almost 2300ft (700m) of climbing in the afternoon heat, sweat pouring, my water bottles tasting like baked plastic by the time we arrived. The rangers stationed near the summit took one look at us and laughed.

The following morning, once more standing and watching mountains emerge from clouds, the world painted in shades of gold and rose, our efforts are rewarded yet again. This is a view that can't be photographed, can't be explained. You have to earn it with your legs, trust that something worthwhile awaits you at the end.

The sun climbs higher. We've still got 93 miles (150km) ahead – through Pai, past the Royal Project (a non-profit established to further protect Thailand's hill tribes), back to Chiang Mai. 'People are going to suffer on this route,' I say. 'That's okay,' Nu replies, wiping his eyes. 'The best things in life make you work for them.'

We turn to descend, the weight of accomplishment sitting warm in our chests. Six days, 207 miles (333km), countless moments of doubt and wonder. Thailand's first long-distance bikepacking route is real – and brilliant. **SR**

Sam Rice

TOOLKIT

Start/Finish // Chiang Mai
Distance // 207 miles (333km)
Getting there // Fly into Chiang Mai International Airport or take trains/buses from Bangkok.
When to go // November to February has excellent conditions, with cool temperatures and dry trails; December to January is perfect.
What to wear // Layers are essential; mountain temperatures drop to 6–12°C (43–53°F) at night, despite daytime highs of 25–30°C (77–87°F). Long sleeves may protect against mosquitos and the sun's UV.
What to pack // Shelter is essential for the remote camping sections; you'll need a lightweight tent.
Where to stay // A mix of ranger stations, camping and homestays, including Thung Yua Homestay.
Where to eat // Village restaurants are abundant; try *krapow moo* and sticky rice to get you up the climbs.
More info // Nu at Triple Cats Cycles (@triple_cats_cycle), for local support and bike hire. It's cash-only outside cities and ATMs may be hard to find, so bring what you need. Route info and GPX files can be downloaded at www.bikepacking.com

Opposite: riding the Tiger Head Mountain Loop in Thailand; refreshments on the way

MORE LIKE THIS
ASIAN ADVENTURES

TIGER HEAD MOUNTAIN LOOP, THAILAND

Northern Thailand's mountains hide another gem just south of the Lanna Kingdom. This 85-mile (137km) bikepacking route circles Doi Hue Seur, or Tiger Head Mountain, weaving through dense jungle, organic plantations, and Karen hill-tribe villages. You'll tackle Thailand's most formidable climbs (some exceeding 25%), but the rewards match the effort: wild gibbons swinging through ancient canopies, crystalline mountain streams for midday cool-downs, and homestays where Karen families share stories over homemade whiskey. The route works for both gravel and mountain bikes, with multiple homestay options meaning you can leave the tent behind and travel light. Starting and ending in Chom Thong, you'll spend three days immersed in tropical heat and cultural encounters that feel worlds away from 'tourist' Thailand.
Start/finish // Chom Thong
Distance // 85 miles (137km)

SHIRETOKO LOOP, JAPAN

Explore eastern Hokkaidō over a week or more, on this mellow and accessible loop along the island's coast and through some of its volcanic national parks. The ride starts from the northeast city of Abashiri, which can be reached direct by train from Hokkaidō's capital, Sapporo. You'll get to know some of Japan's indigenous culture and communities along the way; specifically the Ainu, the first to settle this sparsely populated part of Japan and who, in April 2019, were officially recognised as one of the nation's two indigenous peoples (the other being the Ryūkyūans, of Okinawa). Located at the loop's halfway point, Ainu Kotan is Hokkaidō's largest Ainu community, where you can experience theatre performances and local dishes. After a long day in the saddle spotting Ezo red foxes and red-crowned cranes, soak in hot springs to soothe aching limbs.
Start/finish // Abashiri
Distance // 217 miles (349km)

MAE HONG SON LOOP, THAILAND

If sealed roads and 4000 bends-plus sound like your idea of heaven, the Mae Hong Son Loop delivers 410 miles (660km) of spectacular cycling through northwest Thailand. This is the region's most famous motorcycle route, but cyclists willing to tackle gradients exceeding 20% – and climb the equivalent of Mt Everest one-and-a-half times – are rewarded with stunning views, lush forests, and phenomenal hairpin descents that'll have you grinning for hours. The smooth tarmac takes you from Chiang Mai through tourist-friendly Pai, past hill-tribe villages, and into laid back Mae Sariang, sitting beside a river. With accommodation and food options frequent throughout, you can pack light and focus on the riding. Allocate 5–10 days, bring low gears (28 gear-inches or smaller), and prepare for some of Southeast Asia's most rewarding road cycling.
Start/finish // Chiang Mai
Distance // 410 miles (660km)

Rapha
BASECAMP

THE RINDŌ OF JAPAN'S ISHIKAWA

Explore the magical rindō, the traffic-free forest roads of southern Ishikawa, on the west coast of Japan.

Japan is well known for densely populated cities and efficient, fast transport links. This is handy for the 90% of Japanese citizens who live in cities and urban settlements, and also tourists in search of the real Japan. But the equally good news for cyclists is that this leaves a lot of room for an almost secret network of slow, more circuitous roadways. Known as *rindō*, they lie tucked away in the mountainous interior and the *inaka*, Japan's catch-all word for the countryside, which represents not just the physical space of its less-populated regions, but also their state of mind and being.

Rindō are, literally, 'forest roads'. The characters that make up the word are 林 (forest) and 道 (road), but it's apt to note that 道 is the same as appears in Jūdō, or Sadō (tea ceremony) – it has a deeper meaning, of a life's path, and originates in the Chinese concept of the Tao. To ride the rindō is to travel from point A to point B, but as with many journeys, it's the bits in between that are significant.

To find the *rindō*, you have to travel to the *inaka*. I spent three years living in South Ishikawa, where a narrow strip of towns and cities is lined on one side by the Japan Sea, and on the other by a range of mountains dominated by the 8865ft (2702m) holy peak of Mt Hakusan. South Ishikawa is a region of forests, mountains, lakes, rivers and humidity – high snowfall in winter, a rainy season in June and hot, heavy air throughout summer. It's possible to ride for a day on the *rindō* in these mountains and barely see another human, let alone a car.

My favourite ride in South Ishikawa links two of its most prominent cities. Kagaonsen is a loosely connected grouping

Christopher Tamcke/Alamy

of smaller towns built around bubbling spas and hot springs, though the immediately noticeable landmark is a 240ft- (73m) statue of a female *daikannon* (spiritually enlightened individual) in fading, dirty gold which stands above an abandoned Buddhist theme park and is visible for miles. Kanazawa is the prefectural capital – a cosmopolitan and culturally rich city which is nevertheless mainly ignored by the tourist trade. Like the *rindō*, Kanazawa is a well-kept secret in Japan.

You could ride up the coast from Kagaonsen to Kanazawa in an hour and a half, but the more interesting route is through the mountains; first south, over the 2953ft (900m) Shinmata Pass and for 15 or so miles (24km) in neighbouring Fukui Prefecture, before looping back north at Katsuyama, towards the imposing bulk of Hakusan. Here, the forests are loud with the sound of water and cicadas, and the roadways are narrow, twisting and gravelly in places.

For the most part they are devoid of traffic. There is civilisation, however, and this being Japan, the Katsuyama 7-Eleven is a pitstop for energy-giving *onigiri* (patties of rice wrapped in seaweed), Pocari Sweat, and hot coffee in a can. Just because we're in the *inaka*, doesn't mean a convenience store won't pop up at the right moment. Katsuyama is also the home of the Fukui Prefectural Dinosaur Museum, and even up

"Local friends earnestly informed me that Ishikawa Prefecture's water was famous for being one of Japan's three most delicious waters"

Route 157 north out of the town, there are occasional dinosaur statues, in among the rice paddies and villages. Route 157 is a bigger road than the *rindō*, though a mile or so out of Katsuyama, there's a shortcut, via the *rindō* of Route 135, which is a quieter road and takes cyclists past the Fudōdaki waterfall. Back on to Route 157, and it's possible to take a short diversion on Route 33, all the way to the main trailhead for hiking up Hakusan.

One of Japan's three holy peaks, along with Fuji and Tateyama, Hakusan translates as 'White Mountain', and it remains snow-capped through most of the year. This eminent ranking feeds into a local pride that is also reinforced by the famous Kenroku-en gardens in Kanazawa (see panel), close to the end of this ride, which are also one of Japan's three most important gardens, along with Ibaraki Prefecture's

Joaquin Ossorio Castillo/Shutterstock; Aflo Co., Ltd/Alamy; Mai.Chayakorn/Shutterstock

KENROKU-EN

According to ancient Chinese landscape theory, six attributes and three dichotomies make up the perfect garden: spaciousness and seclusion, landscaping and nature, and flowing water and expansive views. And it is said that nowhere else are all six in such perfect harmony as in Kanazawa's Kenroku-en (the 'garden of six sublimities'). Kenroku-en is considered one of the three great gardens of Japan, and is a haven of peace, meditation and zen in the heart of the city.

Left to right: Kenroku-en gardens; cats in Kaga; Higashi Chaya Gai in Kanazawa; a shrine in Kenroku-en garden; Mt Haku. Previous spread: a forest road in Ishikawa Prefecture

Kairaku-en and Koraku-en, in Okayama Prefecture. Local friends earnestly informed me that Ishikawa Prefecture's water was famous for being one of Japan's three most delicious waters, and that its sushi was also in the country's top three. I never found official confirmation regarding the status of Ishikawa's water and sushi but I can tell you that both are excellent.

Route 157 joins the Tedori river gorges and runs alongside Lake Tedori and its massive dam at the north end, which has spectacular views. The main road has a few tunnels, and though it's not busy, a less-intimidating option is to take the *rindō* up the east side of the lake, which is a tiny road, but quiet. At Tsurugi, in the Kanazawa suburbs, it's possible to take a shortcut but the better route goes back into the *rindō* for two more climbs en route to entering the city, at Kanazawa Gakuin University at the city's eastern tip. From there, it's a more stereotypically Japanese commute to the city centre, with busy roads through the dense urban fabric.

This one ride takes in spa towns, mountains, lakes, forests and one of Japan's great cities. The forest paths of the *rindō* are an indirect, but perhaps a more meaningful way of journeying between and through these places, and, importantly, some of the best cycling roads in the world. **EP**

TOOLKIT

Start // Kagaonsen station
Finish // Kanazawa station
Distance // 90 miles (145km)
Getting there // Kagaonsen is two hours from Shin-Ōsaka station, via a change in Tsuruga, in Fukui Prefecture.
When to go // March–June or September–November, to enjoy spring cherry blossoms or the spectacular colours of autumn in the warmth. July and August are very hot and humid, with a rainy season in early July.
Where to stay // Kagaonsen is famous for its spa hotels and traditional ryokan. The Hoshi Ryokan in nearby Komatsu, established in the year 718, is reputed to be the oldest hotel in the world.
Where to eat // Downtown Kanazawa is packed with cosmopolitan and traditional restaurants.
More info // www.japan-guide.com

MAIH5050/Shutterstock; Bluesnaps/Shutterstock

Opposite: a view of Mt Fuji in autumn; the Shimanami Kaidō cycling route

MORE LIKE THIS JAPANESE GEMS

NOTO HANTŌ, ISHIKAWA

The Noto Peninsula forms the northern half of Ishikawa Prefecture, jutting out into the Japan Sea. It's a sparsely populated maritime/rural region where historically fishing has been a major industry, and which has faced severe challenges in recent years – the slow erosion of depopulation, and the disastrous 2024 Noto earthquake, which inflicted severe damage on the towns of Wajima and Suzu. But it is also one of the most beautiful and idiosyncratic regions of the country, with spectacular summer *matsuri* (festivals) featuring *taiko* drummers wearing devil masks, fire and huge portable shrines. From Hakui, on the southwestern end of the peninsula, all the way round to Nanao, just short of the border with neighbouring Toyama-ken, there's a 175-mile (280km) circumnavigation of the peninsula, comprising mainly flat coastal roads, with the occasional climb over higher headlands. Look out for the terraced landscape of Senmaida ('a thousand rice paddies') and Madoiwa ('window rock'), north of Wajima.

Start // Hakui City
Finish // Nanao
Distance // 175 miles (280km)

SHIMANAMI KAIDŌ, SETO INLAND SEA

Japan is often defined by its two ocean-facing edges: on the western side, the Sea of Japan separates the country from the rest of Asia; on its east, there is the vast, powerful expanse of the Pacific Ocean. However, Japan's 'third' sea is the significant inland stretch of the Seto-nai-kai, which separates, but also connects, three of Japan's four main islands: Honshu, Kyūshū and Shikoku. And in the middle of that sea, between Honshu and Shikoku, an island-hopping network of spectacular suspension bridges, floating bike paths and sea views known as the Shimanami Kaidō, one of the world's greatest bike rides. The bike path has been appended to the series of 55 bridges which make their way across the six islands between Onomichi on Honshu, and Imabari in Shikoku, though one can be skipped in favour of a ferry crossing, to avoid a steep climb. The full distance is 43 miles (70km), doable in one day, or at a more leisurely pace with a stopover on any of the populated islands en route.

Start // Onomichi
Finish // Imabari
Distance // 43 miles (70km)

MT FUJI

There is a saying in Japan that you would be a fool not to climb Mt Fuji once in your life, and that you would be a fool to climb it twice. And while cyclists can't make their way fully to the summit at 12,389ft (3776m), it's possible to conduct a two-wheeled pilgrimage a good way to the top. There are various roads up the mountain, all of which finish at their respective fifth stations (on each approach the summit is the 10th). On the southern side, the Fujinomiya fifth station is accessed by a spectacular hairpinned road, and the Gotemba fifth station is a popular access point from Tokyo. On the eastern flank, there is the Subashiri fifth station. But the most popular approach to cycle is the climb from Kawaguchiko station, north of the mountain, to the Subaru fifth station, at 7546ft (2300m). It's 18.5 miles (30km) of hard climbing but, with the same distance in your descent, maybe you'd be a fool not to try this ride twice.

Start // Kawaguchiko station
Finish // Fuji Subaru fifth station
Distance // 18.5 miles (30km)

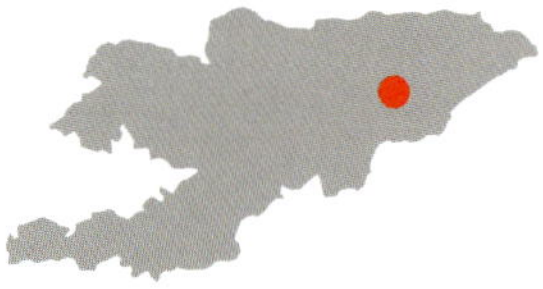

RIDING THE TIAN SHAN MOUNTAINS OF KYRGYZSTAN

A week-long adventure in Kyrgyzstan's Tian Shan mountains transports riders between remote alpine lakes, in a land where ancient customs are observed beneath cobalt skies.

All that separates the blue of the lake from that of the sky is a dark line of mountain peaks, serrated and snow-capped. The lake is Son-Köl, at 9843ft (3000m) above sea level one of Kyrgyzstan's most celebrated water features. Close to its shores is the village in which we have just slept, the stoves in our yurts still smouldering, having kept at bay the chill of an impossibly star-filled night.

It has been 15 years since I looked upon the Tian Shan range from a different perspective, riding across the Kazakh Steppe to the north. Tags such as 'bucket list' seem disrespectful to places like this, making them geographical commodities to be ticked off.

After arriving in Bishkek for our seven-day ride, our group of 10 makes its way across the high plateau and up into haute mountains. En route, our wheel tracks kick up trails of dust, sometimes bisected by the greater clouds pluming from behind herds of wild horses galloping across our path. Kyrgyzstan, like much of Central Asia, provides these sort of rare moments, only possible in locations so utterly remote.

Day one alternates between hard-going gravel and tracks so rutted that we soon wish for the gravel again. For a brief stretch we have smooth, new asphalt that rolls fast and easy but seems to lack, well, soul. In the evenings, exhausted, we sleep;

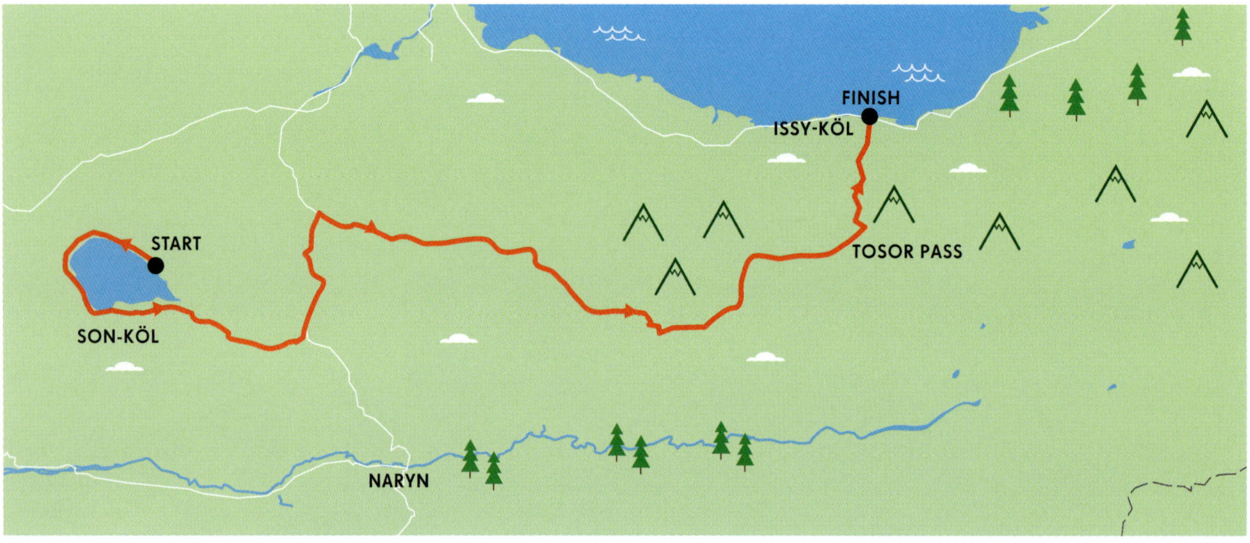

Stefan Amato

sometimes in our own tents, on other occasions on mattresses in the same yurts that have long sheltered the Kyrgyz people. Looking up into the top of our yurt, its radial pattern of wooden supports echoes the bicycle wheels that have brought us here.

Such circular designs seem apt; so close to the top of the world, this feels like a place with fewer of the straight edges that define much of life below, the rigid nature of city living that we all need to escape from time to time. I watch a child play on a small tricycle as his mother places a large-handled kettle on a stove; his father moves wood across a backyard that stretches for 6000 miles (9656km), to Kazakhstan in one direction and to the Himalayas in the other. If borders seem abstract in a land so expansive, our route is pockmarked with the efforts of those who have tried to impose their will upon it.

On the morning of day two, after heavy rains, we find the road ahead flooded. We remove shoes and, in ice-cold water, ford the torrent, carrying bicycles high off the ground before going back for our panniers. Now and then comes the sound of an engine and another echo of Soviet Central Asia skids towards us, in the shape of a 4x4 Lada, its driver hunched behind the wheel and keeping the power determinedly down – lose traction out here and your vehicle will sink deeper with each futile spin.

Over the next few days, we begin to notch up the miles. Forty miles (60km) becomes 60 (100km) becomes 75 miles (120km). Just as Son-Köl sent us on our way, so another of Kyrgyzstan's great lakes, Issyk-Köl, beckons us to the finish. Between them is a sky almost as blue as their waters, while the swim spots we find along the way are so icy they seem to reset your entire cardiovascular system.

DAIRY DEBRIEF

The fermentation of various milks is vital to the diet in the mountains of Central Asia. The word yoghurt derives from the Turkish verb *yoğurtmak*, which means 'to thicken'; while *kumys*, in Kyrgyzstan, has equivalents in the Turkish yoghurt drink, ayran, or the Iranian version, *doogh*. In the high plateau, drunk from a bowl, kumys feels instantly nourishing. The gut-friendly microbes the fermentation process creates have fortified numerous civilisations against sickness, including the ancient Greeks.

Clockwise from top: overnight in yurts beside Issyk-Köl; local traffic; dirt-road descents; roadside snacks

Stefan Amato

On our penultimate night, the approach of our final destination is celebrated with a *plov*, cooked by an Uzbek guide who has met us, intermittently, with a support vehicle. Whole bulbs of garlic are sunk into rice, bubbling in a pan, the carrots, onion and lamb releasing flavours into the pot. We also eat *lagman*, the heavy Udon-style noodle-broth favoured by all the Turkic peoples of the steppe, from the Uyghurs of northwest China to those in Turkmenistan. On our last morning, we meet a vendor selling *kumys*, a fermented horse-milk drink and another flavour of the mountain world. So many miles spent in the saddle teaches us gratitude for everything that comes our way.

The final day brings a final pass, Tosor, at 12,795ft (3900m). None in our group is left behind, of course, but we ascend at different speeds – for those at the front, the biting wind as we climb ever higher is not an easy place to wait for stragglers. At the top, our congratulatory photos are taken quickly, before we force snacks into our mouths and then descend; through the cloud, through the track of rock that becomes gravel, that in turn becomes the rideable earth.

Finally, the sun returns and with it the farmland and smallholdings where people are able to live and cultivate life. In the gardens there are fruit trees and, on the shores of Issyk-Köl, we line up our bikes beside yurts where we'll sleep for a last night.

Translating as 'hot lake', Issyk-Köl is saline and remains unfrozen year-round. The sky is cobalt, the water is sapphire and we step into it from a sandy beach. A wilderness by any definition, but one that never felt so welcoming. **SA & JS**

Stefan Amato

Previous spread: overnight in yurts beside Issyk-Köl; crossing the empty steppe

TOOLKIT

Start // Son-Köl
Finish // Issyk-Köl
Distance // 218 miles (350km)
Getting there // Son-Köl and Issyk-Köl are a five-hour drive from Kyrgyzstan's capital, Bishkek, a regional transport hub.
When to go // June to October.
What to wear // Kit for all four seasons; prepare for highs of 40°C and near-freezing temperatures on passes. Also, riding shoes you can walk in over technical ground.
What to pack // Water filter, swimming kit.
Where to stay // Yurt camps where possible, but you'll need a tent and camping kit for sure. Camp below 11,483ft (3500m) to avoid inclement conditions.
Where to eat // Yurt camps or your own camping-stove..
More info // Son-Köl is at 9843ft (3000m); start slow and steady, spending a night or two at altitude to acclimatise.

Opposite: exploring the Bartang Valley of Tajikistan

MORE LIKE THIS
CENTRAL ASIA DREAMING

KHANGAI MOUNTAINS, MONGOLIA

The lush green rolling steppe of Central Mongolia's Khangai Mountains epitomises the region's nomadic, pastoral wilderness and traditional way of life. Located about 250 miles (400km) west of the capital, Ulaanbaatar, the Khangai's network of doubletrack roads offers a playground for bikepackers, where yurts – known here as 'gers' – dot the landscape outside of villages and towns. The Khangai Mountains stretch for approximately 500 miles (800km), from Zavkhan province in the west, to Töv province in the east. A vast land of plains, forests and extinct volcanoes, the range also acts as a continental divide of water systems, heading north into the Arctic, and south towards the Pacific. Unless you're riding in and out of Ulaanbaatar, you'll need a vehicle transfer to take you out west, to one of the cities and transport hubs like Tsetserleg, Ovorkhangai, or Karakorum, the ancient capital of the Mongol Empire, founded by Chinggis (Genghis) Khan.
Start/finish // Ulaanbaatar
Distance // 250–400 miles (400–640km)

BARTANG VALLEY, TAJIKISTAN

Another bikepacker's dream, the Bartang Valley takes riders far off the Pamir Hwy and onto a moonscape of Bartangi dirt roads, through lesser-ridden valleys and across the high plateaus of the remote, picturesque Pamir Mountains. Expect to spend a lot of the ride following – and crossing – the Bartang river, riding at altitudes in excess of 13,000ft (4000m), which in turn will expose you to unpredictable weather. While the region offers one of the world's finest blank canvases for wild camping, you'll find it hard to turn down Bartangi hospitality at one of the many homestays in villages dotted along the way. In addition to basic accommodation, they invariably offer classic Tajik and Kyrgyz dishes, such as variations of *plov* (the Uzbek rice dish), along with breakfasts of porridge, bread and eggs. The route includes border crossings as well as traverses of national parks and politically sensitive regions, notably the Gorno-Badakhshan Autonomous Oblast (GBAO). Before you travel, confirm which visas and permits are required.
Start // Sary-Tash, Kyrgyzstan
Finish // Rushon, Tajikistan
Distance // 250 miles (400km)

SILK ROAD MOUNTAIN RACE, KYRGYZSTAN

One of, if not the toughest race on the bikepacking calendar, the Silk Road Mountain Race (SRMR) is an adventure like no other. An unsupported, single-stage cycling race through the Tian Shan mountains of Kyrgyzstan, the fixed route is characterised by its remote wilderness, high-mountain passes, unpredictable weather, and warm hospitality. The SRMR showcases and champions these harsh but stunning nomadic lands, creating the perfect setting for riders to test themselves against both the terrain and each other. The exact distance and elevation vary from year to year, but you can expect approximately 1200 miles (1900km), with 98,425ft (30,000m) of climbing. Riders have 14 days to complete the route, which follows gravel, singletrack and doubletrack, as well as old 'Soviet' roads that have long been forgotten and fallen into disrepair. There is very little tarmac, as well as some hike-a-bike, with the distances between resupply points often significant.
Start // Bishkek
Finish // Issyk-Köl
Distance // 1200 miles (1900km)

THE MOUNTAINS OF TAIWAN

With climbs higher than the Alps, dramatic gorges, coastal roads and delicious food, the island of Taiwan is surely a contender for most underrated cycling destination.

To truly explore Taiwan, myself and fellow Global Cycling Network (GCN) presenter Conor Dunne designed a three-day ride traversing the island from north to south. At nearly 430 miles (700km) and with 39,370ft (12,000m) of climbing, it was not for the faint-hearted, especially with one of the world's highest paved climbs on the route. Shooting for our YouTube channel meant we had a tight schedule but, for most riders, a more leisurely approach is sensible.

Our adventure began in Jiufen, a hilltop town overlooking the sea. Locals assured us the views were spectacular, but all we saw was a wall of cloud thanks to a huge storm that arrived at exactly the same time as we did. March, it turns out, is far from the driest season, and October and November are better bets.

Jiufen, with its ornate Taoist temples and lantern-lined streets, is said to have inspired *Spirited Away*, the Oscar-winning film released by Studio Ghibli in 2001 and regarded by aficionados as among the greatest animated movies of all

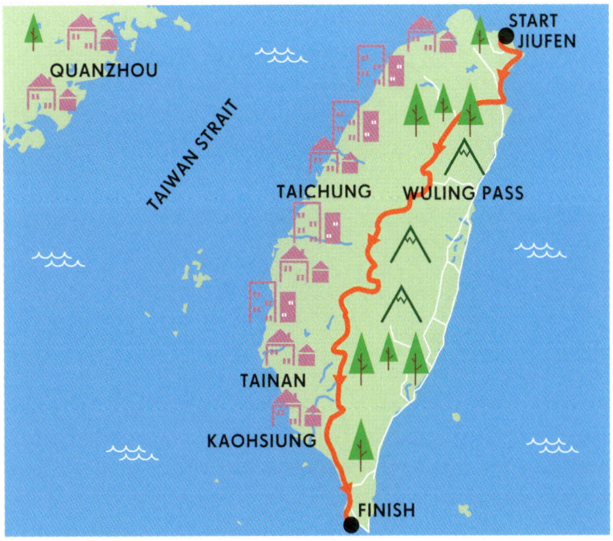

f11photo/Shutterstock

time. It's also famous for its night market where, among other specialities, visitors can try the infamous stinky tofu, a pungent, if divisive, fermented delicacy.

From Jiufen we descended to a coastline dominated by rice paddies, before turning inland to head toward the infamous Wuling Pass, this nation's highest road. As we climbed, the scenery changed dramatically, from paddies to forested peaks, and quiet river valleys framed by fields of cabbages. Even in the pouring rain, it was the kind of place that drew a 'wow' around every corner.

After a long, wet first day, we reached our stop, the Lishan Guest House. Sitting at 6348ft (1935m), it's the highest 'palace-style' hotel in Taiwan, originally built in 1965 as a residence for Chiang Kai-shek. Surrounded by tea and fruit plantations, its imperial grandeur made us feel as though we'd wandered on to a film set. My strongest memory is less glamorous: Conor and I hanging our sodden kit around our hotel room, desperately hoping it would dry before morning.

We would need all the help we could get because our second day included Wuling Pass, a climb that is truly a monster. Starting at sea level, it tops out at 10,745ft (3275m); to put that into perspective, the big European climbs, such as the Stelvio in Italy, peak at 9000ft (2750m), but only begin at 4265ft (1300m). Even allowing for the elevation of our hotel, Wuling would be in another league. Considered one of cycling's toughest road climbs, Wuling is the finishing point for the annual Taiwan KOM Challenge, one of the world's most gruelling one-day races (see p148).

Day two began ominously, with the sound of thunder. We were very much in the storm's path, and the surrounding peaks were hidden behind a curtain of cloud. On what was undoubtedly our toughest stage, we would have to summit not only Wuling, but also the Tataka Pass, the country's second-highest mountain road. For added jeopardy, Tataka had a summit checkpoint which closed at 5.30pm. Miss it, and we'd have no way to reach our next hotel on the other side.

The climb up to Wuling was as brutal as its reputation had warned – 4265ft (1300m) of ascent straight from the hotel, in torrential rain and hail. At an elevation of 9843ft (3000m) the altitude bites, stripping away about a quarter of your cardiovascular capacity, and the cold at the summit chilled me to my core. If you ever ride Wuling, be sure to bring proper gear. But despite the conditions, we couldn't help but smile. Taiwan has an infectious positivity, reflected in the warmth and politeness of its people.

For all that, what followed was the coldest, wettest descent of my life. Fortunately, by the time we reached the base of our next climb, Tataka Pass, the rain had stopped, although we still faced 41 miles (66km) of climbing, with just four hours to make the checkpoint. The first half was spent riding in thick fog, unable to see the road, but accompanied by the

BIKE SECURITY

One of my favourite things about Taiwan is how friendly and secure it is. In the 2025 Numbeo Safety Index, Taiwan scored 82.9 out of 100, ranking it as the fourth-safest territory in the world. Locals are known for their friendliness and visitors often praise the welcoming atmosphere. Anecdotally, you could leave your phone on the pavement in Taipei and come back to find it still there – something that bodes well for bike security.

Clockwise from top: Baishawan beach; Hehuan mountains; pineapple snacks. Previous spread: Jiufen Old Street in Taipei

Oliver Bridgewood

screeches of monkeys in the trees. Then, suddenly, we broke through the cloud. Below us, mist-filled valleys stretched away, with jagged, wooded peaks rising above the lower clouds. The views were spellbinding, the kind of reward that makes every mile of suffering worthwhile.

We reached the checkpoint with just 20 minutes to spare and enjoyed a glorious descent on wide, sweeping bends to our lodgings at a rustic coffee plantation. Having crossed the Tropic of Cancer, we were now on the drier, southern side of the island and at last the weather relented. For the first time in two days, I rode without a wet backside. Small pleasures.

Our final day was long but, mercifully, flatter. The road wound through dramatic gorges reminiscent of Provence, though here the cliffs were flanked by bamboo forests and banana plantations. Emerging onto the plains, we found ourselves surrounded by pineapples, one of Taiwan's signature crops.

With 62 miles (100km) to go and the midday sun beating down, we stopped to refill water bottles. A group of farmers spotted us and waved us over. Expecting to be told off for trespassing, we were instead offered freshly cut pineapples from their fields. Sweet, juicy, and more delicious than any I've ever tasted, it was another reminder of the island's generosity.

The final stretch hugged the coast, flat and fast, leading us to Baishawan Beach in Kenting National Park, a swathe of white sand made famous by Ang Lee's film adaptation of Life of Pi (it's meant to be Mexico). After three days of storms, climbs and unforgettable scenery, there was no better way to end our journey along the length of this amazing island than with a dip in the warm Pacific. **OB**

TOOLKIT

Start // Jiufen
Finish // Baishawan Beach
Distance // 426 miles (685km)
Getting there // From Taipei, Jiufen is a 50-minute drive; by bike it's 27 miles (43km). To get back, we drove to Kaohsiung City, then took the high-speed train to Taipei. Fantastic and inexpensive.
When to go // October to November is best for weather. Summer months get very hot.
What to wear // Bring layers and good waterproofs, the high altitude results in changeable weather and big differences in temperature.
What to pack // Lights! The fog can be thick in the mountains, which are wet and humid.
Where to stay // The Lishan Guest House; there are also lots of Airbnbs and budget hotels. To break the ride up, stay near Sun Moon Lake, Taiwan's largest.
Where to eat // 7-Elevens and FamilyMarts are everywhere, stocking drinks and warm food (plus emergency waterproof ponchos).
More info //www.youtube.com/@GCN

Dave Primov/Shutterstock; aksenovden/Shutterstock

Clockwise from top: Taipei's skyline; cyclists racing the Hualien–Wuling hill-climb challenge; Taiwanese food

MORE LIKE THIS
ONWARDS AND UPWARDS IN TAIWAN

KING OF THE MOUNTAIN (KOM) CHALLENGE

A cyclist's paradise, Taiwan offers scenic loops, coastal adventures and epic climbs. The annual KOM Challenge is a 66-mile (105km) mass-start hill climb held over one day in late October. You'll begin at sea level, in Hualien on the east coast, and ascend 10,745ft (3275m) to the top of the Wuling Pass, via the breathtaking Taroko Gorge. The first miles, along the Qixingtan coastline, are fast and flat, but once the gorge appears there's no respite; steep gradients through marble canyons and up seemingly sheer cliffs will test both legs and lungs. The final six miles (10km) are utterly brutal, with ramps exceeding 15-20% and at high altitude, too, where oxygen is scarce. Expect sudden fog, rain, or even snow at the summit. While professionals finish in just over three hours, most riders take six to seven hours – but simply reaching the top is an achievement.
Start // Hualien
Finish // Wuling Pass
Distance //66 miles (105km)

BUDDHA'S PALM

Located in and around Taipei, this ride features a 90-mile (145km) loop, with more than 9843ft (3000m) of climbing. Traced on a map you can see how the route takes the shape of a giant hand. Starting near the National Palace Museum, you'll tackle five climbs, each representing a 'finger', plus another designated as Buddha's 'thumb'. The 'wrist' comes at Leng Shui Keng, a mist-shrouded volcanic basin and popular tourist spot on the outskirts of the capital. Like so many rides on Taiwan, the route is relentless but stunning. Hot springs, bamboo forests, coastal views and volcanic peaks all feature, and ensure every ascent is memorable. Begin at dawn to avoid traffic out of Taipei, using local convenience stores to refuel. And don't forget to pace yourself; finishing the final 'finger' will bring a sense of accomplishment, just be sure you've enough gas to get there.
Start/finish // Taipei
Distance // 90 miles (145km)

CYCLING ROUTE NO. 1

For a longer and, unusually, flatter adventure, this 746-mile (1200km) ride circumnavigates the entire island and most riders complete it in around nine to 12 days. You'll follow a mix of cycle paths, quiet country roads and busier sections with marked lanes. Starting in Taipei, you'll pass by, or through, Taichung, Tainan, Kaohsiung, Hualien, Jiufen and Keelung, experiencing bustling urban centres, rice paddies, sun-drenched coasts and traditional Taiwanese life. While the terrain is easier than the KOM or Buddha's Palm, you'll still need plenty of endurance, not to mention careful pacing. Daily distances of 50 to 80 miles (80–130km) with overnight stops make it manageable, and Taiwan's bike-friendly infrastructure and support options make the route accessible at all points should you opt to ride certain sections.
Start/finish // Taipei
Distance // 746 miles (1200km)

Matt Munro for Lonely Planet; Sean Pavone/Shutterstock; Robertus Pudyanto/Shutterstock

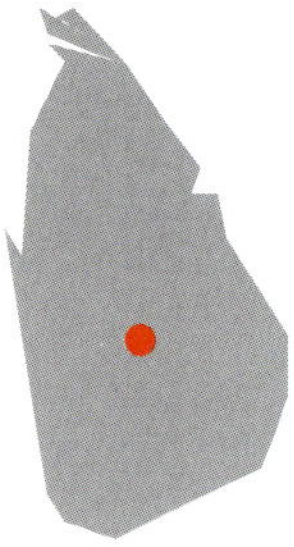

SRI LANKAN SIGHTSEEING

Monkeys, ancient ruins, very big Buddhas and some of the best tea you'll ever taste are the highlights of this two-week cycle tour of Sri Lanka.

Dinner-plate sized footprints? Check. Warm, basketball-sized lumps of dung? Check. 'Yep, we're definitely on an elephant's trail,' confirms my guide, Pete. Many people go to Sri Lanka specifically to see elephants; there are about 3000 in the wild. But when you're cycling around the island's interior, a 3m-tall *Elephas maximus* – 5000kg (5.5 tons) of unpredictability – is not something you really want to encounter. We've had an elephant-alert drill for what to do if we cross paths with one: stand stock still and avoiding meeting its eye, while Pete digs around in the pockets of his combat shorts for some firecrackers. These go off with a bang and, theoretically, scare the beast away – if Pete can find them in time.

While we're not here for the elephants on this 14-day tour, many of the wonders of Sri Lanka's archaeological Golden Triangle are on our itinerary: Sigiriya's citadel; Polonnaruwa, the ruins of a 12th-century city; the Buddhas of Dambulla; Kandy's Temple of the Tooth; and the tea plantations of Nuwara Eliya.

I'm part of a guided cycling tour – seven strangers, one guide, 10 days of riding, around 310 miles (500km) in total. There are pros and cons of joining a guided cycling trip. The advantage is that a lot of the organisational effort is avoided: your luggage is taken from one overnight stop to the next, and your guide will know the tried and tested cycling routes. The downside is that you don't get to select all your companions and the experience is fairly prescriptive. You can't stay an extra day somewhere on a whim, or divert too far from the day's plan.

That might seem contrary to the cyclist's instinctive need for freewheeling independence but it does mean that you can take off with your bike to any number of countries around the world with minimal planning. And on this tour of Sri Lanka's backroads, Pete is happy to fit in some extra mountain biking for those who need more of a fix, which is how I find myself on an elephant's trail while my companions are climbing Sigiriya, a 200m-high (650ft) rock pillar rising out of the jungle with a fortress on top.

Our trip began on a riverside path of the northern central lowlands near Lake Giritale, as we acclimatised to the humidity. Like the changing rooms at a communal swimming pool, the river is divided into sections. In one languid stretch women are washing their long dark hair. In the next, young men, waist-deep in water, are in discussion. In another section, parents are

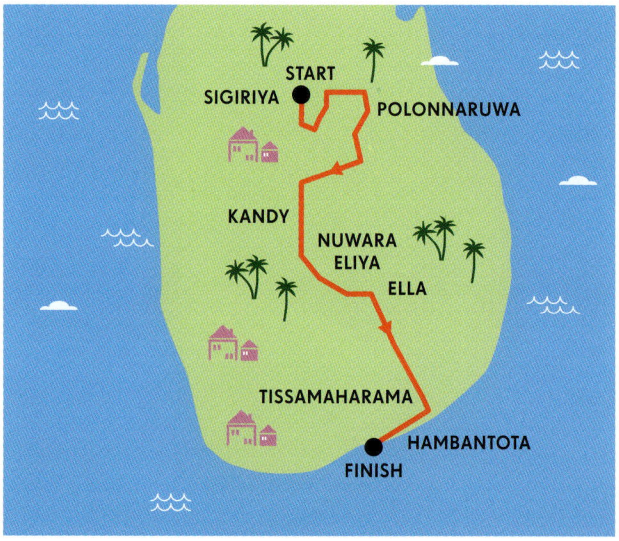

Sajith Perera/Getty Images

washing children, the sudsy youngsters springing like frogs from the riverbank into the water as we pass. Downstream is the tractor and water buffalo washing area.

After my excursion with Pete ends not with a bang but a beer, and we catch up on tales of skulduggery from Sigiriya (see right), our group rides onward to Polonnaruwa, fuelled by lemony, finger-sized bananas. Here the ruins of the 12th-century city are being reclaimed from the jungle, although monkeys – shy grey langurs and bolder macaques – still gambol on bulbous stupas (funerary domes made from millions of bricks). It's worth hiring a local guide to explain the buildings and temples since signposting is thin on the ground; they'll likely have a bicycle, which is the best way to get around the vast site.

Stonework of a spiritual nature is found in Dambulla's mountainside caves, which contain colossal statues of Buddha dating from the 2nd century.

But I've been waiting to get into hill country, south of the Triangle, where the world's finest Ceylon teas are harvested, and the climate is cooler. Our first stop in Sri Lanka's highlands is the city Kandy, and to get to Kandy means, for those who wish, descending 14 miles (23km) down the Knuckles mountain range into the island's cultural hub. Again, there's just one volunteer: me. The first portion of the ride runs through tea plantations, peppered by tea pickers wearing technicolour saris. It was an old tea planter who first showed Pete some routes through the plantations – this is the value of local knowledge.

SIGIRIYA'S HISTORY

In the 5th century, King Dhatusena's first son, Kasyapa, threatened by the arrival of a legitimate heir, bricked up his father alive in his own palace. Kasyapa's half-brother, Mogallan, fled to India, while King Kasyapa built a fortress on Sigiriya's rock pillar. After seven years, Mogallon returned from exile with an army and, in the ensuing battle, Kasyapa's elephant ran amok, causing confusion in his own ranks and allowing Mogallon to triumph.

Clockwise from top: a tea plantation in Nuwara Eliya; Tangalle beach on the south coast; Buddha statues in Dambulla's cave temple. Previous spread: Sigiriya fortress from above

alonanola/Shutterstock

Soon the trail rejoins the road and we race against the setting sun around forested mountainsides and through one-street villages, bunny-hopping over 3ft-wide (1m) potholes, speeding past fume-belching buses and tuk-tuks. Bats as large as tea towels flap along the valley beside us. We make the final climb into Kandy in the smoggy orange glow of twilight.

Kandy is famous for its Temple of the Tooth. The 18th-century building houses one of Buddhism's most sacred relics, a canine tooth of Buddha, which arrived in Sri Lanka for safekeeping in the 3rd century. Every year, in July, the tooth is paraded through Kandy on an elaborately decorated elephant, and there are three *pujas* (blessings) daily at the temple.

The ride continues south to Nuwara Eliya, a colonial hill station at 6500ft (1981m). The rose beds, mist, post office and Hill Club (jackets and ties please, gentlemen) could be an English village circa 1930. English names abound: Horton Plains, Elgin Falls, Gregory's Lake. And then we descend from the highlands all the way to the south coast, hitting the beach after 310 miles (500km) and 238 bottles of water (and uncounted Three Coins beers at the end of each day).

I never did see a wild elephant but being on a bicycle got us close to Sri Lanka's local culture, even if that included the group of children waiting at the top of a pass with homemade bows and arrows, picking off the stragglers. **RB**

TOOLKIT

Start // Sigiriya
Finish // Anhangma
Distance // 310 miles (500km)
Tour // Depending on the tour operator, the terms of each cycling tour may vary – most include accommodation, some food, but not any extras. Flights may or may not be included. Group sizes typically vary from 5 to 15 – generally, the more the people, the lower the cost. An alternative is to get a group of friends and book a recommended local guide independently.
When to ride // December to March.
What to take // A visa is required for most nationalities; it will need to be organised in advance.
Health tips // Some vaccinations are advisable (tetanus, typhoid, hepatitis A) and it's best to avoid bites from mosquitoes.

Opposite: the town of Bellagio on the shore of Lake Como, starting point for a cycling pilgrimage

MORE LIKE THIS
SPIRITUAL RIDES

BALI, INDONESIA

Bali is at its best in the out-of-the-way places. A guided cycle tour here can take in remote beaches, small villages, Hindu temples, markets and rural (and hilly) countryside. Although most cycle tourists arrive via the international airport at Denpasar, Ubud, the culture-rich town in the centre of the island, is the hub for most tours. Set out from here to explore the mountains of the north, coffee plantations and rice paddies, and become absorbed by the ebb and flow of life in villages that never see a coach tour. Some operators offer an optional add-on of a trip to neighbouring Lombok by ferry – the island is far less frequented than Bali and the local people are very welcoming of cycle tourists.
Start // Base yourself in Ubud
Distance // Variable

NEW MEXICO, USA

The Enchanted Circle is an 83-mile (133km) road circuit that revolves around the town of Taos in New Mexico. This part of the American Southwest has long attracted artists, from Georgia O'Keefe and Ansel Adams to author DH Lawrence, whose ranch just north of Taos is a memorial to the man. The region was once hailed as the 'Most Spiritual Place' in the US, maybe because of its deep Native American associations, or its painted historic churches, or perhaps because the stark desert beauty encourages a certain introspection. Cyclists, however, may seek spiritual help for other reasons: the Enchanted Circle Scenic Byway crosses a pair of 9000ft (2750m) passes as it circles 13,000ft (4000m) Wheeler Peak via the Taos Ski Valley. It's a stunning ride through the Sangre de Cristo mountains of New Mexico.
Start/finish // Taos
Distance // 83 miles (133km)

MADONNA DEL GHISALLO, ITALY

This is a short one, in fact, it is not more than a steep hill above Lake Como. But its stature in cycling could not be greater. The story goes that the medieval Count Ghisallo sought refuge from bandits at a shrine on the spot. The chapel memorialises the myth but after its regular appearance in the Giro di Lombardia and the Giro d'Italia, it began to attract pilgrims on two wheels. By 1949, the Pope confirmed a proposal by a local priest that La Madonna del Ghisallo should be declared the patroness of cyclists. The chapel has since become a museum of the sport and a monument to late cyclists. Fausto Coppi donated his 1942 hour-record-setting bike and the remains of the bike on which local boy Fabio Casartelli died during the 1995 Tour de France serves as a reminder of the risks pros take in pursuit of glory. There are several routes to the shrine; the climb from Bellagio is the toughest and best known.
Start // Bellagio
Finish // Madonna del Ghisallo
Distance // 6.5 miles (10.6km)

HOTEL FLORENCE
HOTEL DU LAC

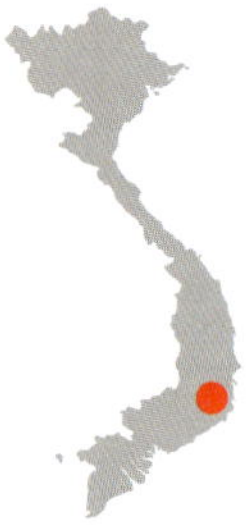

VIETNAM'S CENTRAL HIGHLANDS & COAST

From the punishing Khanh Le Pass to Ho Chi Minh City's hidden road rules, journey from mountain to sea as vibrant Vietnam unfolds in a single, sweeping adventure.

Huy Thoai/Shutterstock

There are countless ways to discover a country by bike, but it always starts the same way: with a map. Maybe someone tipped you off, or perhaps you stumbled on a route during your own late-night research but, in the end, it's you who traces the line. So how did this particular route come to life?

A friend and I had been cycling across southeast Asia for three months, our legs sharper than ever. With Ho Chi Minh City on the horizon and our journey nearing its end, we wanted one last shot at the mountains – not just for the challenge but to explore the Central Highlands, an area we had not yet ventured into. Having started in Nha Trang, from the mountains our plan was to reconnect with the coast, pedalling quiet backroads beside endless beaches, swept along by a salty breeze, the perfect recipe for an unforgettable ride.

We skipped the appetiser and went straight for the main course: the Khanh Le Pass mountain road. This is no easy climb,

"The karaoke machine blared, as we sang and laughed late into the night"

19 miles (30 km) of winding tarmac, rising from lush tropical lowlands to the edge of Đà Lạt's alpine plateau. The elevation gain? A punishing 5577ft (1700m). A full day's effort, the hardest section came early, when the heat and humidity felt suffocating. But as we climbed, the air cooled and the views began to open up, making the sweat worthwhile. In one word: 'gorgeous'. As we neared the summit, a thick fog rolled in, giving the final stretch a mystical, otherworldly atmosphere. Reaching the top isn't just a physical triumph, it feels like entering a different land. The flora and fauna shift, pine trees grow alongside banana plants, greenhouses dot the slopes, and the weather turns spring-like, with colourful flowers blooming along the roadside.

Đà Lạt itself is a stark contrast to the rest of Vietnam. Its cool mountain air, European-style architecture, and relaxed vibe bring a Continental twist to the city. Founded by the French in the early 20th century as a refuge from the Mekong Delta's scorching heat, the city is worth at least a day (your legs will thank you). We spent the evening at DuSam craft beer bar, chatting with local brewers who are putting Đà Lạt on the map. Finding a good IPA in Vietnam is rare; this felt like a true reward.

Leaving Đà Lạt was surprisingly smooth. The road wasn't busy, apart from one short section, and it was mostly downhill. Rain is common, so we geared up accordingly. As for food on the move, a vital part of any bike trip, we relied on bánh mì, Vietnam's legendary sandwiches. They're cheap, filling and delicious, making them perfect for daytime fuel. Since southeast Asia has plentiful food options, there's no need to haul extra kitchen gear, making packing that much lighter. With bánh mì as our go-to, we saved the luxury of sit-down meals for the evenings.

Our next stop was the Bảo Đại Waterfall, named after Vietnam's last emperor, who hunted in the area. It's a short detour, but well worth it. The place feels almost forgotten, with overgrown gardens and winding paths that give it a Tomb Raider feel. The waterfall itself is a 230-foot high, 330-foot wide (70m; 100m) torrent that thunders into a misty basin, shaking both the ground and your eardrums. Best of all, you'll likely have it entirely to yourself since it's well off the beaten path.

The descent continued along the QL28B road, arguably the most scenic stretch of the route. Imagine standing at 3300ft (1000m) on the edge of a sheer drop, gazing out over a lattice of lakes, forested hills, and smoke curls rising from distant villages. With the sun casting a golden glow over everything, it's like cycling through a painting. That night, with no accommodation in sight, we stopped by a roadside restaurant with an open-air seating area and asked if we could pitch our tent in a corner. Not

ROAD RULES

At first glance, traffic rules in Vietnam seem non-existent, but there's an unspoken flow by which everyone abides. The first rule: never stop unless the traffic light says so. Drivers from side roads never look, they just merge into the chaos. Stay alert and anticipate any surprise arrivals, or you'll find yourself slamming on the brakes and cursing under your breath. It's a wild, yet strangely effective system, and one that requires constant awareness.

Viet Su Luoc/Shutterstock

only was it okay, but the staff showed us to a shower room and a spot to charge our phones. Soon we found ourselves sitting at their table, celebrating a family birthday. The karaoke machine blared, the sound echoing through the valley as we sang and laughed late into the night. It was one of those spontaneous, joyous moments that make travelling by bike unforgettable.

Not that it was all plain sailing. In the tropical lowlands, for example, I let my guard down one evening and forgot to zip closed one of my panniers, which I'd left beside the tent. The next morning, as I packed, I found a scorpion nestled inside. I didn't get stung but it was a stark reminder to stay vigilant, and not the kind of wake-up call you want.

In the days that followed, we cruised along quiet coastal roads, passing sleepy fishing villages and golden beaches around Mũi Né. Of course, we stopped for swims and drank from coconuts. The final marvels of our journey included cycling through the Cần Giờ UNESCO Biosphere Reserve, a vast mangrove forest just outside Ho Chi Minh City — a peaceful transition into the coming urban chaos.

So while rolling into Ho Chi Minh City felt surreal, it wasn't overwhelming; it's infamous traffic was surprisingly manageable. From misty mountain passes to bustling city sprawl, one thing had remained constant throughout Vietnam and that was the warmth, generosity and kindness of the Vietnamese people. Smiles, waves, shared meals, and stories – they were the true highlights of this ride. **ND**

Clockwise from left: pausing on the quieter QL28B road; hectic Ho Chi Minh City; Bao Dai waterfall

Previous page: snaking Khanh Le Pass connects Nha Trang and Đà Lạt

Nicolas D'Hoedt; Iryna Hromotska/Shutterstock

TOOLKIT

Start // Nha Trang
Finish // Ho Chi Minh City
Distance // 370 miles (600km)
Duration // 10 days
Getting there // Fly to Ho Chi Minh City, then take the train to Nha Trang. Bicycles travel separately in cargo and can be picked up at the station the next day. It's safe and inexpensive.
When to go // The dry season, from December to April.
What to pack // Rain gear and warmer clothing for the Central Highlands; flip-flops and a swimsuit for the coast. Camping gear can be useful but is not essential.
Where to stay // There are plenty of accommodation options along the route for all budgets. Just be sure to map them out before hitting the road each morning.
More info // www.facebook.com/cyclingfurther

Opposite: the village of Nong Khiaw along the banks of the Nam Ou River

MORE LIKE THIS
SUMPTUOUS SPINS ACROSS SOUTHEAST ASIA

THE HẢI VÂN PASS, VIETNAM

From the ancient imperial city of Huế to the vibrant, ever-evolving city of Da Nang, this is Vietnam in a nutshell. Though relatively short, this ride packs in a lot. Leaving Huế, the road winds through tranquil fishing villages before reaching the breathtaking Lăng Cô Bay, where the waters and sands dance to the rhythm of the tides, all under the watchful gaze of the mountain gods. Beyond the bay, you'll find yourself on the Hải Vân Pass itself, an elegant dragon-shaped road that climbs to 1627ft (496m) above sea level, and which marks the transition between the subtropical north and the tropical south. Though well-known among visitors, the road remains surprisingly quiet, offering cyclists a peaceful experience. After the climb, the thrill of descending into Da Nang awaits. Don't miss crossing the iconic Dragon Bridge on your way. And when your wheels hit the soft sand of Da Nang's beaches, you'll know it's time for a well-earned dip in the sea.

Start // Huế
Finish // Da Nang
Distance // 76 miles (122km)

THE KANCHANABURI LOOP, THAILAND

Thailand isn't just about beaches lined with coconut trees. Leave behind the usual stereotypes and venture into the unforgiving, steep, narrow roads leading deep into Kanchanaburi Province. Head toward Erawan National Park, then continue along the Sinakharin Reservoir, on your way to the Huay Mae Khamin Waterfalls, a natural wonder you won't want to miss. Pack a tent, as this region is becoming a popular escape from the heat of Bangkok; it now offers some of the best campsites in Thailand. A boat will take you across the lake to the untouched wilderness on the other side. Indigenous groups in the area happily showcase their ancestral traditions. When you reach the top of the challenging 4041 road, you'll have conquered Kanchanaburi's toughest ascent, with spectacular views as your reward. Let yourself freewheel down the other side, exploring any of the backcountry roads that effortlessly guide you back to where you started, among blissful agricultural landscapes.

Start/finish // Kanchanaburi City
Distance // 177 miles (285km)

NONG KHIAW TO MUANG NGOY, LAOS

In the heart of the Laotian jungle, along the Nam Ou River, a dirt track connects two of the region's most stunning destinations. Starting in Nong Khiaw, a village nestled in a deep canyon surrounded by towering limestone peaks, this 28-mile (45km) ride is challenging yet rewarding. The track isn't long, but its steep ups and downs can be demanding. A snood is a must to shield your lungs from the dust, especially in dry conditions (avoid when muddy!). Along the way, enjoy gorgeous vistas, remote villages with friendly locals, and water buffalo grazing by the roadside. By the time you reach Muang Ngoy, you'll be covered in dust, but a quick river crossing will help rinse it off. Muang Ngoy may be small but offers plenty, from Western restaurants to a variety of accommodation, with as impressive a backdrop as the one you left behind.

Start // Nong Khiaw
Finish // Muang Ngoy
Distance // 28 miles (45km)

Emad aljumah/Getty Images

EUROPE

THE ALPINA MEDITERRANEAN

This new, three-country route through Italy, Slovenia, and Croatia offers riders a splendidly blended adventure, where history and culture converge with rivers, mountains and sea.

On the second day of the six-stage Alpina Mediterranean Cycle Route, my cycle-mates and I rode into the Slovenian mountain town of Kobarid, the setting for Hemingway's WWI novel *A Farewell to Arms.* We took a break on the stone-arch Napoleon Bridge, across which the French emperor's troops once marched, and realised we were surrounded by quintessential Slovenia. That is, history entwined with monumental natural wonder. The Alps framed an amphitheatre of oaks, firs and beech trees, above a deep gorge funnelling the star of this particular show – the glacial, electric-turquoise Soča River, as it crashed against limestone rocks beneath us.

Since the start of our ride, a couple of days earlier in Italy, I'd kept my eye out for such locations. In my reporter's notebook, I identified them as 'convergences', places where the distinct and particular attractions of the region come together. The first time I scribbled down such thoughts about this new route, the three-country, 185-mile (299km) Alpina Mediterranean, or Alp Med, it felt novel (and not in a Hemingway sense). But spots like Kobarid, where the Alps meet the Soča on land steeped in history, were becoming so regular that I'd begun to suspect the entire route was one big convergence. A point where worlds collide, to the great benefit of those lucky enough to pedal through it.

My journey on this route had, in truth, begun two weeks earlier, when my future cycling companions, the Alp Med's project manager and its lead cartographer, asked if I'd join them on a final, work-the-bugs-out recce ride before they made the itinerary public.

When faced with such a proposition, I generally say yes, regardless of where the route is going. Like most of us committed to adventure on two wheels, I enjoy discovering new places, or even experiencing familiar ones in different ways. I love seeing how, via bike trails, locals showcase the best of their home regions to the rest of the world. So, when asked to test an itinerary that departs from Italy, glides through wine country, heads into the Julian Alps and winds along Slovenian river valleys, before ending on Croatia's Adriatic coast, I of course answered in the affirmative. Yet, as I did so, I was

zedspider/Shutterstock

already thinking of excuses to stick around under the guise of conducting more 'research'.

'This is a solid route with a nice amount of everything,' explained Matija Klanjšček, the Alpina Mediterranean's lead cartographer, when we spoke on the phone before the ride. 'There's culture, great food, beautiful countryside, mountains and rivers, the sea, plus a little mixed-surface riding.' Klanjšček is also co-founder of GoodTrail, a route-development firm based in Ljubljana. 'Our idea was to make it challenging but doable for most riders,' he says. 'Stages are around 80% quiet roads, 20% gravel, and you'll ride about 30 miles (50km) and climb 2100ft (650m) per day.'

The Alpina Mediterranean begins in the commune of Venzone, about 19 miles (30km) north of Udine, in a valley of the Tagliamento river. Squeezed between the Carnic Alps, to the west, and the Julian Alps in northeastern Italy's Friuli-Venezia Giulia region, Venzone has been an important pivot point for travellers through the mountains since Roman times. It was here, in fact, that I noted my first convergence of geographic and cultural forces. At the head of the route. Day one. Thanks to its strategic location, it's also a stop on the Alpe Adria cycle trail, which runs from Austria to Italy's Adriatic coast.

From between peaks, the trail set off south, out of town along the milky-teal Tagliamento, one of Europe's last 'wild' rivers. The route curled east, clinging to the Julian Alps' southwestern edge, and into the medieval, UNESCO-listed town of Cividale

RIVER OF PEACE

One of Europe's most beautiful rivers, the emerald Soča, which begins in Slovenia's Triglav National Park and runs from the Julian Alps to the Adriatic Sea, was once an important front line during WWI. Today, a demarcation of conflict is now a symbol of unity. The Walk of Peace, a network of some 300 monuments located along the waterway, encourages travellers to see the region as one of 'peace, collaboration and friendship among nations'.

Previous spread: the Soča river as it flows through Slovenia

Mazur Travel/Shutterstock; 8_f_roberto8/Shutterstock

del Friuli, at the centre of the Colli Orientali del Friuli wine region. Gradually, the Alp Med found its undulating groove through corduroy waves of vineyards and turned north on the Natisone River, ushering us into Slovenia. In Kobarid, we switched one river for another and, then, for the better part of the next two days, followed the Soča out of the Alps.

On the morning of our fourth stage, in Nova Gorica, we crowded around a cafe table on a terrace overlooking Europe Square (another convergence point I noted), which the Slovenian town shares with its Italian neighbour, Gorizia. We studied the maps and GPX tracks for our upcoming stages. What lay ahead would take us into Slovenia's Karst region, the cave-riddled stretch where, as they say, the mountains meet the sea. We'd then skirt just north of Trieste before diving to the Adriatic.

Instinct kicks in on the last stage; touring cyclists, like migratory birds, are pulled to the end of a route. After crossing the border into Croatia, we could sense the sea before we saw it. The smell of salty air drew us to the 19th-century Hapsburgian resort town of Opatija (a final convergence), where the Adriatic meets with the edge of the Dinaric Alps that rumble into the Balkans.

'A bike trail is a living thing,' explained Jan Klavora, the Alp Med's project manager, as we lifted beers on a patio bar overlooking Croatia's Kvarner Gulf and the islands of Krk and Cres. 'It starts with a desire to connect places, to help cyclists and solve logistics. After it's released to the public, it's no longer ours. It belongs to the locals who live there and those who like to travel using their own power.' **AC**

Matevz Hribar

Clockwise from top: the Ponte del Diavolo in Cividale del Friuli; passing Slovenian vines; Opatija on Croatia's Adriatic coast

TOOLKIT

Start // Venzone, Italy
Finish // Opatija, Croatia
Distance // 185 miles (299km)
Getting there // Trains and buses criss-cross the region, with regular connections to the route's head from the Italian cities of Udine, Trieste, and Venice; and from its terminus via Ljubljana, Slovenia's capital, and Rijeka, on Croatia's coast. The most convenient international airport is Trieste.
What to wear // Regulation cycling gear is fine: jersey, padded cycling shorts, gloves.
What to pack // Windbreaker, waterproof trousers, rain jacket, bathing suit for rivers and coast. A gravel bike is best, tyre widths no less than 1.65 inches (42mm).
Where to stay // The Alp Med's detailed GPX tracks list restaurants and accommodations on each stage ride.
More info // bikeroute.si/

Opposite: wildflowers on the Trans Dinarica as it passes through Montenegro

MORE LIKE THIS
WESTERN BALKAN JOURNEYS

TRANS DINARICA

Since its official launch in 2024, this 3100-mile (5000km), 98-stage route has become one of southeastern Europe's most important bicycle itineraries. Connecting all eight countries of the Western Balkans (the only cycle trail to do so), it links Slovenia, Croatia, Bosnia and Herzegovina, Montenegro, Albania, North Macedonia, Kosovo, and Serbia. Starting in Tolmin, Slovenia, where it intersects with the Alpina Mediterranean, it rolls to the Adriatic before turning east into the heart of the Dinaric Alps, where it forms a loop through the six southernmost countries. Designed to steer adventurers away from over-touristed areas and show off under-appreciated villages and points of interest, the trail also encourages a sustainable-travel economy across the region. The route's GPX tracks provide detailed information about places to stay and eat.
Start // Tolmin
Finish // Tomislavgrad
Distance // 3100 miles (5000km)

ĆIRO TRAIL

Following a network of narrow-gauge Austro-Hungarian train lines built in the late 19th century, this route connects Mostar, in Bosnia and Herzegovina, to Croatia's Adriatic coast. During its day, the Ćiro, a local nickname for the steam locomotives, provided a lifeline to the outside world for remote settlements. Decommissioned in the 1970s, today it offers again a rare opportunity to visit Balkan villages nestled in the Dinaric Alps. Along the way, UNESCO and other cultural sites abound, including the Mostar Bridge, medieval gravesites with monumental tombstones, and the walled city of Dubrovnik. Relatively flat (it was a railway after all), much of the trail is asphalt, with a regular supply of pension accommodation and restaurants. An ideal way to take a closer look at this historic stretch of southeastern Europe.
Start // Mostar
Finish // Dubrovnik
Distance // 98 miles (157km)

TRANS DALMATIA

This brand new, seven-day route takes riders on a loop, of sorts, from Zadar in Croatia, to the surrounding region and across an archipelago that surrounds the northern Dalmatian city. Created to give travellers a more engaged experience around the popular tourism region – beyond the regular, coastal, holiday bottlenecks – the trail actually consists of multiple loops that create flower-petal-like circuits surrounding the central hub. These combined itineraries ride through vineyards and fishing villages, and pass by remote coves. The route also visits three Adriatic islands, rolls into nature parks, and does it all with the majestic Velebit Mountain in the background, providing continual awe-inspiring photo opportunities. Created for all ability levels, the daily stages average around 30 miles (50km) with around 1650ft (500m) of climbing.
Start/finish // Zadar, Croatia
Distance // 211 miles (340km)

BORNHOLM

Make a weekend of this easygoing lap of Denmark's Bike Island and embark on a love-affair with life on two wheels.

Looking back, I realise that my day spent circumnavigating the island of Bornholm was where it all began: the ride that started my love affair with bike travel. That was the summer I travelled to Copenhagen and decided to add a weekend on Bornholm to my itinerary. Bornholm is a small dot in the Baltic Sea, whose white-sand beaches, year-round sun and laidback vibe make it a popular getaway for the already easygoing Danes.

Today a picture of calm, Bornholm has an eventful history, due in large part to its location; a strategic port along key maritime routes, it lies to the east of Denmark, to the south of Sweden, and is north-ish of both Germany and Poland. Thus has the island been occupied by Germanic tribes, Swedes, Danes, the Soviets and, currently, the Danes once more.

Modern Bornholm is held in great affection by Danes, a fact evidenced by its nicknames. Known variously as 'Sunshine Island' or the 'Pearl of the Baltic', others refer to it simply as 'Bike Island', quite the endorsement in this cycling-mad nation. Yet Bornholm is, undoubtedly, a true cycling gem, packing 144 miles (232km) of signposted bike trails into 227 sq mi (588 sq km) of land. Among them are inland trails, dedicated routes for mountain biking, and a 65-mile (105km) loop that circles the entire island.

As a novice rider, my plan that summer was to rent a bike for day trips to explore the island, figuring it would be a good way to get some longer rides under my belt in a low-stress environment. Fortunately, my hostel in Rønne, the island's largest town, had rental bikes. On the downside, they looked to be 50 years old and weigh 100lbs (45kg), but they'd do the trick. So I paid the hostel manager, hopped on and headed

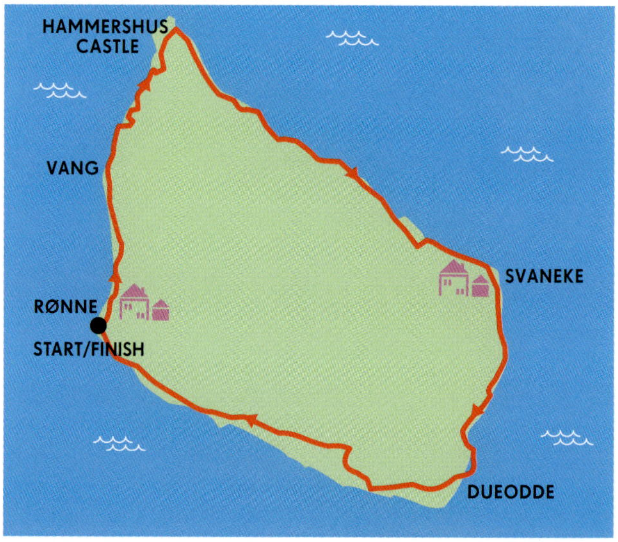

MrPat/Shutterstock

MrPat/Shutterstock

for Dueodde beach, some 20 miles (33km) away. Tack on the return leg and it would be the longest ride I'd ever done.

Biking along the coast on a flat, well-paved path, I couldn't have felt more serene. At around six miles in (10km), I stopped at Nylars Rundkirke, the best preserved of four 'round churches' on the island. Dating back to the 12th century, the thick granite and limestone walls were designed to offer both a place of worship and sanctuary from invaders.

Twenty kilometres later, I arrived at Dueodde. Still morning, and with miles of beach practically to myself, I took a dip in the Baltic. The powdery sands and crystal-clear waters have earned Dueodde a reputation as one of the finest beaches in Europe and it wasn't long before I dozed off, to the sound of my heartbeat returning to its resting rhythm after the shock of a chilly swim. When I woke it was early afternoon, so I packed up and headed back to my bike, which by now I had named 'Susan'. Pointing the front wheel back towards Rønne, I paused; with nowhere else to be, and nothing else to do but ride, I decided to keep going.

I rode on, past windmills and smokehouses and brightly coloured homes. Feeling peckish, I turned into Svaneke Bryghus, an organic brewery, for a pint of IPA and a spiced-herring sandwich garnished, Danish-style, with egg and onions. I kept pedalling. Past fishing villages, wildflowers, oystercatchers and eider ducks. In the course of my ride that day I visited art studios and chatted with passing cyclists. By now I was more than halfway round, the sun still shining and the breeze cool. It was the longest ride I'd ever done – it felt like I could ride forever.

"Powdery sands and crystal-clear waters have earned Dueodde a reputation as one of the finest beaches in Europe"

By the time I hit 50 miles (80km) it was past dinner time and dusk was approaching. I'd been enjoying my excursion so much that I hadn't planned for nightfall. I had neither lights nor food, and my water was running low. I was tired, too, but when I passed a sign for a shortcut back to Rønne – and a well-paved one at that – I chose not to take it. Why come all this way, I reasoned, and not finish the loop?

It wasn't long before I found myself in a darkening forest,

DENMARK'S HIGHLANDS

To sample Bornholm's more challenging road riding, channel your inner Jonas Vingegaard and head towards Vang Hill, ranked among Denmark's toughest climbs at 1.2km (.75 miles), with an average gradient of 7.5%. Alternatively, the road to Hammeren Lighthouse runs for 720m at an average 9%. Mountain bikers head to Almindingen Forest, which boasts singletrack and the island's highest point; or else to Paradisbakkerne, for technical, natural singletrack featuring rocky sections.

Left to right: sand dunes and the Baltic sea seen from Dueodde Lighthouse; Rønne harbour; the town of Gudhjem on the north coast. Previous spread: Nylars Rundkirke is on the west side of Bornholm

where the path switched from flat to rolling, a topography not popular with my old jalopy. I pushed my bike up some rooty climbs and rolled it down the other side, occasionally waving my phone to see if I could get service. The serenity I had experienced earlier that day had most definitely passed. There were moments I wasn't sure where the path was, or even where I was.

After a day of leisure, this felt stressful. In the remaining light I picked out the ruins of Hammershus Castle, built in 1250 as a fortress against rival Scandinavian kingdoms. A beautiful sight but more than a little unsettling, I pressed on.

When I finally pulled back into Rønne, I parked 'Susan' and patted her wide, padded saddle. It was fully dark by now and all the restaurants were closed. I popped the coins I had into the hostel's vending machine and, in quick succession, swallowed three Häagen-Dazs bars and two cans of Tuborg. Concluding that every great bike ride should be capped off with ice cream and a beer, I was beat. The distance, plus a little end-of-day excitement, had turned my plans for a brief, pleasant ride into a two-wheeled adventure. One which ever since has fuelled an inner voice that says: 'Keep going.' **CP**

picture alliance/Getty Images; Janusz Baczynski/Shutterstock

TOOLKIT

Start/finish // Rønne
Distance // 65 miles (105km)
Getting there // Take the train from Copenhagen to Ystad, in Sweden, then transfer to the high-speed ferry to Rønne. The trip takes about five hours. Danish operator DSB has one ticket that covers both the train and ferry.
When to go // April to October
What to wear // Typical summer cycling clothes are fine.
What to pack // Sunscreen, water, a light jacket.
Where to stay // Rønne has the most choice of accommodation, including hotels, bed and breakfasts, hostels, and house rentals.
Where to eat // Svaneke Bryghus, Lille Gadegård Vineyard, or Michelin-starred Kadeau.
More info // bornholm.info

Opposite: the Confederation Trail on Prince Edward Island; the chalk cliffs of the Isle of Wight's south coast

MORE LIKE THIS
REWARDING ISLAND ROUTES

CONFEDERATION TRAIL, PRINCE EDWARD ISLAND

Located on Canada's east coast, Prince Edward Island (PEI) is a dream of red-sand beaches, spectacular seafood, Anne of Green Gables memorabilia – and trail cycling. Established in the 1990s, the Confederation Trail runs along the old Prince Edward Island Railway and provides 170 miles (273km) of off-road cycling. Highlights include St. Peter's Bay, dotted with oyster and mussel beds; Bogside Brewing and the microbreweries of the east side; Summerside's historic waterfront; and Abram-Village, the hub of Acadian culture. You can mix and match parts of the trail or try riding from point to point. Visit in the early autumn to enjoy the harvest season; Islanders are rightly proud of their food heritage and love to share it. Don't miss the chance to stop at COWS, PEI's famous creamery, for a cone and a pack of chocolate-covered potato chips, a true delicacy.
Start // Tignish
Finish // Elmira
Distance // 170 miles (273km)

ROUND THE ISLAND, ISLE OF WIGHT

Located in the Channel just a few miles off the English mainland, the Isle of Wight boasts 200 miles (322km) of cycle tracks and trails. Many riders choose to criss-cross back and forth, visiting attractions such as royal residences, from Norman castles to Osborne House (Queen Victoria's favourite). If you like your history older, drop by Stone Age burial grounds; or for older still, check out the Dinosaur Isle Museum and dinosaur footprints at Hanover Point. Back on the bike, increasing numbers are opting to ride the Round the Island, a circumnavigation whose 64 miles (103km) features close to 6560ft (2000m) of climbing. Be prepared for stunning coastal views along the way, including Alum Bay and its mineral-rich, multicoloured sands. Foodies are well-served too, courtesy of fresh-caught seafood, to say nothing of the island's highly prized heirloom tomatoes, used both in establishments across the island and, further afield, in some of Britain's finest restaurants.
Start/finish // One of four ferry terminals; Fishbourne, East Cowes, Ryde, Yarmouth.
Distance // 64 miles (103km)

TEXEL ISLAND, THE NETHERLANDS

In a region already regarded as a spiritual home of cycling, Texel, off the Netherlands' northern coast, is well worth a visit. Part of the West Frisian Islands, the 63 sq mi (162 sq km) island is easy to navigate by bike, thanks to 87 miles (140km) of cycle paths that run through historic towns and along the coast. There's a wide range of landscapes, from sand dunes to forest to marshlands and you can also explore the island's tidal mudflats, home to sandpipers, oystercatchers and dozens of other bird species, as well as seal colonies (check for tide times). For a full day's outing, a round-island loop runs for 33 miles (53km), with easy terrain that is well suited to a family trip or those just beginning their cycling adventures. And the food and drink – Texel lamb, sheep cheese, fresh seafood and craft beer – make for a tasty post-ride wind-down.
Start/finish // VVV Texel, Den Burg
Distance // 33 miles (53km); various trails

THE PAULINE PORTER POPULAIRE

A three-day adventure on one of Britain's most celebrated endurance rides encounters mountaineering history, iconic cycling ascents, and Wales's beautiful national parks.

When bike builder Tony Oliver moved to north Wales, it presented something of a conundrum for one of his customers. Bryan Chapman owned one of his bikes and, when it needed a little extra care and attention, liked to take it to Tony personally. The round trip to get a quality service now required a ride of over 370 miles (600km), from Bryan's home in Bristol to Tony's new place on the island of Anglesey. Legend has it that Bryan would regularly tackle the ride over a long weekend.

No one knows precisely which route Bryan took, nor how many times he actually made the journey but, after his death in 1989, the Bryan Chapman Memorial ride was named in his honour. A round trip, from Chepstow to Menai and back, it has since grown into one of the most prestigious rides in the long-distance cycling calendar. Also known as the 'Wales End to End', every May it attracts hundreds of riders, who have up to 40 hours to complete the distance. A handful of the very fastest can complete it in an incredible 24 hours – and everyone has to survive on precious little sleep.

So when Will Pomeroy, the current organiser, decided to open the Bryan Chapman up to more riders, he chose to break it over three days, giving entrants time to recuperate each evening. 'This version of the ride has become popular with cyclists who aren't ready to take on 600km in one go,' Will explains, of an event first staged in 2024. 'I've also had great feedback from riders who tackled the Bryan Chapman when they were younger and want to experience it again.'

He named his time-extended version the Pauline Porter Populaire, Pauline being Bryan's regular ride partner, as well

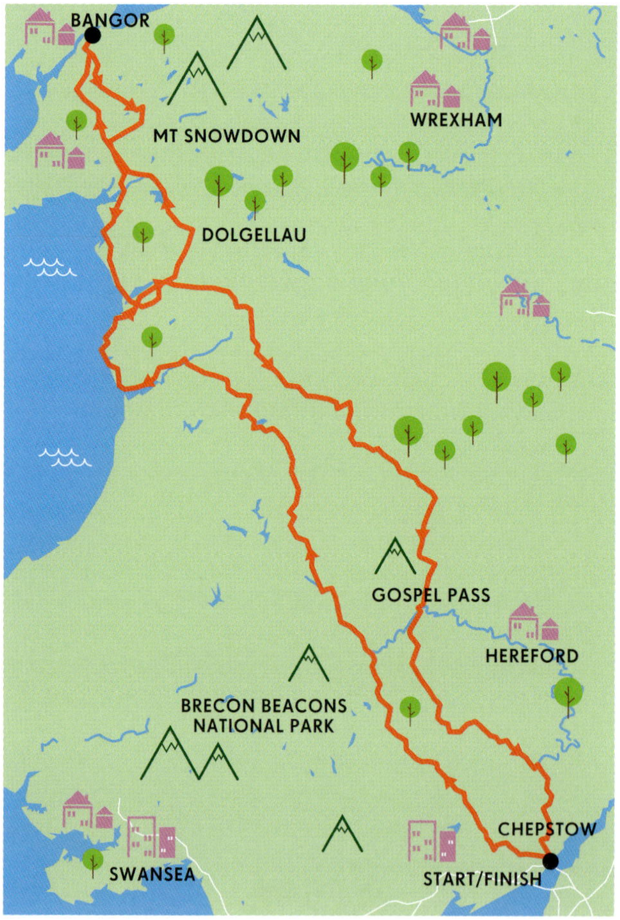

stocker1970/Shutterstock

"Riders on the Pauline Porter invariably pick up a few beers in Barmouth, so their second night at Dolgellau has a party atmosphere"

as the creator of the 'Anglesey & Back', another endurance ride of similarly fearsome distance. The Pauline Porter also runs in May, starting a day earlier than the Bryan Chapman, so that riders on both events pass each other as they circle Snowdonia in opposite directions. Indeed, Pauline has been known to make the occasional guest appearance, stamping brevet cards for riders as they crest the brutal Machynlleth Mountain pass.

You can use Will's flexible approach to create your own multiday itinerary along the route at any time of the year. Starting in Chepstow, the first day's ride is up to 142 miles (228km), through the Bannau Brycheiniog (Brecon Beacons National Park), spotting red kites as you follow the River Wye north towards its source on Plynlimon (2467ft/752m). You then follow the coast road past Aberdyfi and Fairbourne to your first night's rest.

A prolific route planner, Will Pomeroy is known for sending riders over the most challenging hills possible. So, while his second day of the Pauline Porter comes in at just under 107 miles (173km), it starts with a bracing climb up to the waters of the Llyn Trawsfynydd reservoir. To compensate, there's also a visit to the Tan-y-Bwlch Station tea rooms on the Ffestiniog and Welsh Highland Railway, owned by the world's oldest surviving railway company. The route next skirts the western flanks of Yr Wyddfa, the mighty Mount Snowdon (3560ft/1085m), with views of both the Rhyd-Ddu and Snowdon Ranger climbs to the summit.

Crossing the Menai Bridge is a significant milestone, when you know that you have reached the halfway point. Doubling back, head to Llanberis, the outdoor capital of Wales, to take on the climb over Pen-y-Pass. You could book an extra night in the youth hostel at the top of this ascent, spending the evening at the Pen-Y-Gwryd Hotel, immersing yourself in Snowdonia's rich mountaineering history (see panel).

Riders on the Pauline Porter spend two nights at the youth hostel at Dolgellau, one out and one on their way back. Lying in the shadow of the brooding mountain of Cader Idris (2930ft/893m), you can add in extra stops between Menai and Dolgellau if you wish.

But if you are intent on getting back to Dolgellau on day two, your route will include a speedy dash past Harlech Castle, the former residence of Owain Glyndŵr, who led a 15-year revolt against the English in the 1400s. You'll then follow a rolling coastal road down to Barmouth, crossing

SNOWDONIA'S EVEREST CONNECTIONS

Before George Mallory and Sandy Irvine made their fateful attempt on Everest in 1924, they spent time at what is now the Pen-y-Pass youth hostel, and you can see pictures of them if you decide to stop for a night here. The nearby Pen-y-Gwryd hotel was used as a training base by Edmund Hillary and Tenzing Norgay before their own successful ascent, the first, in 1953. Memorabilia is on display on in the Everest Room, where they and others have autographed the ceiling.

Clockwise from top: Harlech castle; climbing through Wales; Cadair Idris in Snowdonia. Previous spread: the Wye Valley

Dan Lambert/Shutterstock; Lukassek/Shutterstock

its iconic bridge. Wales's longest wooden viaduct at 2690ft (820m), it carries cyclists, walkers and trains over the Mawddach river.

Riders on the Pauline Porter invariably pick up a few beers in Barmouth, so their second night at Dolgellau has something of a party atmosphere. It's as good a point as any to celebrate just how far you've come.

Day three takes you back past Cader Idris, where people brave enough to sleep at the top are said to wake as either a poet or a madman. Then it's on to Newtown and Knighton, another stop for tea and cake, this time at the Offa's Dyke visitors' centre on your way to Hay-on-Wye. A town famous for its literary connections and annual book festival, it's convenient for an extra night's stopover, particularly if you want to browse its vast array of second-hand bookshops. But Hay is also the starting point for a climb of Gospel Pass, Wales's highest paved road. It takes grit and determination to make the 5-mile (8km) climb, one that has almost 1640ft (500m) of ascent, followed by an exhilarating descent the other side.

A final run takes you on to Monmouth, where you pick up the Wye Valley to follow the river to Tintern Abbey, another location with literary associations. After the climb back up to the finish line at Chepstow, you can reflect on an adventure that has showcased the very best of Wales's landscape, culture and history. **MS**

Fergus Coyle

TOOLKIT

Start/finish // Chepstow
Distance // 373 miles (600km)
Duration // 3 days
Getting there // Trains run to and from Chepstow: from England via Gloucester; and in Wales, Cardiff and Newport.
When to go // The Pauline Porter Populaire takes place in May. If you're riding independently then summer is best, with more daylight and warmer evenings.
What to wear // Good (padded) cycling shorts; lightweight gear for rain, sunshine and colder nights.
What to pack // The route has long sections with no supermarkets or restaurants, so be sure to plan stops; carry extra water and plenty to eat.
Where to eat // The Honey Cafe in Bronllys is the first 'control' on the PPP, and also has a history serving riders on the Bryan Chapman. Excellent breakfasts make this an essential first stop.
More info // pedalution.co.uk

Opposite: Highland cattle enjoying the NC500

MORE LIKE THIS
ENDURANCE ROUTES TO RIDE AT LEISURE

LAND'S END TO CARLISLE, ENGLAND

While lacking the romance of a John O'Groats finish, if you want to discover the best of England, then this route will take you from the southwest tip of the country to close to the border with Scotland. There are plenty of variations but avoid the record-setting routes that use busy main roads and look online for routes that opt for quieter B-roads. You can use these as inspiration to tailor your own itinerary. Whichever route you go for, it will start with a demanding trek through Cornwall and Devon before you hit the Somerset Levels. The choice from there is yours, but we highly recommend a visit to the Cyclists' War Memorial in Meriden, before heading across the Peak District, through the Forest of Bowland and over the Lake District's highest road, the Kirkstone Pass, before dropping down to Carlisle and your train home.

Start // Land's End
Finish // Carlisle
Distance// 300 miles (483km)

NORTH COAST 500, SCOTLAND

An extensive route that traces the northern coastline of Scotland, this 500-mile journey will immerse you in some of its wildest landscapes and most beautiful beaches. Good train connections make Inverness the perfect starting point (keep your eyes peeled for dolphins in the Moray Firth) before heading clockwise towards Wester Ross to see tumbling waterfalls and yet more dramatic terrain. In Torridon, the route will guide you past some of Scotland's most distinctive mountains, such as Stac Pollaidh, Liathach and Beinn Alligin, before heading towards the highest of the Highlands in Sutherland. Be on the lookout for both golden and white-tailed eagles (Britain's largest), as well as guillemots, razorbills and, if you're very lucky, basking sharks. Follow the coast to John O'Groats and the homeward 'leg', towards Easter Ross, the Black Isle and your finishing line at Inverness.

Start/finish // Inverness
Distance // 500 miles (805km)

DE VOLCANS 600, FRANCE

Starting and finishing in the town of Nevers on the banks of the River Loire, this 373-mile (600km) ride is the perfect way to explore the heart of France. It takes riders into the Massif Central highlands, on a ride that can be a three- or four-day adventure, weaving through a landscape of extinct volcanoes. Weather can be unpredictable, with lightning storms once bringing large numbers of riders to a halt in Mont-Dore. If you are doing this at your own pace, Mont-Dore is good place for your first stop, before tackling the route's highest point, the Col de la Croix Saint-Robert (4760ft/1451m). Day two requires yet more climbing through the mountains, before you drop to the town of Issoire. Day three will take you past Puy-de-Dôme, a classic Tour de France ascent. Once back in Nevers, the Café Vélo offers accommodation, excellent food and reliable bike storage.

Start/finish // Nevers, France
Distance // 373 miles (600km)

David Fitzell/Shutterstock

THE HANSE GRAVEL

Linking the 'Hanseatic' cities of Germany's Baltic coast, this truly historic ride combines pirates with Panzers, and the marvels of medieval architecture with Cold War memorials.

The statue of Klaus Störtebeker sends a ripple of excitement through our group of riders. We're gathering at the base of a monument to the 14th-century pirate who once terrorised this part of Germany, though much of the chatter goes over my head due to a lack of language skills. Nevertheless, I manage to exchange a few words with some of the other riders, along with more contemporary cultural references, such as stickers for FC St Pauli, the Bundesliga football team based here in Hamburg, the starting point for our ride.

The ride in question is the inaugural Hanse Gravel, a 376-mile (605km) route connecting the 'Hanseatic' cities of Germany's Baltic coast and beyond, from Hamburg to Szczecin, in Poland. Featuring 8202ft (2500m) of elevation gain as it winds through forests, fields and along well-maintained trails, the route is named for the Hanseatic League, a historic network of coastal cities and merchant guilds. Founded in Lübeck in the 12th century, the 'Hanse' evolved over subsequent centuries into a powerful commercial and political force, whose role included defending its members from pirates, most notably the aforementioned Störtebeker (see panel overleaf)

From central Hamburg, we ride out past the docks and UNESCO-listed buildings. Unlike most German cities, Hamburg

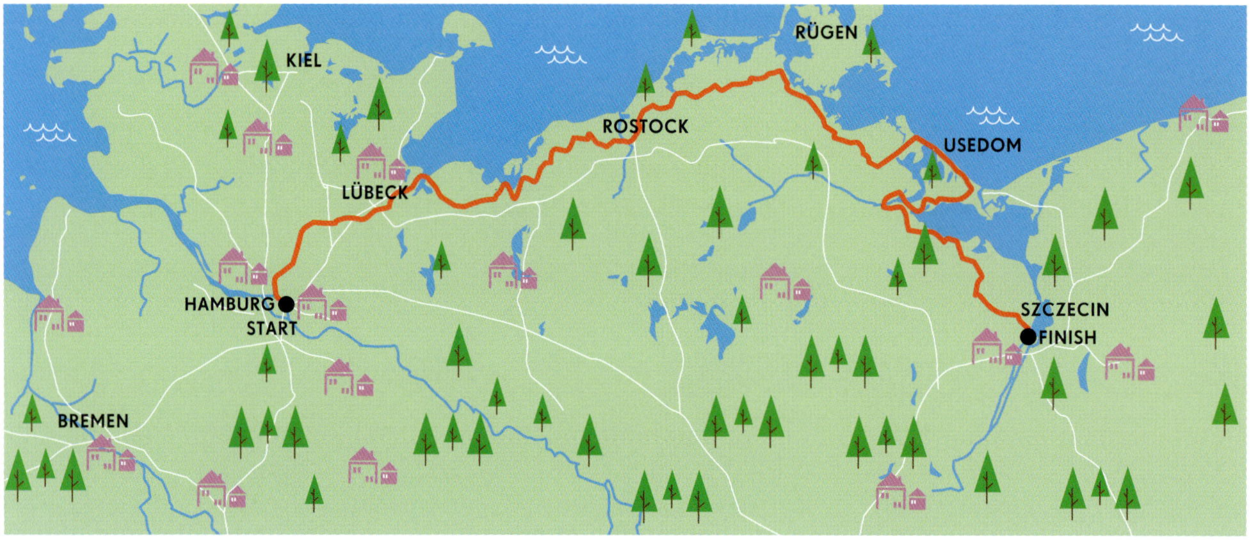

mauritius images GmbH/Alamy

STÖRTEBEKER-HAUS

"I can't help but imagine what stories these ancient bricks might tell: standing sentinel as Störtebeker and his band marauded along the coast"

is devoid of skyscrapers thanks to its Baupolizeiverordnung ('building police ordinance'), a set of regulations established to preserve Germany's medieval architecture.

Riding along the banks of the Alster river, Hamburg gives way to the open landscapes of rural Germany. Twisting singletrack leads, eventually, to the walled city of Lübeck, the largest of this country's UNESCO World Heritage Sites. Named the 'City of the Seven Towers' after the seven churches that dominate the skyline, it was also dubbed the less-catchy, 'Queen of the Hanseatic League'. If that weren't enough, when one of the other riders stops to share some marzipan, I learn that it, too, is another of Lübeck's claims to fame.

Riding east brings us next to the port of Travemünde, formerly the crossing point to Priwall and what was once East Germany. Despite having ridden beside the Alster, it's the first time you feel you're following the shipping route the Hanseatic League was established to protect. Once heavily fortified, Travemünde is now a lovely seaside town, one of whose campsites we bed down in for our first night (there's also a nudist beach, but we steer clear). Echoes of the time before reunification are everywhere, most notably in the shape of the stark, concrete border-posts.

Next morning, we ride out in search of breakfast, into sandy-soiled farmland peppered with small towns and villages, each with its own charm, and whose ancient brick buildings boast ornate stone carvings. It's just after Zierow when the white beaches along the Baltic coastline finally come into view, their cafes and bars the ideal destination for hungry riders. Winding our way into the port of Wismar, a black sailing ship bobs past; it's a traditional 'cog', the emblem of the Hanse Gravel, and somebody jokes that, maybe, Störtebeker's ghost is aboard.

Northern Germany has some of the best cycling infrastructure you'll find, and which also integrates more recent history. While it's mostly traffic-free, the Hanseatic Way boasts sections of Kopfsteinpflaster, the cobblestones that are a legacy of the former communist East Germany. Legend has it that only old Trabants can drive across them; if a modern Volkswagen were to try, it would simply fall apart. These stones are fun to ride, so much so they almost cry out for a Spring Classic to be held here.

On our way to Rostock, we ride along sections of panzer weg, old 'tank roads' and another relic from the days of the DDR. Made up of 'plates', each around 8ft (2.5m) long and 20 inches (500mm) wide, the spaces between these large slabs create a treacherous grid of holes, any one of which will swallow a bike tyre. The art is to ride between them in the hope that, ahead of

HOW THE PIRATE STÖRTEBEKER LOST HIS HEAD

Of the threats that the Hanseatic League was established to repel, none engendered fear quite like the pirate Klaus Störtebeker. Captured in 1401, along with his 70-strong crew, he was sentenced to death by beheading. Legend has it he struck a deal with his executioner, who agreed to free as many crewmates as Störtebeker's headless body could stagger past before it collapsed. He allegedly made it as far as 11, though all were executed regardless.

Clockwise from top: the heart of Greifswald; reaching the Polish border together; the city of Szczecin and the Odra river

you, the upcoming plates haven't moved over time.

From Rostock, the route eventually picks up the old railway line, to the port of Stralsund, another impressive UNESCO World Heritage Site. Like many cities in the region, its railyards suffered heavy bombing during WW2, with Stralsund's medieval architecture sometimes caught in the crossfire. Thankfully, it has been largely restored and I can't help but imagine what stories these ancient bricks might tell: standing sentinel as Störtebeker and his band marauded along the coast; looking out on the Thirty Years' War; then surviving the Napoleonic Wars only to succumb to Allied air raids.

Inland, we ride through more farmland, to Greifswald, an early member of the Hanseatic League, and a town with one of the most beautiful marketplaces in all of Germany. It's also part of the Stolpersteine Memorial Project, a large commemorative artwork comprising brass plaques bearing the names of Jews murdered in the Holocaust and set into the pavements of the suburbs where they once lived.

On we ride, to the island of Usedom, a highlight of the Hanse for its seafront beauty. Yet more fine buildings adorn a part of the coast once known as 'the bathtub of Berlin', housing as it once did the spas of German emperors. We ride along promenades of espalier lime trees and manicured gardens, before the track opens out toward the Polish border, where Szczecin marks the end of our trip. For now, the border feels more like a tourist attraction, yet if this region's tumultuous history tells us anything, it's that the only constant is change. **EO**

Previous page: spot pirate connections in Hamburg at the city's Störtebeker-Haus

TOOLKIT

Start // Hamburg, Germany
Finish // Szczecin, Poland
Distance // 376 miles (605km)
Getting there // Regular flights to Hamburg from most international hubs.
When to go // Best to ride the Hanse Gravel in spring and summer, when average highs are from 15°C to 25°C.
What to wear // Standard trail kit, in spring, ¾-length cycling shorts are fine, paired with breathable layers.
What to pack // This is mostly a coastal ride, so pack a warm jacket for mornings and evenings, a rain jacket, too.
Where to stay // In addition to the route's fine campsites, the towns and cities offer hotels for every budget.
What to eat // A point-to-point ride on which the points are never far apart. Resupply is easy, as is locating hearty Hanseatic fare.
More info // www.hansegravel.com/

Emma Osenton

Opposite: ride alongside the Rhine river on the Trans Germany route

MORE LIKE THIS
HISTORIC GERMAN RIDES, EAST AND WEST

CANDY B GRAVELLEUR

Departing from beneath a C-47 bomber at Frankfurt airport, this annual event follows the route of the 'Berliner Luftbrücke', the Berlin Airlift, to Templehof Airport in Berlin. Used by the Allies to supply West Berlin during the Soviet blockade of 1948, the route pays tribute to Gail Halvorsen, aka the 'Candy Bomber', who shared both his own and his colleagues' candy rations with local children, secretly dropping them from his plane attached to tiny parachutes. Exposed by the journalist who was struck by one such package, the US Air Force then made things official, with the launch of Operation Little Vittles. The route itself climbs though the Riesling wine region, in Hesse, before passing along the former East German border, including Point Alpha. The giant spoil pile of Monte Kali towers above Heringen, before you cross the Havel river just after Potsdam. Weave through the trees before arriving at Templehof, finishing the ride at Berlin's Airlift Memorial.
Start // Frankfurt
Finish // Berlin
Distance // 373 miles (600km)

BIKEPACKING TRANS GERMANY (BTG)

From its most southerly point at the Swiss-French-German border, in Basel, the BTG winds its way diagonally across the country to the most northerly point, on the island of Rügen. Initially following the banks of the Rhine, you'll then climb through Hell's Kitchen gorge before making your way towards the border with Czechia. Dipping in and out of Poland as you wind your way north, you'll encounter traces of former Eastern Bloc architecture and some very quirky border crossings, such as Potůčky with its famous Vietnamese market. Other highlights include the towering limestone formations of Saxony, and there's a multitude of terrain to keep you alert; from hardpacked tracks to the desert of Brandenburg, the Lieberose, and its long sandy stretches. Two ferry journeys bring the journey towards its conclusion, before the spectacular bridge across to Rügen, where the route finishes at the twin lighthouses at Cape Arkona.
Start // Basel
Finish // Rügen
Distance // 994 miles (1600km)

GRENZSTEINTROPHY (GST)

A self-supported route setting off from Höf, near the Germany-Czechia border, and closely following the former Iron Curtain, to the northern coast near Priwall. Not for the faint-hearted, the GST's 373-mile (600km) route takes in some of the same tank tracks that feature on the Hanse Gravel, the infamous panzer weg. Weaving your way through the Grüne Band (Germany's equivalent of the UK's 'green belt'), you'll experience the remarkable change that has seen the five kilometre-wide tract of land that once separated the West and East sections of the Berlin Wall (known as the 'death strip'), transformed into a nature reserve. A route peppered with historical wonders, including museums and former checkpoints; it's humbling to ride past towns which, during the Cold War, were either split in two or simply erased from the map. With other highlights including former surveillance structures, this is also the only bikepacking event to finish on a nudist beach, at Travemünde.
Start // Höf
Finish // Travemünde
Distance // 373 miles (600km)

DaLiu/Shutterstock

LOIRE À VELO: ANGERS TO BEAUGENCY

Take a leisurely spin up the Royal River, past stunning châteaux and rich vineyards, on the family- and cycle-friendly Loire à Velo.

Picture yourself on a bike beside a slow-moving river, beneath broad-leafed trees and the clearest blue skies. That, in essence, is cycle-touring on the Loire. France's longest river has a dreamlike quality, especially in its latter stages, as it flows wide and calm to the Atlantic. Add the largely traffic-free route that is the Loire à Vélo – running for 560 miles (900km) between Nevers and Saint-Nazaire – and you sense the tranquility you might experience as you pass through vineyards and immerse yourself in rural French life.

It's a spell you'd think might be broken if you also added a toddler. Holidaying with a child, it's often said, is simply the same childcare in a different location (especially with a two-year-old). 'Time off' just isn't – or so I thought. For after riding along the Loire with my young family in tow (literally), I'd say it's an ideal way to look after a little one and give parents some time to themselves, even if much of that time is spent in the saddle.

Our small caravan comprised myself and my partner, Daria, along with our two-year-old son, Cosimo, wrapped warm in his trailer for our departure. Leaving Angers, early one chilly September morning, mist hovered over the river and a lazy sun shone weakly.

Surprisingly, it took me a while to warm up, despite hauling

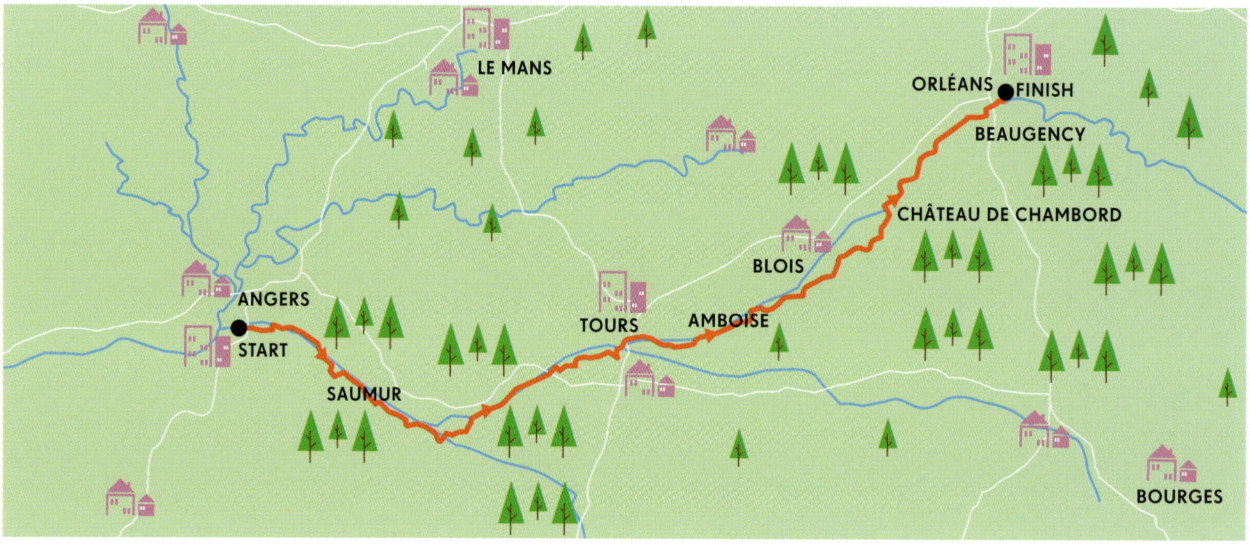

Samuel Jones; AntoineZK/Shutterstock

"The cycle paths here are wide, largely well surfaced and invariably straight enough to allow safe cycling, even for smaller riders"

a trailer packed with a week's worth of camping kit, one 35-pound (16kg) son, and his balance bike. But then the Loire did its thing. Barely nine clicks in, at the small village of La Daguenière, we found our first boulangerie. We raided the pastry counter, washed it all down with cafe au lait, and stocked up on obligatory picnic essentials (baguettes).

On our week-long sojourn from Angers to Orleans, we were barely into the first day's riding but this style of impromptu stopping quickly became its own tempo. Cafes, bistros, bridges – not to mention playgrounds – the staccato nature of our progress meant all in our party were able to enjoy themselves, if not necessarily at the same time. It's an important thing to remember when travelling with small children, this need for compromise. (Unless you're a tired toddler.)

Over the next week, we averaged a bit more than 25 miles (40km) a day, sometimes riding slightly north of the Loire, sometimes south. Crossing its often majestic, historic bridges offered a recurring sense of wonder, not merely at the broad span of the channel (which in places made some UK rivers seem like streams) but also at the engineering capabilities of medieval France.

Indeed, for the budding historian, this stretch of the Loire has much to offer, as you pass beneath the mighty walls of

castles that helped shape French history. Château d'Angers, which dates back to the 9th century, has too many links to mention but counts among its dramatis personae Louis IX and Joan of Arc. Although it's still bustling and vibrant today, albeit with tourists, my thoughts would drift to how such places might have looked hundreds of years ago.

Similarly, the riverside ports. Those we rode past would once have rippled with sails rather than jostling pleasure cruisers, though many towns still retain stern walls to guard their approaches. Such thoughts were not entertained for long, however, when excited young minds had other things on them. ('Stop Babbo, ice cream!')

The ride was a revelation, in ways large and small. Having remained in his trailer for the early miles, the time came, inevitably, when Cosimo wanted to explore himself. The Loire à Vélo enables parents to make this happen; the cycle paths here are wide, largely well surfaced and invariably straight enough to allow safe cycling, even for smaller riders. So, at the end of day three, shortly before we found our treehouse in a campsite outside Villandry, we unleashed Cosimo for the final mile. The delight on his little face as he rode alongside us was wonderful, and it shifted the dynamic.

Now on a tour in which we were all active participants, we adjusted our speed to factor in a two-year-old's desire to ride. Tumbles happened, of course, as did the occasional disappointment when the Loire à Velo's predominantly traffic-free route encountered an infrequent road section. However, it was a pace of travel we were more than happy to accommodate.

As Cosimo's confidence grew, so did his interests, to a pump track spotted from the trailside, or gaps in a hedge, even a picnic spot with a swing. La forêt domaniale de Russy, just outside Blois, saw his little legs clock up a record 4.3 miles (7km), rewarded with an early night at the gîte we'd swapped our tent for. The next morning, our last, Cosimo was once again raring to go as we detoured into the grounds of Château de Chambord.

This Renaissance-era château, the largest and most famous along the Loire, demands your attention. For once, our timing was poor, as Cosimo's eyelids began to droop in the hot afternoon sun. Exploration was thus confined to the extensive deer park, rather than historic hideaways behind elaborate stonework, in which had transpired who knows what intrigues?

We rolled into Beaugency, a town famously freed from English control by Joan of Arc. After seven days of slow travel, some slower still under Cosimo's direction, we celebrated our journey's end with a fire-cooked meal at the Grand Hotel de l'Abbaye. The next morning, figuring the 19 miles (30km) to Orleans for our onward connections might be a bit much for Cosimo, we took the cycle-friendly train for bike-free sightseeing. And, more importantly, planning more Loire cycling adventures for another year. **SJ**

LA LOIRE

The Royal River is home to about 300 royal châteaux, grand houses built between the 14th and 18th centuries. With the end of the Hundred Years' War, in 1453, French monarchs spent more time in the region, known as 'the garden of France'. Inviting such artists as Leonardo Vinci to help with architectural design, the reign of the Loire's royal residences ended in the early 1700s, when Louis XIV completed the Palace of Versailles.

Clockwise from top: packing the essentials for a French vacation; Amboise, where Leonardo da Vinci retired. Previous spread; Château d'Amboise overlooking the Loire; follow family-friendly bike paths

TOOLKIT

Start // Angers
Finish // Beaugency, although nearby Orleans works too.
Distance // 167 miles (269km)
Getting there // Trains from Paris to Angers (1hr20mins); return from Orleans (2hrs20mins).
When to go // Ride either side of peak summer, for quieter trails and to beat the heat.
Where to stay // The route is extremely well served by numerous accommodation options, from campsites to hotels. The treehouses near Villandry are recommended: camping-savonnieres.fr
What to pack // Trailer for camping gear, panniers **for daily/**fresh supplies, maybe a bottle of wine.
Where to eat // Resupply at local stores and chains. Treat yourself at the Grand Hotel de l'Abbaye (Beaugency), whose kitchen dates back to the 19th century.
Things to know // The French rail service puts on special carriages to carry cyclists during peak months. They are popular, so book ahead and arrive in good time.
More info // www.loirebybike.co.uk

Anna Mente/Shutterstock; Samuel Jones

Opposite: vines growing along the Loire river

MORE LIKE THIS
RIDES ALONG THE ROYAL RIVER AND BEYOND

SAINT-NAZAIRE TO ANGERS

Saint-Nazaire, the route's western terminus, is where the mighty Loire finally meets the Atlantic and makes a fitting end (or beginning) to both the famous waterway and cycle route that follows it. Changes in the landscape are subtle as the miles pass, and on this stretch you'll spot traditional fishing huts stretching out into the water, connected to shore by narrow gangways. Of all France's agricultural pursuits, few are more profitable (or popular) than viticulture, and wine production in this region is a relaxed journey of discovery. En route to Angers, this section of the Loire à Vélo passes through Nantes, France's sixth-largest city, and you'll be well served with connections, campsites and other accommodation. Despite such urban detours, the route remains geared towards cycle-tourists, retaining its traffic-free stretches. Perfect for families, it has plenty to offer the seasoned tourer too.
Start // Saint-Nazaire
Finish // Angers
Distance // 107.5 miles (173km)

AVENUE VERTE

This joint Anglo-French project was conceived to connect London to Paris, via a largely traffic-free and waymarked route, in time for the London 2012 Olympics. It seems only the French got the memo, at least on those sections of the English leg that feature dirt tracks and signage that might be generously described as half-hearted. Not so in France, where you can put the map and bike-computer away, and follow a relaxed, traffic-light route all the way from the port of Dieppe to the French capital. Approaching Paris, the route offers two options: riding through the Epte valley, or a slightly more circuitous route along the River Oise in southern Picardy, an area rich in Gothic architecture. Van Gogh fans familiar with this region will be drawn to Auvers-sur-Oise, where the artist lived and spent his last days, painting masterpieces such as *Wheatfield with Crows* and *The Church at Auvers* (both 1890).
Start // Dieppe
Finish // Paris
Distance // 150 miles (240km)

ORLEANS TO NEVERS

At Orleans, the Loire changes course and heads south, towards its eventual source in France's Massif Central. Sauvignon blanc fans will particularly enjoy this stretch as they ride through the famous wine-producing areas of Sancerre and Pouilly Fumé. Unfortunately, the special cycle-carriage trains no longer provide the back-up on offer on other sections of the Loire à Vélo, as they only run between Le Croisic and Orleans. By now, however, you'll hopefully have found your pedalling mojo, so won't need them. The route continues to be a mix of traffic-free and traffic-light and is still relatively flat; in its 560 miles (900km), the Loire à Vélo has just 625ft (190m) of elevation. Hospitality options for the travelling cyclist are numerous, so riders not wanting to stop at Nevers can connect to the waymarked EuroVelo 6 and, some 1864 miles (3000km) later, end up at the Black Sea on the Serbian coast.
Start // Orleans
Finish // Nevers
Distance // 124 miles (200km)

Zatlewg/Shutterstock

KING ALFRED'S WAY

Condensing 10,000 years of history into 217 miles (350km) of off-road trails around Wessex, the ancient Anglo-Saxon kingdom of King Alfred the Great.

Waiting at the Izaak Walton pub in East Meon in August 2020, pint in one hand and map in the other, I entered into conversation with the nearest table. For all of us it was a relatively novel experience; just weeks previously, Britain, like so many other countries, had been in a Covid lockdown.

We swapped experiences of the past four months, sharing now in wonder at the simple pleasure of a beer in the company of strangers on a summer's evening. As that table departed, in rolled the four bikepackers I was here to meet. Legs smeared with sweat-soaked dust, they propped their bikes against the wall of the pub's garden, overlooking the River Meon. They wandered over, tired but elated and brimming with tales of the route we would all soon be riding together – the newly launched King Alfred's Way (KAW).

KAW was the brain child of Kieran Foster, a route planner and 'access specialist', who'd convinced Cycling UK to realise

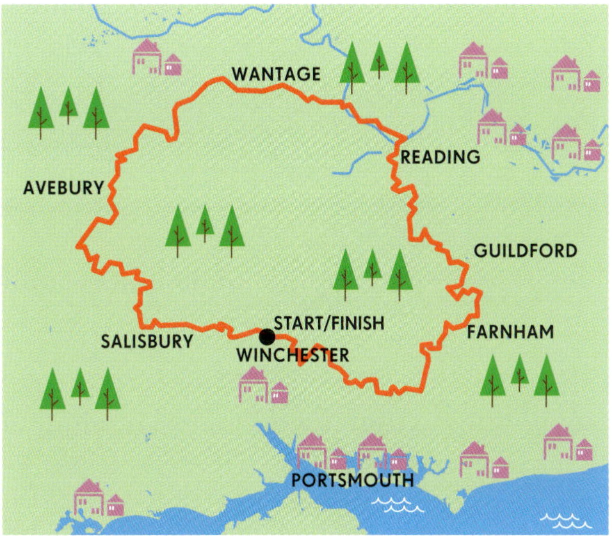

Stefan Amato

his vision of a long-distance circular route linking four of England's National Trails; the North Downs Way, the South Downs Way, the Ridgeway, and the Thames Path.

Together with my colleague Sophie, one of the newly arrived riders, I had spent the past months not just in lockdown but bringing this route to life; wondering all the while when the world would be normal enough to once more allow us to cycle unimpeded through the countryside.

The ride was notable for other reasons, too. Previously, I'd only met the other three riders in the two dimensions of online meetings; the first time meeting Stef, Dave and Katherine in person would also be the inaugural ride of KAW.

The route weaves its way around Wessex, the Saxon kingdom that was once the stomping ground of Alfred the Great, the 9th-century ruler who famously repelled the Danes. Named in his honour, KAW not only transports you through fully 10,000 years of history, it does so without the traffic jams normally associated with this popular tourist region.

Using bridleways and byways – the off-road tracks in England where cycling is permitted – we crossed an ever-changing landscape, from sundried cornfields waiting for harvest to delicate heathland where adders might be spotted in the sun. Whether climbing up steep, loose tracks, or slipping through sunken 'holloways', there was such peace on the trails it was hard to imagine that, variously, more than 17 million people live within an hour of KAW's main route.

This 'accessible remoteness' is part of KAW's charm. Passages through, or close to, the towns and cities of Winchester, Salisbury, Reading and Farnham allow for refuelling and easy train access to London. For all this proximity, these urban areas by no means dominate and, beyond their fringes, the natural landscape rules supreme enough to remain the highlight.

Leaving the city streets behind, we quickly found ourselves in Thomas Hardy territory, of thatched cottages, Iron Age hill forts and stone circles. As a route, KAW provides the ideal spine for a biking adventure, with numerous chances for detours, including various ways to take in the views over Stonehenge.

The legendary monument stands sentinel on Salisbury Plain, a vast expanse where skylarks rise up in song. Negotiating your way across this ancient chalk plateau is made slightly easier by the presence of the British military, who use it to practise manoeuvres and have thus kept it free from urban sprawl.

On the other hand, while you're safe from the risk of live ammunition, Salisbury Plain is not without its hazards, as we discovered chatting to a crew of off-road motorcyclists. Having set off from Cornwall earlier that week and riding the trails ever north, their journey had been delayed by a spent mortar shell ripping a tyre to shreds – and along the same byway we'd ridden earlier in the day. We counted ourselves lucky for dodging – pun intended – that particular bullet.

WHO WAS KING ALFRED?

From the 5th to 11th centuries, England's Anglo-Saxon 'monarchs' were regional rather than national rulers. Of these, King Alfred of Wessex is the most well-known. Governing an area covering much of southwest England, it was Alfred who famously held back the invading Viking hordes. Born in the town of Wantage and buried in Winchester, Wessex's capital, Alfred earned his honorific through valour on the battlefield and, just as importantly, his enthusiasm for education.

Clockwise from top: approaching the highest point of the route, Butser Hill; the standing stones of Avebury; the statue of King Alfred in Winchester, a potential starting point for the route

SeraphP/Shutterstock

Riding up over the Vale of Pewsey, in Wiltshire, we dropped down to Stonehenge's less famous cousin, the prehistoric monument at Avebury. In Avebury village, we stocked up on local produce and wandered freely among the stones, before mounting up once again and tackling the chalk and flint of the Ridgeway.

Arguably Britain's oldest road, the Ridgeway was likely one of the many herepath used by Alfred to move his army against the Viking invaders (here is Old English for 'armed host' and path means, well, 'path'). More than a thousand years on, we made good use of it too, taking in the views until storm clouds chased us from the heights, or the slippery, un-rideable chalk sent us scurrying to the market town of Wantage, Alfred's birthplace.

Three days of riding more than 50 miles (80km), with laden bikes on uneven terrain, saw most of us wake with leaden legs. By the finish, however, our hearts were just as heavy, sad that our pioneering journey was ending. It saw us eke out our last day, the pace more congenial to talk, our rest-stops longer. One included a demonstration from Dave on how to ride a skatepark half-pipe on a cargo-heavy gravel bike.

It led to reflections on events both ancient and modern. A route that once helped this country repel fearsome invaders had more recently brought together five relative strangers during one of the strangest times any of us had experienced. In the years since I first rode King Alfred's Way, there may have been more epic rides but few which have packed so much into so little time, and with such fine off-road riding. **SJ**

Previous page: King Alfred's Way covers chalk downland and deciduous woodlands

Stefan Amato; Valery Egorov/Shutterstock

TOOLKIT

Start/finish // Winchester
Distance // 217 miles (350km)
Getting there // Good rail connections to London and Portsmouth, plus main roads to the Midlands.
When to go // Late spring to September is an ideal time to ride. Try to avoid the route after prolonged periods of rain, unless you enjoy slogging through mud, or over (very) slippery chalk.
What to pack // Prepare for all weathers and consider gloves for sections with overgrown vegetation. Gravel bikes are ideal for this route, preferably with a wide range of gearing and a lightweight bikepacking setup; for off-season riding, a hardtail will be better suited and more comfortable.
More info // For up-to-date GPX files, free online guides, and a helpful Facebook group, visit cyclinguk.org/kingalfredsway

Opposite: Balmoral Castle in the Cairngorms; enjoy oysters in Whitstable on the Cantii Way

MORE LIKE THIS
RIDES WITH HISTORICAL CONNECTIONS

CANTII WAY, ENGLAND

Cycling UK's fifth designated bikepacking route takes you on a journey through the best Kent and southeast England has to offer. The region was once occupied by the Celtic Cantii tribe, from whom both the route and area draw its name. Julius Caesar, when he landed in 55BCE, thought the Cantii by far the most civilised of the British tribes he met, and you'll feel not much has changed as you journey through the garden of England. Highlights are the seasonal fresh produce: Kent is famous for strawberries and other soft fruits; the vineyards here are increasingly giving the Champagne region a run for its money; and the oysters in Whitstable Bay are renowned among chefs. Largely off-road and with good rail links along the loop, this is a more relaxed route that will appeal to both the bikepacking-curious and seasoned riders alike.
Start/finish // Canterbury
Distance // 145 miles (234km)

TRAWS ERYRI, WALES

Traws Eryri (pronounced Tr-ouse Eh-ruh-ree) is Welsh for 'Trans Snowdonia', and plunges you into the heart of a landscape made famous by Wales' tallest mountain, Yr Wyddfa (Mount Snowdon). Unlike the popular mountain, with its crowds of inappropriately dressed climbers, this route offers the chance to experience the natural beauty of this national park in peace and tranquility. Cycling UK's seventh bikepacking route starts in the mid-Wales town of Machynlleth and ends on the shores of the Irish Sea, under the shadow of Conwy's majestic medieval castle. A hardtail will see you best along the ancient tracks, Roman roads and deserted lanes, as you pass through the lush valleys and rugged peaks of this majestic landscape. The route is remote, so pack your tools and be ready too for the 'best' of Welsh (wet) weather.
Start // Machynlleth
Finish // Conwy
Distance // 122 miles (196km)

CAIRNGORMS NATIONAL PARK LOOP, SCOTLAND

Created by Markus Stitz, the man behind Bikepacking Scotland and thus many of the UK's most interesting off-road adventures, the Cairngorms National Park Loop uses old military and drovers' roads. The Arctic-like landscape means no extreme climbs or descents, so gravel riders will thrive on this extensive loop. But don't be fooled, that doesn't mean it's easy. There are long stretches into the wild where, despite opportunities for resupplying and accommodation, riders will want to be confident in their own self-sufficiency. The rewards can be mighty, as you ride through some of Scotland's most beloved national scenery. Fans of the British Royal family – or just the Highlands generally – will also enjoy the opportunity to ride close to Balmoral, the country estate that is home to King Charles' Scottish retreat.
Start/finish // Aviemore
Distance // 165 miles (266km)

cktravels.com/Shutterstock; Elizabeth O'Sullivan/Shutterstock

THE SUPERMARATONA

Be wowed by the views, food and Ladin culture of this mountainous tour of the Dolomites on road bikes, featuring 13 high passes in three (or more) days.

'That's the Sassolungo,' says our guide, Richard Feichter, better known by his nickname Boksic. 'It's beautiful at this time of day.' I know what Boksic is doing: because I've dropped behind our group of five fit fifty-somethings on the Passo Gardena, our last climb of this three-day tour of the Dolomites, he's trying to distract me from the fatigue slowing my legs. But today, with a cumulative 28,000ft (8535m) of ascent weighing on me, Boksic's hope is misplaced. I continue grinding uphill at a glacial pace.

Our adventure had started two days ago when we'd arrived – two English and two German riders – at the Hotel Melodia del Bosco in Alta Badia, deep in the Italian Dolomites. Our aim was to ride the route of the Supermaratona over three days in June. This road cycling challenge climbs and descends 13 mountain passes over about 180 miles (290km). It's the big brother of the Maratona, a popular gran fondo (or sportive, a fast-paced mass ride on closed roads) in the region. The first Maratona was staged in 1987 with 166 participants who rode 109 miles (175km) over seven passes in the Dolomites, incuding the Gardena, the Valparola, the Fedaia and Passo Duran. Today, the number of riders is capped at 8000, from 30,000 applications.

However, in 2024, Italian alpinist Hervé Barmasse, a legend of the Matterhorn and Mont Blanc, didn't think the Maratona was sufficiently challenging so he set out on the 180-mile (290km) route that we're tackling. But Barmasse aimed to complete it in day, cycling up (and down) the equivalent of Mt Everest. For perspective, a tough day in the Tour de France would encompass about one third of the Supermaratona's elevation. Barmasse finished his superhuman feat in about 18 hours, and since then only a handful of cyclists have completed the Supermaratona in fewer than 24 hours.

By giving ourselves three days, it seemed like a difficult but doable trip for experienced road cyclists. We'd spend three days on our lightweight carbon bikes, covering between 50 miles (80km) and 77 miles (125km), staying one night at the Rifugio Palafavera and the next at Hotel Villa Argentina near Cortina d'Ampezzo. Our added advantage was that our off-the-bike kit – a change of clothes, phone chargers and

Manuel Glira

Manuel Glira

so on – would be carried ahead of us. The intention behind this loop is that it can be ridden at any time (once the snows have melted), over as many days as required, independently or supported.

Leaving Alta Badia early on a bright morning, we headed up the valley before turning right towards our first ascent, the Passo Gardena. Two things became apparent: I was comfortable on the climb but a lot less confident on the downhill, lacking practice at long, fast descents. Also, we'd timed the trip to perfection. For all three June days the weather was perfect and spring's wildflowers were still blooming in the alpine meadows.

At the top of the second climb, Passo Sella, as we had a coffee break surrounded by the Sella Towers, pinnacles of pale, fractured dolomitic limestone, I realised that there is not a dull view anywhere in the Dolomites. Local tourism hosts are keen for visitors to stay longer and experience the local Ladin culture rather than dash from one photo op to the next but it's impossible not to whip out a camera at every turn.

Lunch at the Rifugio Castiglioni at the summit of Passo Fedaia introduced the local speciality that was served everywhere: a venison ragu served with fresh tagliatelle. It's a warming dish, perfectly suited to a mountainous region

"At the top of Passo Sella we had a coffee break surrounded by the Sella Towers, pinnacles of pale, fractured dolomitic limestone"

peppered with ski stations where winter snow persists well into the summer months.

The final climb of the trip's longest day was up Passo Duran. Propelled upward by the thought of a beer and bed I raced Andreas, one of the German pair, along the wooded slopes and up to the barren plateau and the waiting rifugio.

On the agenda for the second day of our Supermaratona was Passo Giau. In my ignorance, I was unaware of this giant's reputation but the maths is memorable: it's 10km (6.2 miles) long with an elevation gain of 1000m (3280ft) and an average gradient of 10%. It didn't take long for us to all shift into our lowest gears as Richard glided between us, offering encouragement and taking photos of us plodding away, with vast views of cliffs and a hazy nothingness beside us. Of all the ascents in the Dolomites, the Giau is the one that has

MEET THE LADINS

The five valleys around Alta Badia are the historic home of the Ladin people, a community of around 30,000 people. Given the inaccessibility of this region, the people spoke their own language, Ladin, a Rhaeto-Romanic tongue that predates Italian by centuries and is one of the three official languages of South Tyrol (German being the third). Ladin is taught in schools and is an important part of local identity; you'll certainly hear it so try learning a few words. 'Vives!' (cheers!) as the Ladins say.

Left to right: climbing the Passo Giau; a coffee break at the top of Passo Sella; in the shadow of mountains. Previous spread: climbing the Passo Gardena

featured most in the Giro d'Italia grand tour, first appearing in 1973. One more climb and it was time for a late lunch before an arduous descent into Cortina d'Ampezzo, dodging construction traffic as the town prepared to host the 2026 Winter Olympics.

On our final day we were joined by the wiry owner of Hotel Melodia del Bosco, Klaus Irsara, for our return journey to Alta Badia via the passes of Falzarego, Valparola, Campolongo, Pordoi, Sella and the other side of Gardena. When he can escape the office, Klaus guides guests on rides and also takes off for short bikepacking trips, exploring the many trails through the Dolomites forged by soldiers and shepherds through the millennia.

By this day of the route, essentially a loop of the famed Sellaronda circuit, I was struggling. A restorative barley risotto at Rifugio La Tambra on the Passo Campolongo was perhaps the most delicious dish of a trip packed with memorable meals. But not long after, Richard was dropping back to coax me up the final metres of the Gardena before the final descent back to Alta Badia and a debrief over locally brewed beer at the hotel.

So, who is this trip for? Those not opting for an e-bike ought to be fit, experienced road cyclists. But it's a sociable challenge that can be enjoyed over as many days as it takes. **RB**

TOOLKIT

Start/finish // Alta Badia
Distance // 180 miles (290km)
When to go // Late May to September; avoid August.
What to wear // Padded cycling shorts, **a baselayer, jersey and helmet as a minimum.**
What to pack // Check the forecast and carry at least a windproof jacket or gilet and gloves for chilly descents. If you're not on a guided tour, also bring maps and tech for navigation. Carry water bottles and sunscreen on rides.
Where to stay // Hotel Melodia del Bosco in Alta Badia is a well-equipped base for cyclists, with laundry and secure storage, and can organise rental bikes, guided tours on road or gravel routes, snacks and more.
Things to know // E-bikes are gaining charging stations so it's feasible to use one in the Dolomites.
More info // www.altabadia.org, www.maratona.it

Opposite: visit the Val di Funes in the Dolomites

MORE LIKE THIS
MOUNTAIN ADVENTURES

LA ROUTE DES GRANDES ALPES, FRANCE

For over 100 years an official tourist route, the Route des Grandes Alpes, has linked Lake Geneva and Nice, on the Mediterranean coast. In some 450 miles (725km), it crosses the Cols de Colombière, Aravis and Saisies, then the Cormet de Roselend and the highest road pass in the Alps, the 9068ft (2764m) Col de l'Iséran. From there, it descends to the foot of the Col du Télégraphe and the oppressively mighty Galibier – and then hits the cols of Izoard Vars, Cayolle, Valberg, Couillole, Saint Martin, Turini and Castillon, before one last bump, the 1663ft (507m) Col d'Èze, and the official finish in Nice. Phew! Cycling the Route des Grandes Alpes is an unforgettable journey – one that every serious road cyclist should consider, whether it's with a company carrying your luggage from hotel to hotel, or more purely touring in the tyre tracks of heroes.

Start // Thonon-les-Bains
Finish // Nice
Distance // 448 miles (722km)

TRANS-DOLOMITI, ITALY

If you prefer trails to tarmac, explore the exceptional beauty of the Dolomites on this challenging off-road loop on history-rich trails through mountain meadows, which gives the perfect excuse to fuel up on Italy's delicious food and drink. The Trans-Dolomiti route was finessed by the nomadic German couple Franzi Wernsing and Jona Riechmann, also known on social media as Tales on Tyres. Beginning from the town of Brixen, close to Italy's border with Austria, the riding is best suited to mountain bikes, rather than gravel bikes. Fitness is a factor, given the steep ascents; the highest point of the route is at 7700ft (2347m). There's no lack of villages in which to buy food and water for the day so you may not wish to carry a full cooking setup, but if you're planning on overnighting in mountain refuges, you'll need a sleeping bag and bivvy for back-up, remembering that wild camping is forbidden in this region.

Start/finish // Brixen, Italy
Distance // 163 miles (262km)

THE WOLF'S LAIR, ITALY

Staying off-road, the Apennines are the spine of Italy, running down the centre of the country. This wild route, just east of Rome, plays around on some of these mountainous vertebrae, circling three national parks in the little-visited region of Abruzzo. The Wolf's Lair ride was designed by bikepacking buddies Francesco D'Alessio and Giorgio Frattale, also known as filmmaking duo Montanus. They were living in the city of L'Aquila when the earthquake of 2009 hit; several years later they started exploring their backyard wilderness on bikes, eventually composing the route they christened the Wolf's Lair after the local lupine inhabitants. The wolves are thriving but seem more interested in the abundant deer and boar than bikepackers. In this depopulated region, there are places to camp and refill water bottles, but fewer opportunities to pick up food supplies – so plan ahead.

Start/finish // L'Aquila, Italy
Distance // 241 miles (388km)

Matt Munro for Lonely Planet

PARIS-BREST-PARIS

Take a gentler approach to this endurance-riding classic and be transported back to the earliest days of the bicycle on this trip across northern France.

Few of the tourists flocking to the Palace of Versailles notice the small monument on a traffic island on the outskirts of the city. You need to cross a busy road to read the inscription: 'Route of the Paris-Brest-Paris. Last stop of the winner Charles Terront... He completed the 727-mile (1170km) route in 71 hours 16 minutes without rest.'

It was near this spot, on Wednesday 9 September 1891 at 5.45am, that Terront's mother handed him a fresh set of clothes for his triumphant arrival back in Paris. His eyes were clogged with dust from three days of solid riding but, convinced his nearest rival was just minutes behind him, he set off at speed for the Bois de Boulogne, where a crowd of 10,000 had gathered before dawn to see him cross the finish line.

The 'Paris Brest et Retour', was the brainchild of Pierre Giffard, a journalist with *Le Petit Journal*, a leading newspaper. A few days earlier, some 207 riders had set out from its offices at 61 Rue Lafayette, with bands playing as they rode up the Place de la Concorde and along the Champs-Élysées. Fewer than half the starters would finish; of those, some took almost two weeks.

Today, the 745-mile (1200km) Paris-Brest-Paris (PBP) is among the world's oldest 'audax' events, with each edition drawing thousands of riders. Held every four years, entrants

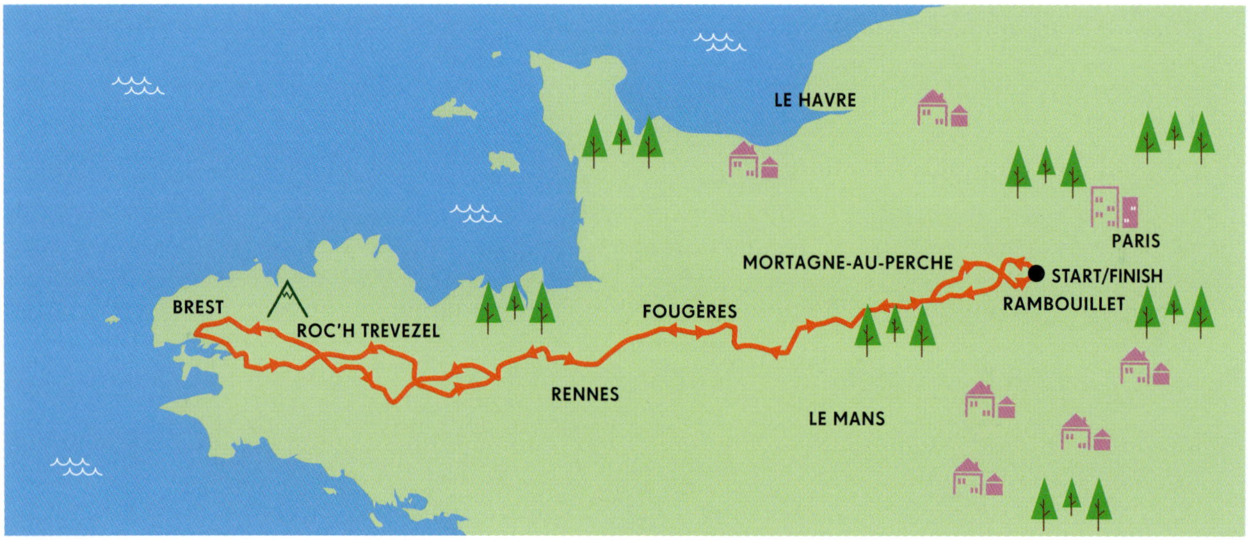

Mistervlad/Shutterstock; miloks50/Shutterstock;

"Small towns such as Tinténiac or Saint-Méen-le-Grand offer plentiful options for lunch, and a chance to catch up on world events"

have up to 90 hours to finish, which means little sleep and arduous night-riding.

For a more sedate alternative, many opt to tackle one half of the famous route, breaking the outward leg into sections as they ride out of Paris, across northern France and all the way to the Atlantic Ocean at Brest. Helpfully, you can plan your overnight stops at towns that host 'controls' during the official PBP, and where riders must have their 'brevet' cards stamped as proof of passage.

Cycling out of Paris, ride through Versailles to Rambouillet, where the modern event starts. The route then winds through arable farmland and pretty villages. Terront tackled these roads on a fixed-gear, British-made Humber, quickly building a 15-minute lead on his nearest rival, Joseph Jiel-Laval. By Mortagne, at 160km, that lead had narrowed to 10 minutes.

Mortagne-au-Perche is situated on a hilltop and features a cluster of historic sites, such the 15th-century church of Notre-Dame, famed for its ornate carvings and stained-glass windows. And while Terront and Jiel-Laval had to race on, here you can find somewhere to eat, sleep and even add in a day of sightseeing.

The next section of PBP, to Fougères, is 109 miles (175km) with a smattering of gentle climbs. Terront and Jiel-Laval rode much of the inauguaral event together, mostly in silence according to reports, though they knew each other well. Jiel-Laval had come fifth in that year's Bordeaux-Paris (350 miles/560km), behind four exceptionally strong British riders, and Terront had been his pacesetter for much of that ride.

It was on the Fougères section that Terront suffered a series of punctures and Jiel-Laval pulled ahead. With the majority of the field on solid tyres, Terront was using innovative Michelin pneumatics that could be changed by the roadside. Enabling his quick return to the fray, Michelin paid handsomely for sponsorship and were richly rewarded. Terront's eventual success in the race meant that, just two years later, an estimated 10,000 cyclists in France were using Michelin's patented technology.

On the 90-mile (146km) section to Loudeac, small towns such as Tinténiac or Saint-Méen-le-Grand offer plentiful options for lunch, and perhaps a chance to catch up on world events. Back in 1891, crowds would gather to read the stage reports posted at regional offices of *Le Petit Journal*, with the race being followed more widely across Europe and in the USA.

Pierre Giffard was already a winner. In the 1890s, *Le Petit Journal* became the first paper in the world to hit a daily circulation of more than one million copies. For Giffard, it

LET THEM EAT CAKE

It's a 12-mile (20km ride) from Paris to Maisons-Laffitte, home to Pâtisserie Durand, where in 1911 a circular cake was commissioned to mark the third PBP (following a 10-year gap between the first and second races). Today, its creator, Louis Durand, looks down from the back wall of the bakery. You can visit, then ride with your own choice of cake to the bench, a mile or so hence, that honours Pierre Giffard, the PBP's founder.

Clockwise: the Bois de Boulogne; Maurice Garin winning the 1901 race; riders on today's event

Fergus Coyle

Le Petit Journal

SUPPLÉMENT ILLUSTRÉ

Huit pages : CINQ centimes

DIMANCHE 1er SEPTEMBRE 1901

MAURICE GARIN

Vainqueur de la course Paris-Brest

endorsed his belief in the power of the bicycle to change the world. In an editorial after the race he wrote: 'For the first time we saw a new mode of travel, a new road to adventure, a new vista of pleasure. These cyclists averaged 80 miles [129km] a day for 10 days, yet they arrived fresh and healthy... Aren't we on the threshold of a new and wonderful world?'

The final challenge before Brest is a 1260ft (384m) ascent of the mighty Roc'h Trevezel, part of the Amorican Massif and the highest point on PBP. It's a long but steady climb, with views across Brittany. It is followed, unsurprisingly, by a speedy descent into Brest, where you can dip your toes in the Atlantic and celebrate your achievement with local specialities such as shellfish, mackerel and lobster. While you're washing them down with a well-earned glass of Breton cider, you might consider the resolve required to make the return trip on those early fixed-gear bicycles.

Back in 1891, Jiel-Laval was first to arrive in Brest and turn back for Paris. The decisive moment in the race came on that return leg, when Jiel-Laval was sleeping in a hotel. Taking a longer way round to avoid being spotted by opposing riders, Terront's strategic masterstroke gave him the lead for the rest of the race.

Terront rode on to the finish line, on the Blvd Maillot, with a police escort and in the company of 100 riders who had joined him for the final section. Newspaper reports later described Terront's cry of victory as he crossed the line, a man of 'prodigious energy who has just manifested himself with so much audacity and beautiful valour'. **MS**

Pierre Laborde/Shutterstock; Photo 12/Alamy

Previous page: the port of Brest and its castle; the gardens of the Palace of Versailles

TOOLKIT

Start // 61 Rue Lafayette, Paris
Finish // Brest
Distance // 407 miles (656km)
Getting there // Eurostar to Paris, but bikes need to be booked (and boxed). You can also book a train for the return, from Brest to Paris.
When to go // Spring and summer are best; early September coincides with the PBP's anniversary.
What to wear // Good cycling shorts are vital, you also need gear to cope with varying weather.
What to pack // Charles Terront's autobiography is available in the original French, Les Memoires de Terront.
Where to eat // Le Crabe-Marteau is a great place to sample the best Brest seafood: crabemarteau.fr
More info // For the PBP you'll need to complete qualifying rides of 200km, 300km, 400km and 600km.
Details // paris-brest-paris.org.

Opposite: passing Richmond town on the LEL and then riding through the Scottish Borders

MORE LIKE THIS
ADAPTABLE ENDURANCE RIDES

LONDON-EDINBURGH-LONDON (LEL), GREAT BRITAIN

Like Paris-Brest-Paris, this 930-mile (1500km-plus) ride runs every four years and is an out-and-back. Easily adapted to ride one leg, the route starts to the north of London and takes you across the flatlands of Lincolnshire and over the Humber Bridge, before you reach the Pennines and an ascent of Yad Moss that delivers you to 1968ft (600m). The route then heads over the border, through countless small villages and into the Scottish Lowlands. Just like the PBP, you can plot controls from the actual event as your potential overnight stops, in places like Boston, Richmond and Moffat. Although LEL doesn't go into Edinburgh, you can ride triumphantly into the city before boarding a train to whisk you effortlessly back to London, happy in the knowledge you've seen some of the best of Britain's countryside.

Start // London
Finish // Edinburgh
Distance // 466 miles (750km)

GRANDONNÉE HOKKAIDO, JAPAN

With increasing numbers of Japanese riders heading for PBP and other classic European events, this Grand Randonnée, or Grandonnée, was developed to meet the demands of this nation's growing audax community. Outside of race time, the route can easily form the basis of a two-week adventure to discover the best of Hokkaido's pristine nature and unique culture. The first leg takes you from the island's capital of Sapporo to more than 2789ft (850m) of ascent, as you ride over Mt Shiribetsu on a 47-mile (75km) climb that starts in Asahikawa. Thereafter, a bit like PBP, you could simply content yourself with riding half the total mileage, the 373 miles (600km) to Nemuro Bay where summer arrives late in the year. However, unlike PBP (or LEL), the Grandonnée has a very different return leg, one that runs to the south of Daisetsuzan National Park. It's well worth taking on the extra distance to fully experience the best of Japan's northernmost island.

Start // Sapporo
Finish // Nemuro Bay
Distance // 373 miles (600km); 745 miles (1200km)

BOSTON-MONTREAL-BOSTON, USA/ CANADA

This 745-mile (1200km) ride from New England to Canada and back used to run every year as an organised randonnée. Considered to be North America's answer to Paris-Brest-Paris, it was only in PBP years that this event took a break. Since 2006, it no longer operates as an organised event but lives on as a 'permanent'; that is, a route riders can follow at any time of the year, completing within a time limit of their choosing. The ride takes you through Massachusetts and then north through Vermont, cycling through the beautiful landscape of New England. You'll clip the corner of New York State, before heading over the border into Canada for a short foray to Huntingdon, Quebec, your finish line unless you fancy the ride back. Route information, basic mapping and background on the ride is available from Randonneurs USA (rusa.org).

Start //Boston, USA
Finish // Montreal (Huntingdon), Canada
Distance // 373 miles (600km), or 745 miles (1200km)

rightclickstudios/Shutterstock; Rebecca Cole/Alamy

PIRINEXUS

Hop the border of Spain and France and explore the Pyrenean mountains and the Costa Brava on this engaging loop of Catalunya from Girona, which is suitable for novice bikepackers.

Girona, less than an hour north of Barcelona by train, is a city in Catalunya, as Catalans call their autonomous community of northeast Spain. It's a difficult place to leave because, for people who enjoy riding bicycles, it's pretty much perfect. For some years now, Girona has been a preferred habitat of numerous pro cyclists, influencers and enthusiasts, drawn by its beautifully beguiling old town, compact size, unbeatable cafes and restaurants, mild climate and the varied riding routes on road and gravel on its doorstep. It was one of those routes that I wanted to do: the Pirinexus, a clockwise bikepacking loop of more than 200 miles (320km) up into the foothills of the Pyrenees mountain range, westward along the border with France and then south back to Girona via the Costa Brava.

The Pirinexus route was the brainchild of the Girona Vies Verdes (greenways) consortium with the cross-border support of local administrations in Spain and France. It was designed to celebrate Catalan cultural heritage, gastronomy and landscapes, which is what most intrigued me. With admirable foresight, the route planners plotted itineraries for two-, four- or six-day trips so, as someone who averages 15mph (24km/h) over a few hills, I decided on four days, which meant overnighting in Llanars in the Pyrenees, Capmany in the agricultural flatlands near Figueres and Torroella de Montgrí on the coast.

Having reacquainted myself with Girona, I packed some kit onto my gravel bike (lightweight stuff on the handlebars, heavier items under the top tube) and set off under drizzling skies. First impressions of a bike ride are important and I was immediately impressed by the signage of the route and every other cycling or walking route. The initial stages were on those aforementioned greenways, typically repurposed former railways now coated with a fine gravel but still even and flat. This was enviable cycling infrastructure.

First impressions are subject to change and within a couple of hours the drizzle had become heavy rain that sprayed my drivetrain with grit and I'd lost track of the signposts I was

Robin Barton; Sergi Boixader/Alamy

"This nunnery was founded during the time of Count Wilfred the Hairy, a legendary leader who united a lot of Catalan regions"

following in the towns. Thankfully, I'd loaded the route's GPX files into my phone and I quickly grew to love its cheerful chirrup when I found my way back on course.

Continuing towards Olot, the road started climbing as the rain fell. At the summit, the mist-wreathed views extended over green hills towards the mountains. A perfectly cambered descent led me to Olot and then the town of Sant Joan de las Abadesses, which expanded around the first monastery for women in Catalunya. This nunnery was founded during the time of Count Wilfred the Hairy, a legendary leader who united a lot of Catalan regions before being killed in battle in 897 CE.

After Sant Joan de las Abadesses, I still had a way to go before my stop for the night in Llanars, most of it uphill. After 63 miles (100km) and 5000ft (1525m) of ascent, I arrived at my Swiss chalet-style hotel. The next day promised even more climbing so after a plate of tagliatelle and an attempt at drying some cycling kit, I had an early night.

Day two and the Coll d'Ares lay ahead. The day is simply the climb to the highest point of the route, which is also on the border with France, and then it's downhill for many miles until the Coll de Panissars, where we cross back into Spain. It's a comfortable gradient up the Coll d'Ares so I found my rhythm and only realised that I'd crossed into France when the language on the signposts changed. The summit of the Coll was a hive of activity with horse riders and motorcyclists enjoying the views.

On the way down, I picked up the Tech river and followed this through the French towns of Prats-De-Mollo-le-Preste, Arles-sur-Tech and Amélie-les-Bains-Palalda, where I stopped for a galette. Such artists as Picasso, Matisse and Chagall passed through this region, centered on the town of Céret where the Musée d'Art Moderne is one of France's finest, with an extensive collection of Picasso's pieces. It's cherry season so I buy a bag for the next stage.

After following flat bike paths through orchards, the route climbs back into Spain over granite mountains and through woodlands of cork oak and wildflowers. The prettiest part of the trip is followed by the most rugged section, a surprisingly steep off-road descent to La Jonquera. Then it was a head-down sprint against the setting sun to Jordi Angrill's farmhouse in Capmany, Mas Martí, where I'm staying the night. At dinner with Jordi, his daughter and family friends I apologised for my rusty Spanish.

GIRONA FOR AMATEURS

You don't have to be a professional cyclist to enjoy Girona. Yes, there are big climbs if that floats your boat but east of the city the flat countryside is latticed with lanes all the way to the coast. Vies Verdes, Catalan for 'greenways', are former railways converted to cycling tracks and they connect several towns and villages. And the greenways consortium has installed 25 e-bike charging stations along Pirinexus.

Clockwise from top: a 12th-century Gothic bridge in Sant Joan de les Abadesses; find menhirs; the Greek statue of Asclepius at Empuries ruins

RogerMechan/Shutterstock; Lenar Musin/Shutterstock

'We don't speak Spanish either,' they laughed. Conversation turned to Catalan politics and the quest for independence from Spain. I began to understand more of the significance of the Pirinexus route and the fluctuating historic borders of Catalunya. But we also touched on topics that include the best olives for oil, the state of the local wine industry and ham – 'the only thing the Spanish do well', according to Jordi.

After a breakfast of cheese, eggs and some irresistible Spanish ham, Jordi handed me a couple of bananas and I set off for the coast. Thunderstorms were forecast and it was barely half an hour before the skies darkened and the deluge began but with Greek ruins and grape vines on the day's itinerary it really didn't matter. Around Figueres, famous for being the hometown of Salvador Dalí, lies the Empordà wine region. I was now in a rural Spain of stone-walled fields, rust-red soil and quiet lanes.

I reached the Mediterranean sea at Sant Martí d'Empúries, which was also the gateway to the Iberian Peninsula for the Greeks and Romans. Here, the Museu d'Arquelogia de Catalunya preserves the ruins of a Greek town and a Roman settlement, including ancient mosaics, a Roman Forum and a statue of the Greek god of medicine, Asclepius, looking out over the bay. The cycle path passes beside the ruins but you'll need to stop and pay for a ticket to get a closer look.

My last stop was at the Molí del Mig hotel just outside Torroella de Montgrí. From here, I turned inland and back towards Girona along yet more well-signposted paths. **RB**

Previous page: a view over the Pyrenees from the Coll d'Ares; Girona's old town

TOOLKIT

Start/finish // Girona
Distance // 211 miles (340km)
Getting there // There are fast, frequent trains from Barcelona (the nearest international airport) to Girona.
When to go // This is a region with a mild climate so the route is rideable almost year-round but spring (March to June) and autumn (September to November) are ideal.
What to wear // Padded cycling shorts, a baselayer, jersey and helmet as a minimum. Gloves if you like. Waterproof clothing, including overshoes, is recommended according to the weather forecast.
What to pack // Foolproof navigation tech, chargers and a paper map. Sunscreen. Camping kit if needed.
Where to stay // Options on the route range from hotels to homestays. In Girona, Hotel Ciutat de Girona and Hotel Carlemany are bike-friendly and central.
More info // www.viesverdes.cat/en/

Opposite: Albarracín, regularly voted one of Spain's most beautiful towns; and a bridge crossing on Montañas Vacias

MORE LIKE THIS
SPANISH ADVENTURES

MONTAÑAS VACIAS

For experienced bikepackers, the Montañas Vacias loop is an escapist's dream. It ranges over an inland region east of Madrid known as Spain's Lapland – not for the climate (though it can be cold) but for its depopulated desolation. Devised by Spanish bikepacker Ernesto Pastor; his hope was to encourage riders to a stunning region of Spain that has missed out on the benefits of tourism. The loop starts from the town of Teruel, around two hour from València or Zaragoza by direct train. From Teruel, the route climbs steadily on an off-road track towards Albarracín, which is regularly voted one of Spain's most beautiful towns, clustered along a ridge and shielded by medieval fortifications. The highest point of the ride is Pico de Peñarroya at 6653ft (2028m), with views across the Sierra de Javalambre being the reward. Here the route turns west again back to Teruel.
Start/finish // Teruel
Distance // 423 miles (680km)

PYRENEAN TRAVERSE

Pedalling between the Atlantic and the Mediterranean along the length of the Pyrenees mountain range is dream challenge for many cyclists. You'll be exploring distinct regions of France and Spain with their own languages, customs and food: the Basques to the west and the Catalans in the east. The mountain scenery is epic but you're never very far from a town or village. And you can test yourself against some of the biggest names in road racing: the passes of the Tourmalet, the Aubisque and more. There are multiple methods and routes to choose from, including events such as the unsupported Transpyrenees ride, the supported Transpyr race for 300 entrants and multiple trips with tour operators. Most, but not all, depart from near Bilbao (often Irun on the French border) and head to Cadaqués on the Mediterranean coast.
Start/finish // Irun/Cadaqués
Distance // approx 560–700 miles (900–1125km)

THE TRAKA

Also starting from Girona is The Traka, one of Europe's premier gravel races. The event takes place over a long weekend in April or May and offers a range of distances to competitors, from 62 miles (100km) to 223 miles (360km). Riders on the blue riband long route typically set off at dawn on Friday and finish by dawn the next day. Pro riders show up and in 2025 they included former Girona resident and World Tour pro Lachlan Morton. 'It's a pretty idyllic destination to come and ride,' he explained on the EF Pro Cycling blog. 'You can go towards the coast, where it's smooth and fast on flowy gravel roads. Or you can go into the hills where it's more chunky and make it as gnarly or as adventurous as you'd like.'
Start/finish // Girona
Distance // from 62 miles (100km) to 348 miles (560km)
Info // www.thetraka.com

Ernesto Pastor

NORWAY'S RALLARVEGEN

Swooping from wild and windswept mountain passes to serene blue fjords, the so-called 'Navvies' Road' unlocks the Norwegian landscape at its most majestic.

The Bergensbanen and the Flåmsbana are two of the world's most revered railways. Pilgrims cross continents to board these two Norwegian mountain lines, to ride their iron rails through glacial valleys and beneath thundering waterfalls, and gaze at the fells with noses pressed reverently against a carriage window. But, wonderful though those railways can be, these landscapes are arguably even more sublime when unimpeded by a pane of glass, when you feel the rush of Norwegian mountain air against your cheeks, and when you have the freedom to hit the brakes – to stop and take it all in.

The Rallarvegen – the 'Navvies' Road' – was originally an artery used to construct the Bergensbanen and the Flåmsbana routes; it was along this gravel path that weary labourers trudged, and picks were heaved to chisel tunnels through the stubborn bedrock. Those navvies could not have guessed that their humble service road is now an attraction in its own

Nowaczyk/Shutterstock

right, a 50-mile (82km) bike route traversing a tapestry of landscapes, from the mountain plateau of the Hardangervidda where glaciers creak, to the alpine meadows of the Flåm valley, where wildflowers sway. The denouement comes at the tip of the Aurlandsfjord, where saltwater laps at the base of the mountains and where road and rail can go no further, with the only way onward by boat.

I start my ride at Haugastøl, a short distance from the Norwegian outdoor capital of Geilo, where the Rallarvegen begins its gentle westward ascent, passing a succession of glacial lakes and turf-roofed cabins hunched on the shore. Vegetation thins as I push on up the contours and birch forests turn to boulder fields and beds of moss; snow patches cling to the north faces, lingering relics of winter just past.

For certain stretches the only sign of civilization is the Bergensbanen itself, the sleek modern trains occasionally sweeping past, their passengers sometimes waving smugly at cyclists from warm seats. The railway is the Rallarvegen's constant companion – swooping over our path on a bridge, or else tunnelling below us and setting the ground quaking – but always at its side as the miles unfurl, like two snakes coiled together. The history of the Bergensbanen, and the Rallarvegen that accompanies it, is a quietly revolutionary one.

For a long time, the only practical way to travel between the Norwegian capital Oslo and its second city of Bergen was a five-day steamship journey along the coastline. The 1870s heralded the construction of a rail link between the cities, no mean feat given the mountains, fjords and forests that lay in between them.

Nowaczyk/Shutterstock; my nordic/Shutterstock

The most formidable obstacle was the Hardangervidda, Europe's largest high-mountain plateau, where rails would have to scale dizzying elevations, and power through shoulder-high drifts. Thanks to a stoic workforce, the railway opened in 1909, and modern trains still follow that century-old route, snow ploughs keeping the line open on winter days. But any bike ride along the Rallarvegen must seize on a narrow window between mid-summer and early autumn, when drifts wither on the high passes and the path beneath emerges, and when the railway builders of old seem a little more present.

A literal and metaphorical high point of the Rallarvegen comes as road and rail approach Finse, a remote mountain hamlet perched at 3937ft (1200m), and where I dismount at the end of my first day of riding. This outpost has historically been a staging post for expeditions into the sub-Arctic wilderness, with cramponed outdoors-folk alighting for the Hardangerjøkulen glacier (a training ground for both Amundsen and Scott). For most, Finse is perhaps better known as the location for the ice planet Hoth in *The Empire Strikes Back*, whose filming coincided with one of the most severe storms in living memory. The cast and crew lodged and filmed at the hotel Finse 1222, where I spend the night, soothing my weary limbs beside blazing hearths.

The following morning, it's a bracing two-hour ride over a fog-bound plateau to Myrdal, and here the Rallarvegen reaches a crossroads. Many Bergensbanen passengers change here for the famous Flåmsbana, a branch line which although only measuring a measly 12 miles (20km), eclipses its big brother for scenery, including a 2841ft (866m) descent to the mouth of the Aurlandsfjord. The Rallarvegen impetuously swerves off from the Bergensbanen to accompany the Flåmsbana, and here reaches its swashbuckling finale, the gradients steepening, the switchbacks tightening – and the speed picking up.

My ears pop as the Rallarvegen dips below cloud level, and the landscape of barren rock turns into a lush green valley. The churning water of the Flåmselvi river appears, a series of whitewater cascades, sometimes visible but almost always audible above the whirr of the bike chain. Miles pass, the river broadens and slows and the air warms. Pine forests appear, and crimson farmsteads too, clinging to precious pockets of flat terrain. Soon there are signs of humanity and the spire of the 17th-century church heralds my arrival in the port of Flåm. Here, road, rail and river all culminate at the mouth of the Aurlandsfjord, one of Norway's most celebrated landscapes, where 4600ft (1400m) mountains drop almost sheer and a little village sits on the shore.

Here again, I come to a crossroads. Those hungry for more adventure can load their bikes on a ferry, and putter on into the fjord system. Those with calves of iron (and a streak of masochism) can pedal all the way back up to Myrdal. But I load my bike onto a return Flåmsbana train, admiring the switchbacks of the Rallarvegen from a warm, window seat and waving smugly at the cyclists on the road. **OS**

RIDING THE BERGENSBANAN

The Rallarvegen shadows a section of the Bergensbanan, running some 37 miles (60km) from Haugastøl to Myrdal. The full 308-mile (496km) train route, from Oslo to Bergen, is one of the highlights of any trip to Norway. Westbound trains leaving the capital first skirt the Oslofjord, before climbing into the mountainous interior. The stretch west of Myrdal is also wonderful, with the train navigating a series of valleys to reach Bergen.

Opposite from top: passing waterfalls on the plateau; descending towards Flåm. Previous spread: traditional homesteads viewed from the Rallarvegen

TOOLKIT

Start/finish // Haugastøl/Flåm
Distance // 50 miles (81km)
Getting there // Bergensbanen trains run from Oslo to Haugastøl in around 4hr30min and bike spaces can be booked in advance. A return from Flåm to Oslo will take around six hours, with a connection at Myrdal. Bike rental is available in Finse and Haugastøl.
When to go // The Rallarvegen typically opens from July to September, and August is when the weather tends to be at its most forgiving. But be warned, the mountain weather can be remorseless at any time of year.
What to pack // A good raincoat is essential even in the height of summer. Be sure to pack plenty of snacks for the ride as shops are almost non-existent between Geilo and Flåm.
More info // flamsbana.no, visitnorway.com and vy.no

Opposite: goats blocking the Jotunheimvegen; the MS Henrik Ibsen on the Telemark Canal

MORE LIKE THIS
NORWEGIAN GEMS VIA CANAL AND COAST

MJØLKEVEGEN

The Mjølkevegen translates as the 'milk route' and it was along this thoroughfare that farmers once heaved pails from highland dairy farms to market. Today, cyclists can also travel Norway's most scenic milk round. The journey begins outside the town of Gol, (conveniently served by a Bergensbanan station), renowned for its medieval stave church. You soon find yourself pedalling northward across rugged country, with the snow-capped peaks of Jotunheimen, Norway's loftiest range, rearing to the west. The gravel path passes through a few villages with accommodation and shops but, for many, the attraction is wild camping along the 142-mile (230km) route, pitching for the night beside lakes where the only sound is the hiss of a stove. The finishing line comes at the village of Vinstra, the reputed home of Norway's wandering folk hero Peer Gynt, from where you can wander back to Oslo via the scenic Dovrebanen railway.
Start // Gol
Finish // Vinstra
Distance // 142 miles (230km)
Info // www.golinfo.no

KANALRUTA

Just as the Rallarvegen shadows the Bergensbanen, the Kanalruta follows the banks of the Telemark Canal, a pioneering 19th-century engineering project to link a chain of serpentine lakes and create a historic logging route out of the Norwegian interior. The starting point is the old sawmilling village of Ulefoss, from where cyclists push west, passing chains of locks, forested foothills and misty fells. Beyond the village of Lunde, settlements thin out and solitary cabins and tiny chapels guard the lake shore, though you will likely see other travellers on the waterways. Built in the 1900s, the MS Henrik Ibsen and its sister ship, MS Victoria, shuttle tourists up and down the Telemark Canal, occasionally docking to pick up cyclists keen to swap graft in the saddle for idle hours on deck. The endpoint for both boats and bikes comes in the village of Dalen, famed for its extraordinary wooden hotel, built to serve well-heeled 19th-century travellers.
Start // Ulefoss
Finish // Dalen
Distance // 70 miles (113 km)
Info // www.telemarkskanalen.no

KYSTRIKSVEIEN

The Kystriksveien (Coast Road) is a contender for Norway's most epic road trip, stretching some 403 miles (650km) north, from the outskirts of Trondheim to the town of Bodø, set just within the limits of the Arctic Circle. It's mostly done by car but intrepid cyclists with an abundance of time and energy tackle it too, looping their way along the succession of fjords that fracture Norway's Atlantic shore. Cycling days quickly fall into a rhythm, with shoreside rides bookended by ferry hops over narrow straits. Detours to offshore islands, meanwhile, such as little Leka, rugged Vega or remote Lovund, only serve to enhance any Kystriksveien odyssey.
Start // Steinkjer
Finish // Bodø
Distance // 403 miles (650 km)
Info // www.kystriksveien.no

HENRIK IBSEN

TAKING IT SLOW IN ITALY'S ABRUZZO

The shepherds who once roamed the high pastures of Abruzzo, occupy a special place in Italian history. Ride in their footprints and follow in thousands of years of tradition. And sheep.

Too steep, too steep, don't fall. I'm in the middle-rear of the pack, far enough from the rest of my cycling group on our The Slow Cyclist tour that I cannot see the riders in front of me and can't hear those behind. It's a lucky thing too, because this not-terribly drastic incline – on a quiet country road – has struck within me a level of panic that is best unseen by other eyes. Already today I have displayed my characteristic 'agility' by catching my leg underneath the hulking frame of my rented e-bike; the changing colour-scheme on my shin promises an impressive bruise by day's end. New to cycling, I am not yet at peace with my purpose-bought, padded cycling shorts, nor am I yet convinced that I know what a gear actually does. All I can think about is my face and a rock, colliding. I'm terrified – and I love it.

I'm just outside the meticulously restored town of Santo Stefano di Sessanio, in the Abruzzo region of Italy, and although I have lived in this country for over a decade I feel far, far away from home. To call Abruzzo 'wild' is not quite accurate, although it has become popular to do so; to call it 'untouched' is worse, given its popularity stretches back centuries. Instead, the region that sprawls across the eastern spine of the Italian peninsula sings with its own identity, fiercely connected to a still-present past.

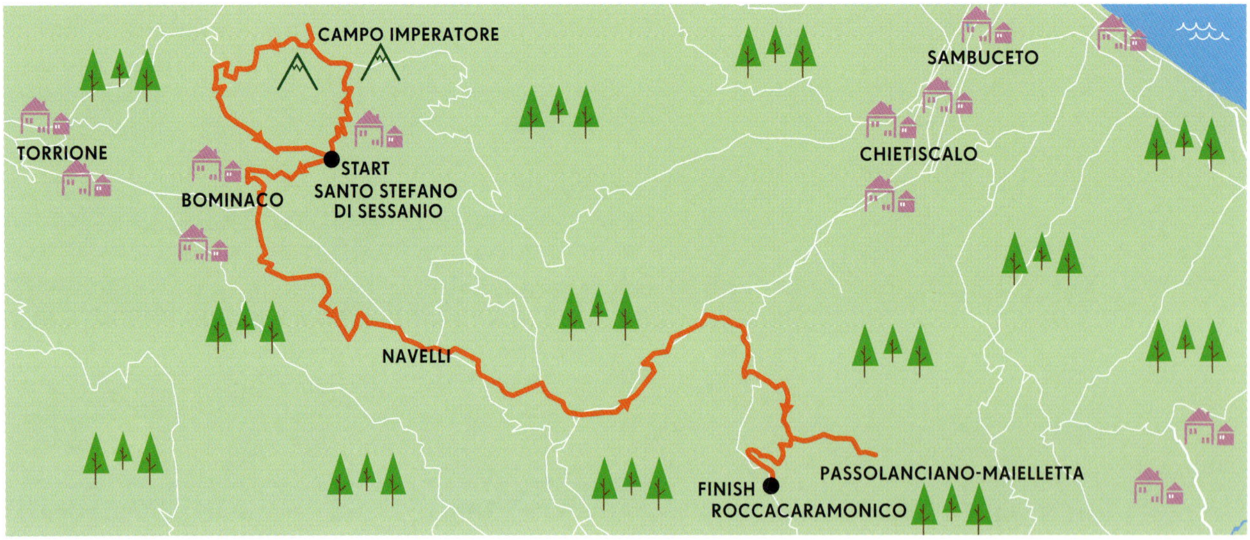

Daisy Wingate-Saul

"I come to realise that cycling is perhaps the best way to experience a place like Abruzzo, sharing something without having to articulate it, to breathe it in"

Any trip to Abruzzo has to begin in the Gran Sasso d'Italia, a massif in the Apennine Mountains, the range that stretches through central Italy and holds it taut, like a prehistoric backbone. You can see the range from Rome on a clear day but until you're up close, it's hard to understand just how imposing these peaks are. But it's far from a desolate, forbidding place: every cliff bears traces of 'transhumance', an ancient method of pastoralism that involved the seasonal movement of livestock between summer and winter pastures, by nomadic shepherds. And so, all along these jagged crags are signs that someone passed, someone stopped, someone lived here.

Everywhere you go, the venerable Corno Grande that anchors the Apennines and is their highest point, gazes back with, conditions depending, a subtly changing expression – a Mona Lisa in limestone. And while I might not have thought of it before, I come to realise that cycling is perhaps the best way to experience a place like Abruzzo. It allows you to share something without having to articulate it, to breathe it in. Indeed, while I'm travelling with a fantastic group, my favourite parts of the days are those stretches where we ride in single file yet don't make conversation. The silences, the interludes that give you time to yourself, where you don't feel the need to fill the bus or van with your own voice, where every inch of sky seems to belong to you alone.

When we reach Campo Imperatore, the sense is of a somewhat noisier history. It was on this vast plateau that, every September, as many as five million sheep once gathered before being led along the coast, to Puglia. Today, the only chorus that surrounds you is one of green, punctuated by ancient stones and faraway mountains that tease you to come ever closer. In the days of ancient pastoralists, however, this plain and its attendant peaks would have echoed to the cacophony of that livestock.

From Campo Imperatore, we ride on to Maiella National Park, where the slopes curve more subtly and the hills around our temporary home, at the family-run Case Catalano, are blanketed in downy yellow flowers. Cristina and her father welcome us into their delightful gardens and immediately take to grilling *arrosticini*, the unctuous lamb skewers that have become the worldwide ambassador for Abruzzese cuisine. It's not hard to understand why, especially for this cyclist; the

ARE WE TRANSHUMAN?

'Transhumance' played a fundamental role in the history of Abruzzo and continues to be one of its most revered cultural traditions. The route shepherds would take with their sheep stretched from L'Aquila in Abruzzo to Foggia, in Puglia, a road known as the Tratturo Magno (roughly the 'King's Path') and which spanned almost 155 miles (250km). While transhumance has largely disappeared, much of the music, literature, and folklore of Abruzzo celebrates this history.

Clockwise from top: a church on the Campo Imperatore; the hermitage of Santo Spirito; cycling around the town of Caramanico

Daisy Wingate-Saul

combination of the miles completed and calories burned turn every bite into a reward.

By the time we reach our last day on the road, where we'll ride our steepest inclines to visit the spectral Hermitage di Santo Spirito, I feel a pang of sadness that my cycling journey is coming to its end. By now I've got the hang of switching gears and have finally managed to dismount without catching my leg beneath the chassis of my increasingly familiar bike. If I can just about imagine a situation where I won't need padded shorts, I definitely cannot see a way forward in life that doesn't involve a near-constant flow of *arrosticini*. As I head back to Rome the following day, the knobbly contours of the Apennines begin to fade until they are just a line on the horizon. But I know that somewhere, among those crags that carry the evidence of the lives (and livestock) that came before, the Corno Grande still presides over all, with its ever-changing gaze.

And what better way to connect with lines back through history than by tracing them with the wheels of a bicycle? If the challenge of sustainable travel is to make it something more than a picturesque backdrop to our own self-indulgence, then surely it is aboard a machine that lets us engage with the landscape as we move through it. Because, somewhere in the deepest part of Abruzzo, I became a cyclist, ready to take on the steepest climbs and unafraid to fall (well, maybe just a little afraid). And I'm not sure I would want to do it any other way. **VD**

Daisy Wingate-Saul

Previous page: autumn colours on the Campo Imperatore plains; the castle of Rocca Calascio

TOOLKIT

Start // Santo Stefano di Sessanio
Finish // Roccacaramanico
Distance // 105 miles (170km)
Getting there // Santo Stefano di Sessanio is a 2-hour drive from Rome, but if you're bringing your bike you can take a train from Roma Termini station to L'Aquila. From there it's a 20-mile (30km) ride.
When to go // May and September are optimal, but June and July offer cooler nights and warm days.
What to wear // Padded cycling shorts are a must, but pack layers for temperature changes.
What to pack // Sunscreen and a jacket for evenings.
Where to stay // Case Catalano inside Maiella National Park.
Where to eat // Cantina Chiesamadre, carved into the rocks of Santo Stefano di Sessanio.
More info // Book with www.theslowcyclist.com

Opposite: the Parenzana rail trail; the facade of St Peter's Basilica where Via Francigena finishes; riding L'Eroica towards Siena

MORE LIKE THIS
ITALIAN RIDES WITH HISTORIC CONNECTIONS

VIA FRANCIGENA

Originating in the 7th century, this ancient path begins in Canterbury in southern England and finishes, by way of France and Switzerland, in Brindisi in the heel of Italy's boot. It was in this Italian port that pilgrims would once board ships to sail onwards to Jerusalem. The cycling portion doesn't cover quite as much ground, but a challenging route nonetheless adheres to the majority of the footpath. Beginning deep in the Alps at the Great St Bernard Pass in Switzerland (8100ft/2469m), the predominantly Italian section of the Francigena passes through the Val d'Aosta, Piedmont, and Emilia Romagna before descending into the Eternal City via Tuscany's rolling hills. The 23 stages will have you averaging riding 30 miles (50km) per day, which is more than enough to work up an appetite.
Start // Great St Bernard Pass, Switzerland
Finish // St. Peter's Basilica, Rome, Italy
Distance // 590 miles (950km)

THE PARENZANA TRAIL

Fancy riding the rails between three countries without ever boarding a train? Then saddle up and follow the Parenzana Trail. Following the long-defunct Parenzana railway line, which ran from 1902 to 1935, the route connects Italy, Slovenia, and Croatia along an almost entirely traffic-free track. While the stunning natural landscape is reason enough to plan a journey here, the Parenzana is also an open-air museum, preserving relics from a crucial transport system that once transported salt, oil, wine, coal and people through the Istrian Peninsula, a region which has undergone countless dramatic changes throughout its history. Make it an overnight journey in the summertime and reward yourself with multiple dips in the clear and tranquil waters of the Adriatic Sea.
Start // Trieste, Italy
Finish // Poreč, Croatia
Distance // 76 miles (123km)

L'EROICA

Started in 1997 as an annual event celebrating vintage bicycles (those manufactured before 1987), L'Eroica has not only gone from strength to strength but has also added editions to accommodate more recent machines (Nova Eroica). If that weren't enough, the route has, additionally, become a year-round feature of the roving rider's calendar by virtue of the fact it passes through some of the most breathtaking landscape in Tuscany. The twelve 'stages' of the original event connect historic villages, castles, and plenty of vineyards, through a combination of paved and unpaved roads. Cyclists can tackle the entire route, or sections of their choosing along the many, well-signposted trails. For even more time amongst the rolling fields of the Val d'Orcia, tackle the extended Eroica Montalcino route that dips south, towards Siena. From there, you'll have no trouble at all finding a wine tasting or two (or three).
Start/finish // Gaiole (classic); Nova and Montalcino, various
Distance // 130 miles (209km)

POST PAVLVS·V·BVRGHESIVS·ROMANVS·PO

TENERIFE'S VOLCANIC RIDES

Tenerife's unique volcanic terrain and high-altitude climbs serve up explosive multiday adventures for professional Tour de France cyclists and ambitious amateur riders alike.

James Cannon

Pedalling through the psychedelic landscapes of Tenerife's Teide National Park is like cycling on another planet. In the high-altitude Las Cañadas caldera, the collapsed crater around the island's iconic 12,198ft (3718m) Mount Teide volcano, I cycle past Martian-red sand dunes, silvery pumice gravel, fragments of glistening black obsidian and pinnacles of mustard-yellow rock. The volcanic terrain here is so otherworldly it has been used by NASA to test their Mars-exploring Perseverance rover, and by the European Space Agency to train its astronauts.

But this wild volcanic terrain is also a secret playground for elite Tour de France cyclists, who come here to sharpen their fitness and climbing skills on the high-altitude slopes – and for amateur riders, like me, who want to follow in their tyre marks. Elite squads such as Ineos Grenadiers, Visma-Lease a Bike and Movistar are regulars here. 'No other environment can beat Mount Teide,' declared 2012 Tour de France champion

"I can feel the blowtorch heat of the sun and the metallic chill of altitude"

Sir Bradley Wiggins. Four-time Tour de France winner Chris Froome says it is like 'travelling to Mars'.

At 785 sq mi (2034 sq km), Tenerife – a saddle-shaped island in the Atlantic Ocean around 186 miles (300km) from Africa – is the largest of Spain's Canary Islands, making it perfect for training camps and multiday adventures. You can cycle from sea level to over 6562ft (2000m), and while Mount Teide tops out at 12198ft (3718m), the highest road reaches to the cable-car station, at 7730ft (2356m). Those high-altitude climbs boost the body's oxygen-carrying red blood cell count. And as Tenerife is on the same latitude as the Sahara Desert, it enjoys year-round sunshine.

But with the intense summer heat, mind-scrambling altitude and strange volcanic geology, cycling in the Teide National Park soon becomes a hallucinatory experience. The phantasmagorical terrain drains the body and tricks the mind. Climbs look flat. Flats turn out to be climbs. I can simultaneously feel the blowtorch heat of the sun and the metallic chill of altitude. There are white clouds pooling in the valley below me and desert sands lining the roads above me. Nothing makes sense. As I grind along the grey road, which stretches across the volcanic landscape like a solidified river of lava, the ominous cone of Mount Teide (still active, but dormant since 1909) looms on the horizon but never seems to get closer.

James Cannon

I feel gloriously giddy, as though I've had too many bottles of the local Dorada lager. I'm sweaty but spellbound. Exhausted but excited. So, this is how the pros must feel when performing killer training sessions here before the Tour de France. They just ride a lot faster: on previous trips I have seen Geraint Thomas, Fabio Aru and Primož Roglič fly past in a blur of bright Lycra. There was no point giving chase.

On my two-day 'Rings of Fire' adventure, I tackle two loops through volcanic terrain from my base in Puerto de la Cruz in the north of the island – a good launchpad for exploring the Teide National Park. On the first day, a 119-mile (192km) loop, I spin along the dramatic northern coastline, past deep ravines, banana plantations and palm groves to the pastel-toned fishing village of Garachico. After diverting along glistening black sea-cliffs to the isolated Punta de Teno lighthouse, I dive inland, through terraced farmland, to the mountain village of Masca, where I grind up a brutal 11% climb which even the pro riders fear. I then explore the western segment of the Teide National Park before returning to the hotel.

My second day, a 77-mile (124km) loop, begins with an unrelenting climb from sea level to the ancient lava flows, red cinder cones and sparkling dunes in the eastern part of the Teide National Park. In the afternoon, I descend through pine forests on a mountain road which swirls downhill like the slides at Tenerife's Siam water park. The drop in altitude is so rapid my water bottles implode. I then trace the sun-drenched coastline westwards, where palm trees explode into the sky like frozen fireworks, before arriving back in Puerto de la Cruz.

For multiday rides, getting help from a cycling tour company means you don't have to carry kit and food, so you can ride fast and free like the pros. My own adventures were supported by Alberto and Marcos Delgado of Tenerife Bike Tours. The local brothers know every road, cafe, and microclimate (there are 11 different climate zones in Tenerife, so you can always find blue skies). 'It is great to see this island where I grew up become so popular with cyclists,' Alberto tells me. 'The scenery is so good you forget you are working hard.'

Cyclists who want to feel like they are racing in a professional peloton can ride many of the same roads in the Vuelta al Teide sportive, held every May. I took part in 2022, and thanks to the road marshals and feed stations I enjoyed a wonderfully smooth and zippy ride experience. But the volcanic landscapes here are worth savouring over several days.

Anybody can enjoy the geological wonders of Tenerife on a bus tour or with a rental car. But nothing beats the environmental intimacy of cycling. To arrive in this volcanic landscape by leg-power alone, so you can taste the volcanic dust on your lips and smell the perfume of the pine trees, is a uniquely rewarding way to experience Tenerife's beauty. And if you visit in the months before July's Tour de France, you'll share the roads with the best cyclists on the planet. Good luck trying to catch up with them. **MB**

HOTEL PARADOR

Hotel Parador de Las Cañadas del Teide is the only hotel in the Teide National Park, and it's the preferred base for most professional cycling teams when they visit the island. Whether you stop there for lunch, or just to nose around, it's your best chance for bagging a selfie with a world-famous cyclist or banking a signed bidon. Pro riders also enjoy restorative coffee stops at local cafes, so keep an eye out for any riders in pro team jerseys and their branded support vehicles as you explore the island.

Top to bottom: exploring Teide National Park; Previous spread: find spectacular volcanic terrain on Tenerife

TOOLKIT

Start/finish // Puerto de la Cruz
Distance // 196 miles (315km), over two days
Getting there // Most international flights arrive at Tenerife's South Airport. From there it is a one-hour transfer or drive to Puerto de la Cruz.
When to go // Tenerife has warm year-round temperatures, but between March and May you'll avoid the summer heat and be more likely to see pro riders prepping for July's Tour de France. Ride some of this route on the challenging 113 miles (182km) Gran Fondo course of the annual Vuelta al Teide sportive in May (vteide.com)
Where to stay // The north is the best base for exploring the nearby Teide National Park. The cyclist-friendly Hotel Alua Tenerife in Puerto de la Cruz offers secure cycle storage and post-ride massage services. Tenerife Bike Tours offer guided tours and bike-rental services.
More info // webtenerife.co.uk

Opposite: sinuous Sa Calobra in Mallorca's Tramuntana mountains

MORE LIKE THIS
OTHER PLACES TO PEDAL LIKE A PRO

GIRONA, SPAIN

The Catalan city of Girona has been the adopted home of professional cyclists ever since Lance Armstrong moved here in the 1990s. As with the popular pro cycling destination of Tenerife, Girona is a great place to share quiet roads and cosy cafes with the world's finest riders. And thanks to the Spanish region's punchy climbs and eclectic landscapes, you're guaranteed some memorable road rides. In a 103-mile (166km) clockwise loop from Girona, passing through Amer, Olot and Banyoles, you can explore rugged Catalan countryside, sleepy villages and the volcanic terrain of Garrotxa. The big tests come with the leg-flaming ascents of Sant Martí Sacalm (2057ft/627m) and Rocacorba (3212ft/979m) – the fabled training climb of the professional peloton. But with local climbs such as Sant Hilari Sacalm, Els Àngels and Sant Grau all within touching distance of Girona, it is the perfect base for a multi-day adventure.
Start/finish // Girona
Distance // 103 miles (166km)

MALLORCA, SPAIN

With its quiet roads and smooth climbs, the Spanish island of Mallorca is a popular training location for professional cyclists, especially the Olympic riders who represent the British Cycling team. The annual Mallorca 312 sportive, which takes place in April, is one of the most iconic events in the amateur European road cycling calendar. The event is so popular that even former pros like Sean Kelly, Annemiek van Vleuten, Vincenzo Nibali and Alberto Contador have taken part. But the legendary 194-mile (312km) route can easily be broken up into a more leisurely multi-day trip for those who wish to stretch out the journey. The anti-clockwise loop begins and ends in Playa de Muro, on the island's northeast coast, and circles the ruggedly beautiful Serra de Tramuntana mountain range, serving up a colossal 16,568ft (5050m) of climbing overall.
Start/finish // Playa de Muro
Distance // 194 miles (312km)

NICE, FRANCE

Nice is the launchpad for some devilishly difficult climbs stretching from the sparkling Mediterranean coastline to the foothills of the Alps. The French coastal city has become the preferred training base for many elite cyclists, in particular those who race for Ineos Grenadiers, who have a team base there. And the American bike brand Trek still name their flagship bike after the iconic Col de la Madone. On a 64-mile (104km) anti-clockwise loop, you'll enjoy the best of the scenery, including a coastal dash around glamorous Monaco, and a slog up the vicious climbs of the Col d'Èze (1634ft/498m) and the Col de la Madone (3024ft/922m) – a storied training climb for pro riders living in the area. With many other scenic coastal roads and sharp climbs in the region, Nice is an ideal choice for a long weekend of cycling.
Start/finish // Nice
Distance // 64 miles (104km)

Mazur Travel/Shutterstock

THE HOPE 1000

This brilliantly designed route through the Swiss Alps is long-distance bikepacking made easy, says champion adventure rider Lael Wilcox.

'Switzerland calling.'

Willi Felix is calling me in Tucson, Arizona, from the other side of the world. He wants to invite me to his race in Switzerland on a route he designed after decades of riding research. It's called the Hope 1000 (previously the Navad 1000) a 620-mile (1000km), self-supported mountain-bike race across Switzerland from Lake Constance to Lake Geneva with a staggering 96,218 feet (29,327m) of climbing.

'How do you fit that much climbing into such a short distance?'

'It's the Alps,' replies Willi. 'They are steep.'

Five months later, mid-May, I'm on a plane from Alaska to Zurich. I've planned to ride the entire route, for fun and in preparation for the race.

I pack light because I'll be living on my bike. Summer in Switzerland is warm and sunny for the most part, and though the route tops out at 6800 feet (2070m), most of it is much less elevated. For the race, my upper-body layering system is a long-sleeved shirt, a cycling gilet and a rain jacket. I don't even pack a pair of trousers.

Willi picks me up from Zurich Airport and takes me to his home in Bettwiesen, a 30-minute drive from Zurich. I unpack and rebuild my bike, trying to stay awake to beat jet lag. A few days later, I'm out on the Hope 1000.

The route is broken into 11 segments, each a solid day's ride, and each starting and ending in a town with at least a grocery store, but typically also a hotel, restaurant, train station and possibly a bike shop. So it's a simple adventure to plan, mount and complete – and you can shorten it with ease. For instance, a great option for a week-long trip is to begin in Sursee and ride the western half of the route in the higher mountains.

I leave early morning after coffee and a croissant, riding through farm fields and along a creek. The road turns up; first it's paved, then dirt, then trail. I'm spinning my easiest gear, cranking slowly up the steep pitch (a couple of sections have to be walked). I'm alone. The view opens up. A chairlift, static, hovers above the trail. I'm surrounded by mountains with a

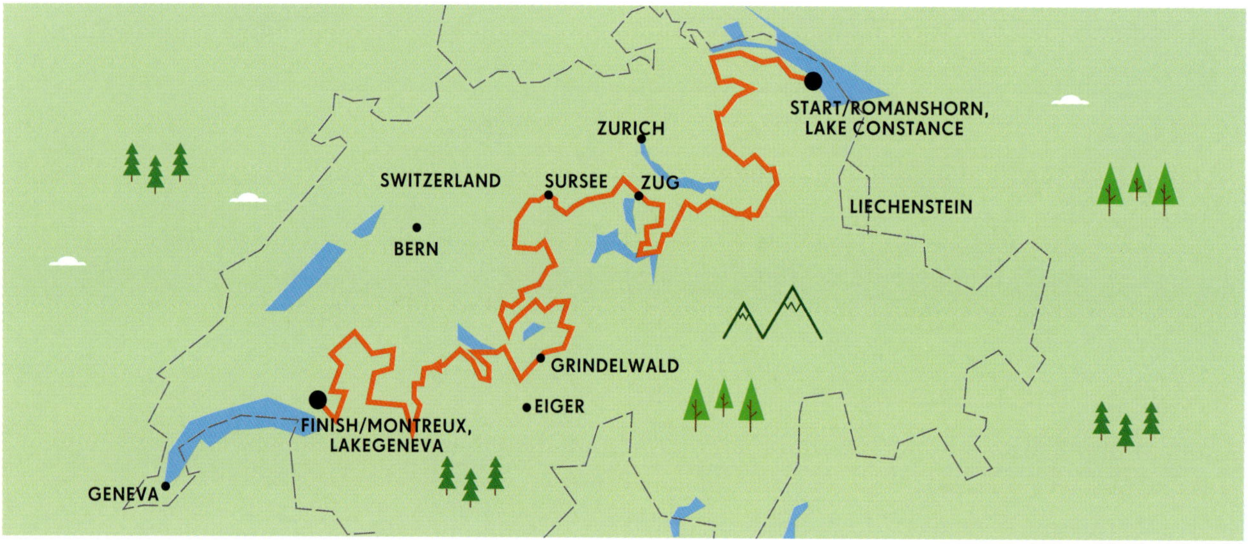

Rugile Kaladyte

direct line of sight to the next lake, crystal blue. This is the Switzerland of postcards and calendars, pristine and peaceful.

Then I descend, stopping at a spring to fill up my water bottles and a shop to buy lunch: a slice of pizza and a container of cabbage salad. The local language is German and I don't speak it, but it's easy to get by. The village stores are plentifully stocked with baked goods and yogurt drinks, sandwiches and snacks.

The day continues. If I'm not climbing, I'm descending. In the intended direction, riding west, many of the climbs are either paved or well-graded roads; Willi has ensured trails are reserved for the descents.

Past dark, I make it to a small mountain hut. It's a three-sided building, public and free for hikers and cyclists. I spook a sleeping German hiker awake. I tell him about the Hope 1000 route and that I'm riding to prepare for the race. He's hiking the Camino de Santiago de Compostela, spending three months walking to Spain. 'Your bike looks like a rocket ship', he says.

Next morning, I'm up with the sun before six. I pack my sleeping bag and mat and I'm back on my bike. The German rubs sleep out of his eyes: 'Are you already racing?' he asks.

This is how I want to spend all of my days.

In the mountains, I'm mostly alone. I encounter smiling farmers and cows, cyclists and hikers. I never go more than 9 or 10 miles (15km) between fresh water fountains or 25 miles (40km) before finding a restaurant or shop. I don't have to worry about food or water until I'm hungry or thirsty. It feels like

THE MONTREUX JAZZ FESTIVAL

The Hope 1000 ends in the handsome city of Montreux on the shore of Lake Geneva, which for two weeks each July is home to what has become the second-biggest jazz festival in the world. The festival still has its roots in jazz, but has expanded to include every style of music, with celebrated artists from around the world performing. If that blows your flute, time your ride appropriately and make sure to secure your accommodation well in advance.

"The Hope 1000 is a masterpiece of bikepacking design. I never have to worry about where to find food or water"

From above: the Hope 1000 climbs over 98,000ft (30,000m); Lael finishes with a dip in Lake Geneva. Previous page: the Hope 1000 provides picture-postcard Swiss scenery

Rugile Kaladyte

an adventure without concern – which is the ultimate freedom. Most nights are clear and I sleep in fields. To avoid getting wet, I take shelter under a barn during an afternoon shower and sleep under the porch of a cabin. (There are always options for hotels and guesthouses, but I'd rather sleep out. Bivouacking on public land away from protected areas and populations is generally acceptable in Switzerland.)

The second half of the Hope 1000 route, I discover, is both better and harder than the first, with climbs up the Grosse and Kleine Schedeggs past Grindelwald, with views of the Eiger, Jungfrau and Mönch, singletrack traversing craters through Stübleni, and the final climb over the Col de Jaman to Montreux on Lake Geneva. The route ends at a statue of Freddie Mercury. After 620 miles (1000km) and 98,000ft (30,000m) of climbing, Freddie is always waiting.

There are many ways to cross Switzerland, but the Hope 1000 is a mountain masterpiece. After 20 years of research, Willi published the route and organised the race to encourage more people into self-supported adventure riding. Thanks to its logistical ease, he sees it as a beginner-friendly bikepacking race.

Willi is nearly 60 and rides his own race every year. In addition, before the grand depart each June, he verifies every kilometre to make sure the Hope 1000 is both rideable and challenging. Mountain biking wasn't invented in Switzerland, but maybe it should have been. **LW**

TOOLKIT

Start // Romanshorn, Switzerland, on Lake Constance

Finish // Montreux, Switzerland, on Lake Geneva

Distance // 632 miles (1017km)

How to get there // Zurich Airport is half-an-hour's train ride from Romanshorn. Geneva Airport is the closest to Montreux.

When to ride // The end of May and October.

What to take // A mountain bike (hardtail or full suspension) with 2in tyres, disc brakes and easy gearing.

Where to stay // The Hope 1000 is designed to pass hotels and official campgrounds.

What to eat // Croissants, sandwiches and drinkable yogurt, if you're like me.

More info // The Hope 1000 was previously the Navad 1000: full GPX track www.bikepacking.com/routes/navad-1000/. Willi Felix hosts a free race on the Hope 1000 route every June: www.hope1000.ch/.

Opposite: eating up trail on the 1000 Miles Adventure; racing the Bike Odyssey in Greece

MORE LIKE THIS
LAEL-APPROVED BIKEPACKS

THE BIKE ODYSSEY, GREECE

This mountain race, held each June, connects small, peaceful villages in Northwest Greece, via high pasture and mountain passes, verdant forest and arid Mediterranean landscapes. The route is 80% trail and 20% road, and if the gradients are occasionally demanding (you'll gain 55,000ft/16,800m over the entire route) and the surface loose, it is entirely rideable. Fresh water is abundant; camping is easy. Northern Greece is a land of feta, walnuts and honey. Away from cities, packable food and stores can be hard to source, so be sure to stock up when passing through larger towns. However, nearly every village has a cafe and place to have a meal. Race in June or tour the route between April and October. It is a particularly attractive touring destination in the spring and autumn when European weather elsewhere is less friendly.

Start // Smixi
Finish // Kato Tithorea
Distance // 385 miles (620km)
Info // www.bikeodyssey.gr

LA TRAVERSÉE DU MASSIF VOSGIEN, FRANCE

An official French mountain-bike route running north-south through the Vosges Mountains in eastern France, the signed Traversée du Massif Vosgien follows primarily well-graded dirt roads and trails in forested Alsace. You'll meander through many small villages and past castle ruins, with ample opportunity for lodging, camping, and sampling local cuisine and Alsatian wines along the way. The region's culture, on the border with Germany, is quite distinct and the Vosges Mountains are a quiet, natural retreat for its residents. Best ridden in the summer months (May to September), the route is 90% trail and a slice of France not often seen by visitors. The local *tarte flambée*, white wine and Munster cheese are not only justly celebrated, they're great fuelling options for the mountainous trail. A well-connected rail network makes this route easily accessible.

Start // Wissembourg
Finish // Thann
Distance // 252 miles (406km)
Info // www.alsaceavelo.fr

1000 MILES ADVENTURE, CZECHIA AND SLOVAKIA

Starting in 2011, the 1000 Miles Adventure was one of the first bikepacking races in Europe. It travels through the beautiful mountains and forests of Czechia and Slovakia from the German border to the Ukrainian border (the direction changes each year). And though it feels remote, you're never far from populated areas, and your next hot meal and cold beer. The route developer and race organiser, Jan Kopka, wanted to bring home his extensive experience of adventure racing around the world. Due to his efforts in part, bikepacking is popular in Czechia. The race start is in July and 7 to 27 days are recommended for completion – NB, significant sections of the route are open for the race alone, so to ride its entirety, sign up for the race.

Start // Hranice, Czechia
Finish // Nová Sedlica, Slovakia
Distance // 1000 miles (1610km)
Info // www.1000miles.cz

The Bike Odyssey; 1000 Miles Adventure

105

WEST KERNOW WAY

Discover lost ways, sandy beaches, fishing villages and industrial remnants on a bikepacking loop of Cornwall's far west coast, fuelled by fish and chips.

For more than 40 years my family would holiday in St Mawes, a pretty harbour town on the south coast of Cornwall that was once supported by fishing but today reels in tourists. We'd rent houses, chalets and, one year, a caravan on a dairy farm where creamy Cornish milk was left on our doorstep every morning. But it wasn't until 2021 that it occurred to me to take a bicycle down for the family trip, an idea sparked that year by the inauguration of Cycling UK's West Kernow Way bikepacking route, which follows a figure-of-eight course around the west of Cornwall, skirting Land's End, looping down to the Lizard peninsula and then circling back around Redruth to Penzance.

And so it was that my Dad dropped me off at Truro train station with my laden bike for the short hop down to Penzance. With the railway line approaching along the coast, I quickly got my bearings and set off clockwise with the sea over my left shoulder.

Jordan Gibbons

Kernow is the Cornish name for Cornwall, deriving from the Celtic word for 'headland' or 'horn'. Since the 1970s, hikers have enjoyed a National Trail, the South West Coast Path, that guides them around the beach-scalloped fringe of this gorgeous county at the tip of the UK. Cyclists looked on with envy. But in 2021 Cycling UK, formerly known as the Cyclists' Touring Club, launched another in their series of multiday, mostly off-road routes. The West Kernow Way was intended to be an accessible introduction to the west of Cornwall, covering not only quaint villages, coves and such famous landmarks as Land's End and the Minack Theatre, but also fascinating and unexpected features of Cornish history. The route touches on a lot of the region's mining heritage and includes several so-called 'lost ways'. These are former public paths, such as the Tinners Way, a track used by horse-drawn carts for centuries and marked on 17th-century maps, but long since disused and forgotten. The West Kernow Way knits these historic tracks into the route's patchwork of lanes, bridleways and other trails as a way of restoring access and encouraging their use once more.

But it starts on the lanes that weave along the coast to the tiny port of Mousehole (pronounced 'mowz-ul'), once raided by Spanish galleons in the 16th century. About 10 miles (16km) later there's a detour to the first beach of the trip, Porthcurno, and the amazing open-air Minack theatre, first developed by Rowena Cade in the 1930s in order to stage a production of Shakespeare's *The Tempest* on the Cornish clifftops. After I'd been riding for 20 miles (32km), I reached the junction leading to Land's End and met an older couple on comfortable bikes.

'Are you going far today?' I asked.

'We've come from John O'Groats,' they replied. They were just a couple of miles from completing the feat of cycling the length of the UK, from the northernmost point of Scotland to England's southern tip.

I wasn't planning on cycling quite so far. My intention was to split the West Kernow Way into two 75-mile (120km) sections and stay overnight somewhere between Porthleven and the Lizard. So far, progress was brisk. I passed Land's End, rode through the seemingly sub-tropical Cot Valley and then entered the town of St Just, epicentre of the region's tin mining. Here there are vestiges of that industry in the shape of disused engine houses overlooking the sea; one, the Levant Mine and Beam Engine, has been restored, with a working 1840s steam engine.

Turning east, I joined the Tinners Way, an age-old track that's in the process of becoming an official right of way once more. This section of the route climbs up onto moorland, which is somewhat eerie if fog has come down. It's also where I started to go wrong: with many conflicting tracks disappearing over the moors, it's a navigational challenge. If you pass Mên-an-Tol (two upright menhirs flanking a hollow, ring-shaped stone) and the Nine Maidens stone circle, you're going in the right direction.

Jordan Gibbons; Ian Woolcock/Shutterstock; PaolaVi/Shutterstock

A GLOSSARY

Decode some local Cornish placenames:
Als, alt – a cliff
Bal – a mine
Bron – a hill
Dinas – a hill fort
Enys – an island
Goon – moorland
Lan – a monastic enclosure
Maen, mēn – a stone
Mēn-an-Tol – a stone with a hole
Nans – a valley
Pen – a headland
Pol – a pool
Porth – a cove
Praze – a meadow
Ruan – a river
Towan – a sandhill
Tre – a dwelling
Wheal – a mine
Zawn – a chasm

Clockwise from left: Cadgwith Cove on the Lizard Peninsula; the south coast; mining ruins near St Just; Minack Theatre; Mên-an-Tol on the moors. Previous spread: sandy Loe Bar on the WKW

Rough trails descend to St Erth via Nancledra, where the crossover in the figure-of-eight route comes. By St Erth I'd done about 45 miles (72km) and was behind schedule. I decided to push on for 10 miles (16km) to the harbour town of Porthleven for the night, where I ordered fish and chips at The Ship Inn.

The next day promised the best of Cornwall, conveniently packaged in the Lizard, a rounded headland that feels like a world unto itself. To reach it, I rode along the coast with the sea a sparkling distraction over my right shoulder. This also means cycling up some steep and sandy slopes as the route swoops down to tiny coves and back up the other side. It's hard work on a loaded bicycle, but there's often an ice-cream as a reward. The fishing village of Coverack made a perfect spot for lunch, 35 miles (56km) beyond Porthleven. Then I turned inland on lanes that led towards Helford. Rather than taking a dogleg inland, I hopped on a local ferry across the Helford River to the Ferry Boat Inn. Note: it's a tiny boat with space for at most two bicycles.

From here, the official route heads towards the north coast of Cornwall at Porthreath and then veers diagonally down to Marazion, from where it's easy to ride back to Penzance. But along the way I noticed how close I was to the maritime town of Falmouth, protected by Henry VIII's Pendennis Castle, now a creative hub for Cornwall. Embracing the freedom of being on a bicycle, I decided to divert to Falmouth from where I took a second ferry back to St Mawes. **RB**

TOOLKIT

Start/finish // Penzance (Marazion)
Distance // 147 miles (237km)
Getting there // Penzance train station is on a direct railway line from London Paddington, with stops also at Reading, Exeter and Plymouth.
When to ride // The best time is from May to October. Short sections of the route can be waterlogged after rain or in winter, but much of it is rideable year-round.
What to wear // Padded cycling shorts, a baselayer, jersey and helmet as a minimum. Waterproof or windproof clothing depending on the season plus waterproof overshoes if rain is forecast.
What to pack // Camping and cooking kit if not using accommodation. Otherwise, foolproof navigation tech and a paper map. Plus battery chargers as required.
Where to stay // Plenty of accommodation options from hotels to campsites. Peak season is July and August when advance booking is essential.
More info // www.cyclinguk.org

Jordan Gibbons

Opposite: taking the Tarka Trail through Devon; approaching Mont-Saint-Michel in Normandy

MORE LIKE THIS
CELTIC CONNECTIONS

TOUR DE MANCHE, ENGLAND/FRANCE

Separated by the English Channel but bound by a related language (Breton, Cornish and Welsh are members of the Brittonic language family), Cornwall and Brittany have much in common. Similarities extend beyond placenames to the granite stone and the steep descents down to coves and inlets. Explore both the Breton and Cornish coasts on this inventive route that runs along England's south coast between Plymouth and Poole and uses two ferry rides to link to a route along the Norman and Breton coast between Roscoff and Cherbourg that takes in the distinctive profile of Mont-Saint-Michel. On the French side, the Tour de Manche uses more than 143 miles (230km) of traffic-free greenways. The English stretch follows parts of the National Cycle Network.
Start/finish // Plymouth
Distance // 435 miles (700km)

DEVON COAST TO COAST, ENGLAND

The classic Devon Coast to Coast route offers a pleasant couple of days' cycling through the west country. The route connects Plymouth on the south coast with Ilfracombe on the north coast by piecing together existing bike paths, such as the Tarka Trail, with some of the lanes and former railway lines on the signposted National Cycle Network. With modest elevation gains, it's a trip suitable for families. Setting off from either Plymouth or Ilfracombe, you'll skirt Dartmoor National Park, follow the Taw and Torridge estuaries on the Tarka Trail (named after the local otter in Henry Williamson's book) and ride Drake's Trail between Plymouth and Tavistock, which now includes the exciting Gem Bridge. There are a couple of electric bike charging stations along the way.
Start // Plymouth
Finish // Ilfracombe
Distance // 97.5 miles (157km)

LÔN LAS CYMRU, WALES

The Lôn Las Cymru (Welsh Green Lane) is the perfect way to discover Wales' wonderfully hilly hinterland. This 253-mile (407km) route runs from Cardiff in the south to Holyhead in the north. The route follows the Taff Trail railway path, then crosses the Brecon Beacons, the Wye Valley and over to the sea at Machynlleth. From here, Snowdonia offers tough climbs and seaside views before crossing onto Anglesey via the magnificent Menai Bridge. This is one of the toughest routes on the National Cycle Network, even if you start in Chepstow rather than the Welsh capital and stay on tarmac for most of the ride. The reward for traversing hundreds of miles of mountains is a special insight into the great beauty of Wales, and a sense of satisfaction for having travelled across it.
Start // Cardiff/Chepstow
Finish // Holyhead
Distance // 253 miles (407km)

3
Coast Path
Tarka Trail

VÍA VERDE DEL ACEITE

Originally a railway line built to transport olive oil, this beautiful greenway now uncorks some of Andalucía's virgin landscapes for two-wheeled travellers.

Millions come to Andalucía to spend days by the sea, to slump in deckchairs along Europe's busiest holiday coastline. But in the Andalucían hinterland lies a different 'sea', one much less familiar. One of silvery branches rather than blue waves, noisy with the rustling of foliage rather than the rush of tides. A place where tourists are notably few but which, in its own distinctive, dusty way, is just as compelling.

This is the Mar de Olivos, the 'Sea of Olives', where almost every contour is dotted with rows of ancient, knotty olive trees, some of them millennia old. Winding through their midst is the Vía Verde de Aceite, the 'Greenway of Olive Oil', which cyclists can use to glide through unsung Spain, rolling past towns at siesta-time, soaring over parched canyons, or passing wayside cafes where they can stop to drizzle the lustrous liquid on their salads.

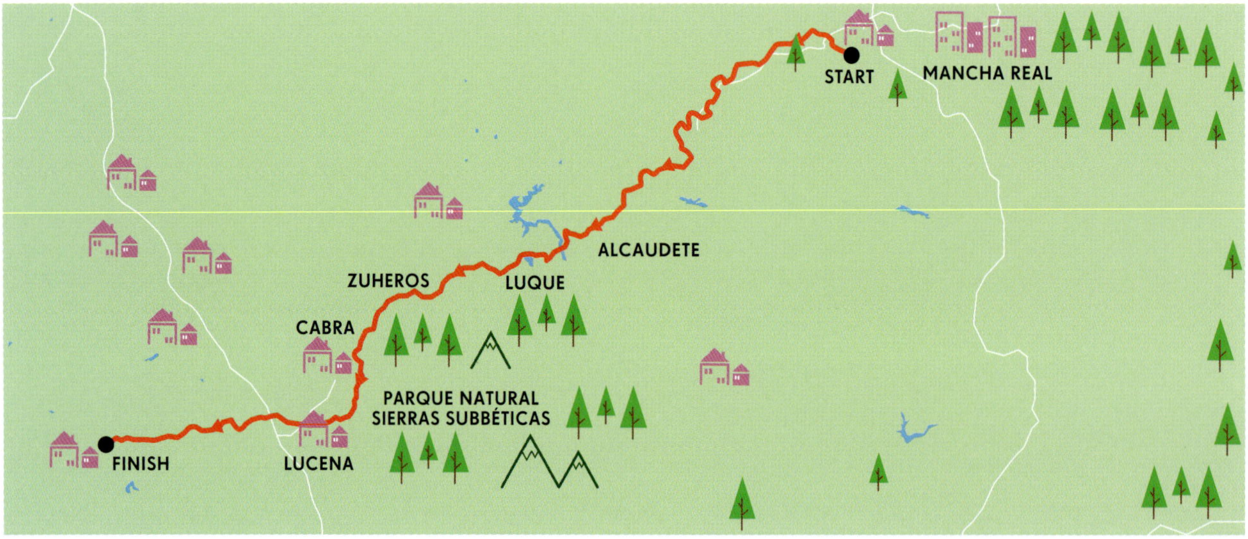

My journey on the Vía Verde de Aceite starts in Jaén, among Andalucía's more overlooked cities. Rising over its rooftops are the stout ramparts of the Castillo de Santa Catalina, a hilltop stronghold of Moorish origins. From the vantage point of the castle hill I can start to triangulate the 80 miles (128km) that lie ahead of me, the greenway slicing across the plains, meandering among low-slung foothills before vanishing into the haze.

I set out in earnest the following morning, riding a thin strip of gravel that's trodden only occasionally by dog walkers and picnicking pedestrians, but which remains off limits to motorised transport. The only sounds here are the song of the crickets, the crunch of loose stones under bike tyres, and the putter of faraway tractors embarking on the olive harvest. Up close, you soon spot clues that the Vía Verde once had a very different life, before the coming of cyclists. By the wayside are mustard-yellow stations with weed-strewn platforms, and water towers that have not seen a drop for decades.

In the late 19th century, the olive oil producers of Andalucía needed a way to export their product to the kitchens of Europe, and thus was born the Linares-Puente Genil railway. Steam trains huffed through these parched landscapes, the golden cargo slopping about in their trucks before being loaded onto waiting ships at the port of Malaga (passenger trains also travelled the route). By the mid-20th century, the railway was in decline, finally grinding to a halt in the 1980s. Only in 2001 was the Vía Verde del Aceite repurposed, for a new smokeless, soundless kind of travel. For cyclists today, the area's railway heritage is inescapable and indeed part of the appeal.

There are tunnels through which you can freewheel – and savour some respite from the Andalucían heat – while little, lineside huts also offer precious slivers of shade for pit stops. Most impressive of all are the viaducts, built by disciples of Gustave Eiffel no less, and that remain in service for cyclists. Notable examples are the Viaducto del Río Víboras, whose iron span soars haughtily beside a medieval humpbacked bridge; and the Viaducto del Río Guadajoz, where you can look down through the sleepers and see the rushing river far below your pedals.

But it is as it approaches its midpoint, looping beneath the Subbética range, that the Vía Verde del Aceite is at its most wildly beautiful. Here, I ride under a limestone escarpment, swiss-cheesed with bat caves, its heights crowned by old watchtowers where birds nest in crumbling masonry. A succession of towns appear almost like islands in the sea of olives. First comes Luque, its station now a restaurant, with croquettes, gazpacho and bacalao served within the cool of the old ticket room, or else alfresco in the shade of retired goods wagons. Some miles on comes Zuheros, where a steep path runs up a hillside to a maze of whitewashed alleyways. I lock up my bike to wander among them, inhaling the scents of jasmine and rosemary, planted in ceramic pots of glazed blue.

Andreas Werth/Alamy; Margaret Stepien for Lonely Planet;

LUCENA

Almost always bypassed by holidaymakers rushing between Córdoba and Malaga, the peaceful little town of Lucena is a good choice for a night's rest on a Vía Verde itinerary. In the Middle Ages this was a bastion of Sephardic culture – 20 years ago an extensive Jewish necropolis was unearthed beneath the city. A walkway gets you close to the rediscovered tombs, some of which date back as far as the 8th century.

Left to right: a signpost on the cycle path at Dona Menica village; a refreshing bowl of salmorejo; passing below Zuheros castle. Previous spread: crossing a bridge at Zuheros village on the Vía Verde Del Aceite; Luque's castle and town

More wonderful aromas follow along the greenway. I catch a whiff of a bakery one dewy morning, and scents of sherry late one afternoon, before stopping on a whim at a nearby bar. Such is the liberty you enjoy when cycling the Vía Verde del Aceite. Built as a railway line, it is devoid of steep inclines, sudden turns and the track-bed is one you can wholly trust in, freeing your gaze to take in the sierras and olive groves all around you. It is impossible to get lost and impossible to go hungry, such is the abundance of cafes that have taken up residence in the many stations that, albeit in a different way, are still places of comings and goings.

Towards the end of the greenway the mountains retreat, the country flattens further and more towns appear: Cabra, whose archaeological museum houses a wealth of Roman sculpture and mosaics; and pretty Lucena, famed for its Jewish heritage. The Vía Verde del Aceite terminates, rather abruptly, on the outskirts of the humdrum town of Puente Genil, not far from where modern high-speed trains thunder between Madrid and Malaga at speeds in excess of 220mph (350kph). And though dedicated road cyclists can occasionally be found thrashing up and down the Vía Verde, it is for me – and I imagine most others – a route best suited to slow, wistful days in the saddle. You can watch the silent miles roll by, looking out over that sea of olives just like the train passengers of old, with the notable difference that you are travelling under your own steam. **OS**

Andreas Werth/Alamy

TOOLKIT

Start // Jaén
Finish // Puente Genil
Distance // 79 miles (128km)
Getting there // Jaén's mainline station can be reached on direct trains from Madrid, taking about four hours. Puente Genil-Herrera is set on the high speed AVE line, taking 3hr30min to return to the capital.
When to go // Summer heat means that most cyclists ride during the 'shoulder' seasons, from September to November or from March to May. In midwinter the route also has its appeal, with some snows on the highest peaks.
Where to stay // Part of the Spanish government's chain of historic hotels, the sublime Parador de Jaén perches beside the Castillo de Santa Catalina (paradores.es).
Where to eat // The great cafes in railway stations all deliver a similar repertoire of chorizos, *patatas bravas* and cool *salmorejo* soup. Try La Cantina in Dona Mencia, El Tren in Cabra, and Restaurante La Estación in Lucena.
More info // viasverdes.com

Opposite: Teruel on the Vía Verde de Ojos Negros; the interior of San Pedro church in Teruel

MORE LIKE THIS
GREEN AND PLEASANT SPANISH RIDES

VÍA VERDE DE LA SIERRA, ANDALUCÍA

Shorter though more spectacular than its olive-country cousin, the Vía Verde de la Sierra cuts a 22-mile (36km) course through Andalucía's southern cordilleras, taking flight over viaducts, and charging through shadowy tunnels burrowed into limestone bedrock. However, this so-called 'Greenway of the Mountains' never actually served as a working line. WWI and the subsequent Civil War meant construction was halted, and no rails were ever laid. Today it's often done as an out-and-back day trip by cyclists, although there's good reason to linger in the towns which bookend the route. Olvera, in the west, is one of Spain's prettiest pueblos blancos, its lilywhite houses cascading down the contours beneath a neoclassical church. Equally sublime are the landscapes along the trail, with rushing rivers, scrubby *barrancos* and jagged monoliths, in whose uppermost crags griffon vultures nest. Sleepy Puerto Serrano marks the eastern terminus.

Start //Olvera
Finish ///Puerto Serrano
Distance // 22 miles (36km)

VÍA VERDE DE LA VAL DE ZAFÁN, ARAGON AND CATALUNYA

The Ferrocarril del Val de Zafán, in Aragon and Catalunya, is a line with a dark past – sections of it were built with forced labour during the Spanish Civil War, as the Nationalists used it as a supply line to advance on the Republican-held coast. In modern times, it enjoys a happier chapter, and the Vía Verde de la Val de Zafán now follows the abandoned track-bed through the foothills of the Sistema Ibérico. Along the way are shadowy orchards, deep ravines and, of course, more station cafes. Best of all you can extend your ride eastward by joining the Vía Verde del Carrilet de la Cava and the Cami Natural de l'Ebre, following the Rio Ebro on its final meanders to the blue Mediterranean.

Start // Valdealgorfa
Finish // Tortosa
Distance // 52 miles (83 km)

VÍA VERDE DE OJOS NEGROS, ARAGON AND VALENCIA

'The Greenway of Black Eyes' may sound ripe territory for an injury, but in reality this is another serene and beautiful ride. It traces the course of an old narrow-gauge railway, from near Valencia up to the iron-ore mines of Aragon, on a course roughly parallel to the Val de Zafan route. It's also the longest of all Spain's Vía Verdes, with an abundance of fine architecture along the way. Soon after departing you reach Segorbe, with its shadowy cathedral, after which the great Mudéjar bell tower of Jerica reigns over the horizon. Close to the route's northern terminus comes the likeable city of Teruel, renowned for its own Mudéjar wonders, as well as the abundance of dinosaur fossils in the hills all around.

Start // Algímia de Alfara
Finish // Santa Eulalia
Distance // 99 miles (160km)

trabantos/Shutterstock; StockPhotoAstur/Shutterstock

WEST CORK'S WILD COAST

Cycle above cliffs, around peninsulas and beside beaches along West Cork's coastline to discover big Atlantic seascapes, a maze of country lanes, and whales.

When I'm back home in County Cork and feel like a break I'll often stuff a sleeping bag, a few harmonicas, some rain gear and a pair of sunglasses into my bike's venerable panniers and pedal west for a week or so. I'm prepared for all weathers, ready to join in pub music sessions and able to sleep out if that's the way things go. Navigation? All I have to do is keep the sea on my left. It's an easy approach to cycle touring.

Three times, so far, I've ridden the 186 miles (300km) between Clonakilty and the tip of the Beara Peninsula to the west, following in the tyre tracks of Irish travel writer Peter Somerville-Large. In the snows, rains and wind of early 1970 Somerville-Large set off on a 3-speed bike, carrying a canvas tent and an umbrella, to research his book *The Coast of West Cork*. His writing ranges across history, conjuring up cattle raids, sword'n'shield battles, pirate fleets and eccentric landowners, as he pedals between ancient ring forts, medieval castles, ruined manor houses and village ports. Cycling half a century ago, he describes a rural Ireland still focused on small farms and close-tied villages. Food then was, by his account, far from inspiring.

Cyclists in West Cork today – far better fed – can still enjoy the meandering spirit of Somerville-Large's inspiring trip, not least because the small roads of coastal West Cork now form

Fotogro/Shutterstock; Mystic Stock Photography/Shutterstock

CASEY'S
GOOD FOOD
LIVE MUSIC
COURTYARD

the most southerly section of the Wild Atlantic Way, a 1533-mile (2500km) 'signed route' designed to lure travellers off busy arterial roads and into the quiet veins and capillaries – the country roads and *boreens* (lanes) – that network the 'Next Stop America' seaboard of Ireland's west.

West Cork attracts and rewards cyclists of all stamps. A peloton of hard-cranking English friends raced the route from west to east in miserable summer weather that drove them into one pub after another for shelter; they loved it. At different times I've lent an old single-speed bike, and the Somerville-Large book, to a guitar-toting Frenchman, to an Israeli student and to a German woman. Each disappeared for a week or two and each had totally different adventures; one sitting in with musicians and cycling from gig to gig, another camping out on remote beaches cooking self-caught fish, and the third island-hopping across Roaringwater Bay before ending up in a Buddhist retreat centre on the Beara.

It's all about the quality of the distractions rather than the mileage, I reckon. Will Clonakilty's street music, or guitar- or cycling festivals change your plans? Will you be tempted by country-market day in any one of the towns along the coast, with stalls of local cheeses, home-baked breads, organic vegetables and cakes? Or a day heading out to sea on a whale-watching boat? An evening sea-kayak trip while phosphorescence lights up the waters? A pub lock-in, as accordions, fiddles, pipes and banjos pepper the air with machine-gun-fast riffs? Things happen when moving at pedal-speed in West Cork.

On the most recent of my cycle 'de-tours' – so-called because of their haphazard nature – to the Beara, I started by riding through a chill autumn night to watch the dawn sun rise over the eastern sea and light up the miniature Stonehenge of Drombeg Stone Circle. Then I freewheeled – mostly – down to Union Hall for a full-Irish breakfast in The Coffee Shop. Bacon, sausages,

WHALE WATCHING

Harbour porpoise and common and bottlenose dolphin are present year round in West Cork, blue whale and orca are rare sightings, but it's the minke, fin and humpback whales that are the real attraction. Though they can sometimes be seen from high cliffs with binoculars, for the full marine Jurassic Park experience take a specialist boat trip (www.whalewatchwestcork.com) to get out among the whales as they lunge, dive and breach spectacularly while feeding.

Clockwise from top: Bantry Bay and the town; Kealkill Bronze Age stone circle, cycling on Sheep's Head Peninsula. Previous page: Casey's Bar in Clonakilty; the coastline of the Mizen Peninsula

markferguson2/Alamy; Martin Hesketh/Shutterstock; Corey Macri/Shutterstock

eggs, toast, and famed Clonakilty black pudding, as well as apple tart: the fuel I needed for a day of grinding up hill after hill.

As always, I was making route choices as I rode. If the early morning sun hadn't given way to drizzle, I'd have cycled on to Baltimore to take the ferry across to Cape Clear Island, where Irish is spoken, traditional jigs and reels (Irish folk dancing) played, and I could have pedalled out to the seaward cliffs, where I'd been told there was a good chance of seeing a pod of minke whales feeding close inshore. But with visibility poor I headed around Roaringwater Bay, across the Mizen and onto Sheep's Head instead. By evening I was sitting in a friend's clifftop cabin sipping tea and watching the sunset.

For cyclists, the Sheep's Head is like the whole coast of West Cork, or even the Wild Atlantic Way, in miniature. A coast-teasing 50-mile (80km) circuit following small roads, many so little used they have a strip of grass down their centre. Big cliffs and, in storms, even bigger seas. Hidden stone circles, smaller than Drombeg. Pubs where conversation easily sparks into song. The 'needle-to-an-anchor' old-style shop, post office and sometime wine bar that is JF O'Mahony's in Kilcrohane. Few cars. Perfect riding country.

The next morning from the Sheep's Head I could see the length of the Beara Peninsula far across Bantry Bay. On a rigid-inflatable boat you'd be across in 20 minutes, but by bike there's another couple of relaxed days to go, and more distractions. Bantry, with its Friday market. Cafes in touristy Glengarriff. The Caha and Slieve Mishkish mountains inland, Hungry Hill wreathed in cool mist. A pint of Beamish in MacCarthy's in Castletownbere, enjoyed among fishing crews from half a dozen nations' trawlers. Then the long haul to the peninsula's end, cranking out the miles, until there was only air and water ahead and I'd run out of land. All I had to do now was turn around and head home. This time keeping the sea on my right. **JW**

"I'd been told there was a good chance of seeing a pod of minke whales feeding close inshore"

TOOLKIT

Start // Clonakilty
Finish // The tip of Beara Peninsula
Distance // 186 miles (300km)
Getting there // Fly to Cork Airport, cycle 12 miles (20km) to Kinsale and you're on the Wild Atlantic Way. Irish buses will usually take one, maximum two, bikes if there's room.
Bike hire // O'Donovan Cycles in Bantry (www.bikenbeara.ie/hire.php) offers rental bikes. See also www.ireland.com/what-is-available/cycling/bike-rental/destinations/republic-of-ireland/cork/all.
When to ride // Early autumn offers good weather, enough evening light, open restaurants, cafes and accommodation, and less tourist traffic.
Where to stay // For hotels, B&Bs and campsites, see www.ireland.com; for independent hostels, see www.independenthostelsireland.com
Where to eat // See www.westcorkmarkets.com for details on country markets.

Opposite: riding the Gap of Dunloe on the Ring of Kerry

MORE LIKE THIS
IRISH RIDES

DUBLIN & THE BARROW

This classic three-day journey traces the Grand Canal Way from central Dublin, wending west along the historic waterway to Robertstown in County Kildare. Hang a left here and cycle south along the towpath of the Barrow Navigation, which skirts Ireland's second-longest river. Hug the banks of the much-storied and beautiful Barrow as it meanders betwixt several counties, past castles, around woodlands and through ancient towns, including Monasterevin, Athy, Carlow, Borris and Graiguenamanagh, until you reach the last lock in St Mullins, where the river becomes tidal and the towpath evaporates. As you'd expect from a canal-based route, there's no climbing, but there are muddy sections, so a hybrid or mountain bike is recommended.
Start // Dublin
Finish // St Mullins, County Carlow
Distance // 93 miles (150km)

CONNACHT CLASSIC

There's been a huge surge in the popularity of cycling in Ireland over the last decade, but nowhere has embraced the bike revolution more than the beautiful and charismatic County Mayo town of Westport. Myriad routes meander along the coast and into the Connacht countryside from here, including the popular Greenway, but the loop out towards Connemara and delightful Doolough and back is arguably the perfect cycling circuit, taking in the super scenic Sheeffry Pass, Tawnyard Lough and 585m of climbing en route. The outride is mostly along quiet country lanes, past several tempting pubs, while the return route sidles past Croagh Patrick – a stunning peak where St Pat apparently sat for 40 days of fasting in the 5th century. It's a rapid finish along an R-road and then a cycle path back into the embrace of Westport, where Matt Malloy's legendary bar awaits.
Start/finish // Westport, County Mayo
Distance // 42 miles (67.5km)

RING OF KERRY

A back-route version of the famous Ring of Kerry starts from Killarney, heading out along the quiet country lanes and ultra-remote roads of the Iveragh Peninsula to the wild west coast. The outbound route rolls past Lough Acoose and Glencar, traverses the Ballaghasheen Pass and hits the Atlantic at Waterville, opposite the Gaeltacht (Irish-speaking) village of Ballinskelligs. If you have the legs for it, return via Castlecove and Sneem, pedalling alongside delightful Derrynane Beach, across the Coomakista Pass (a Ring of Kerry highlight) and through the Gap of Dunloe, a gorgeous glaciated valley, on your way back to the many welcoming pubs of Killarney. Examples of ogham stones (standing pillars engraved with an early Irish alphabet), lie close to this route, as does the Staigue Stone Fort. With over 1500m of climbing, and scenery that refuses to be rushed, this ride is best spread across two or three days.
Start/finish // Killarney, County Kerry
Distance // 95 miles (153km)

ROLLING THROUGH BAROQUE SICILY

When an earthquake all but destroyed Val di Noto in 1693, its aristocracy rebuilt – and how. A short tour reveals its architectural (and culinary) hits.

Everybody, I am sure, has their own preferred way of appreciating Baroque architecture. Mine is after a couple of evening beers. It's then that Baroque's excess seems to make the most sense. Why finish a corner with a boring right angle when you can add some curlicues and a gargoyle? At night the shadows seem to accentuate the drama.

Some of the world's best examples of Baroque towns are in Sicily and it so happens that they can be strung together on an easy clockwise loop starting from Syracuse on the east coast over three or more days. The other corners of this compact triangle are Noto and Ragusa (with a side-trip to Modica, famed for its chocolate, and a fly-by through Palazzolo). I'd also heard great things about Sicilian cuisine so this ride was as much about epic food as architecture.

From my base at Hotel Gutkowski on Syracuse's island of Ortigia, I headed south and west to Noto, a short ride of 19 miles (30km). It's a gritty, wind-blown road along the coast to Avola's marina but here I turn inland and then climb up to Noto. I'm staying at Il Giardino del Barocco, a B&B with rooms set around a quiet courtyard in the centre of town.

This region is known as the Val di Noto. On 11 January 1693, a massive earthquake devastated the towns and villages of southeast Sicily. Tens of thousands died and disease and plundering was rampant in the weeks after the quake. But by May of 1693, a reconstruction commenced that was largely funded by the local aristocracy and Benedictine monasteries and led to the most vivid flowering of late-Baroque art in the world.

An innovation of post-quake Baroque urban planning was a linear layout. Noto is arranged along three strata with, naturally, the rich living at the top of the hill and the poor at the bottom. This has the convenient effect of aligning many of the town's Baroque big-hitters along its main street, Corso Vittorio Emanuele. After a Sicilian-style pizza (more like two crêpes sandwiched together) and a Noto-brewed Belgian ale by Birra Vendicari at the *salumeria* Sabbinirica à Putìa d'Ercole, I wander over to the church of San Domenico. It's a pure expression of 18th-century Sicilian Baroque and the masterpiece of Syracuse-born architect Rosario Gagliardi (who

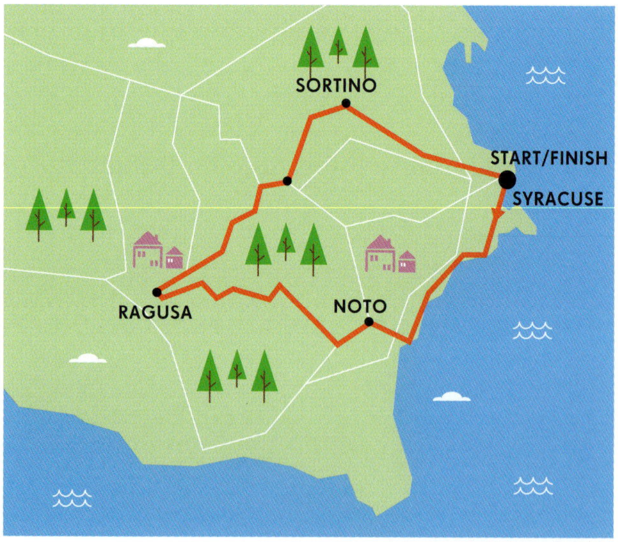

Westend61/Getty Images

died in Noto in 1762), the dominant figure of the Val di Noto, and one of the most original architects of 18th-century Italy.

Further along this pedestrianised street is a fusion of Baroque and Neoclassical at La Cattedrale, dedicated to St Nicholas of Myra, the patron saint of a rag-tag bunch including students, brewers, prostitutes, merchants, sailors and children. He was the inspiration for Santa Claus (Saint Nick). At the Palazzo Nicolaci di Villadorata, built in 1737, I get a glimpse of the lifestyles of Noto's nobility on 'Prince's Street'.

The next day, after a breakfast beneath citrus trees, I set out for Ragusa by riding southwest along a main road then turning right on to a road that is wider than the little white line on the map suggests. This is suddenly a more rural Sicily, which means that none of the names nor roadside chapels marked on the map are signposted on the road. But I keep faith and am rewarded with my first signpost to the town of Frigintini – next stop Ragusa.

Ragusa, like Noto, was destroyed during the earthquake of 1693. The Old Town, Ragusa Ibla, was rebuilt on a promontory, now adjoined by suburban Ragusa Superiore. I'm staying in its Baroque heart, with about 60 churches around me. But first things first: food. I park by Salumeria Barocco for a platter of cheese and salami. The star *formaggio* is called *tuma persa*, the 'lost cheese'. Cheesemaker Salvatore Passalacqua found the recipe for a hard, savoury cows' milk cheese that hadn't been made for a century, and resurrected it. As I'm nibbling the last of it, thunderclouds unleash grape-sized hailstones and lightning. A dozen people cram into the tiny shop, surrounded by Sicilian wine, cheese, salumi, artisanal ales and chocolate from Modica. An hour later I leave, enlightened but a little heavier.

The spine of Ragusa Ibla is the flagstoned Corso XXV Aprile, which leads from the Giardino Ibleo Belvedere uphill to the Duomo, another of Rosario Gagliardi's masterpieces.

MONTALBANO

Almost as great a pull to southeast Sicily as Baroque architecture and crunchy-oozy *arancini*, is the fictional detective Montalbano. The creation of writer Andrea Camilleri, Salvo Montalbano solves crimes in almost 30 novels, but always finds time for his early-morning swim and a long lunch. The hit TV series uses Ragusa as the setting for many scenes (Montalbano's restaurant is actually A' Rusticana) and his house on the show is, of course, now a B&B.

Clockwise from above: St Nicholas Cathedral, Syracuse; the canyons of Pantalica; Ortigia island and old town in Syracuse. Previous page: riding up to Ragusa's old town

DaLiu/Shutterstock; Giacomo Augugliaro/Getty Images

siculodoc/Getty Images

From Ragusa, the route retraces its way up the valley then continues uphill to Giarratana and east to Palazzolo, the next Baroque town on the itinerary. An aggressive feral dog apart, this section offers the most scenic cycling.

Lunch at Palazzolo proves that slow food isn't just about the ingredients. I continue onward to the Anapo Valley, where 15ft (5m) tall rushes sway in the humid air. Vincenzo, the host of the Sacre Pietre agriturismo, gives me a tour of his farm: he grows numerous varieties of lemon, including one that you can eat raw (delicious with a bit of olive oil, chilli and herbs), kiwi fruit, pomegranate, figs and oranges. After my hot ride he pours me a glass of sweet, home-made (and grown) almond milk. He shows me an ancient Greek well in his orchard, which was part of an irrigation system that took water down to Syracuse, but I'm distracted by trying to find fresh figs in his trees.

The Valle d'Anapo is on the Dell'Antica Grecia cycling route from Syracuse and that's the way I'll return to the Sicilian coast after breakfast: fresh eggs from Vincenzo's hens, bread made from an ancient grain, local ricotta (try it with Vincenzo's marmalade). The final day is generally downhill with a couple of climbs, one to Belvedere for a first sighting of the sea. Back on Ortigia, I refuel with *pasta alla Siracusana*. Cycling in Sicily has been not only a way of getting from one amazing building to another but from one great meal to the next. **RB**

TOOLKIT

Start/finish // Syracuse
Distance // Up to 150 miles (240km)
Where to stay // I travelled with Inntravel (www.inntravel.co.uk) who booked bike-friendly hotels in each town and organised luggage transfers and airport transfers.
Where to eat // In Noto, the Sabbinirica à Putìa d'Ercole at Via Emanuele 93. In Ragusa Ibla, the Salumeria Barocco (www.salumeriabarocco.it) at Corso XXV Aprile 80. In Syracuse Casa Trimarchi at Via Laberinto (www.casatrimarchi.it).
When to go // Avoid June to August due to heat; September and October are ideal.
More info // Book at www.inntravel.co.uk; rental bikes can be provided or bring your own. If you wish to be independent, a pannier or large saddle or frame bag would be sufficient to carry everything.

Clockwise from top: the mosque-cathedral of Córdoba; the Bauhaus school in Dessau, the Duomo of Siena

MORE LIKE THIS
ARCHITECTURE TOURS

BAUHAUS, GERMANY

By convention, cyclists prefer curves, contours and crests to straight lines. But when the straight lines belong to a building designed by the founder of the Bauhaus, Walter Gropius, and constructed in the 1920s, then our hearts skip a beat. The Bauhaus Building in Dessau, a perfect example of the Bauhaus principle of utilitarian harmony, is the destination of this 82-mile (132km) bike ride. After a visit to Berlin's Bauhaus Archive (in its temporary home), pedal southwest out of the capital and pass through pretty Potsdam and continue in a straight line to Dessau: the Komoot app can plot a route that is mostly on cycleways. The prize for reaching the Bauhaus Building is an overnight stay there. Yes, you can sleep very inexpensively in the very studios where the likes of Josef Albers, Herbert Bayer and Gertrud Arndt worked. Breakfast is not included but the bicycle garage is free. More information: www.bauhaus-dessau.de
Start // Berlin
Finish // Dessau
Distance // 82 miles (132km)

GOTHIC ITALY

Gothic architecture – all flying buttresses, ribbed vaults and pointed arches – gestated in the Late Middle Ages in northern France, spreading down to Italy and Tuscany, where it employed Tuscan marble to great effect. The cathedrals of Florence and Siena are classic examples, both built during the 13th century and decorated with frescoes. A five-night tour of Tuscany might start in San Gimignano, where 14 of its original 70 towers erected as status symbols by wealthy families still stand, and end in Siena. The route would pass through quiet valleys and hamlets before arriving in Siena where you can admire the magnificent black-and-white Duomo, dating from the 13th century. Check out the western facade, which features elements of French Gothic, Tuscan Romanesque, and Classical architecture.
Start // San Gimignano
Finish // Siena
Distance // From 85 miles (135km)

ISLAMIC SPAIN

The Moorish architecture of southern Spain has several headline acts, including Seville's Giralda, Córdoba's mosque-cathedral and the Alhambra of Granada. But Andalucía's smaller towns and villages also demonstrate the influence of the region's Islamic rulers from the 8th century onwards. This tour starts from the town of Antequera, just north of Málaga, the nearest international airport. Head northeast to the Moorish village of Iznájar then make for Lucena and pick up the Via Verde de la Subbética rail trail to Zuheros and its 9th-century Moorish fort. From Zuheros, pedal past the Parque Natural de las Sierras Subbéticas to Priego de Córdoba and its fascinating Islamic quarter. Continue through the hills of the Sierra Nevada to Montefrío and then follow the path of the Catholics as they marched to conquer Granada in 1492. Granada's Alhambra and Albayzín, its Muslim quarter, remain.
Start // Antequera
Finish // Granada
Distance // 165 miles (265km)

BAUHAUS

OCEANIA

'BREADPACKING' ON BRUNY ISLAND

Some bikepacking trips are about climbing mountains while others are concerned with racking up the miles. One, on Tasmania's Bruny Island, is all about bread.

Soon after I moved south to Tasmania, or lutruwita, a friend sent me an Instagram Reel of a quiet back road featuring handmade wooden signs. Stencilled with the word 'Bread', they pointed the way along a leafy gravel stretch to three chunky, retro-style fridges perched on an old pallet. Inside, a surprise: fresh loaves of woodfired sourdough wrapped in brown paper bags, left daily by the 'Bruny Baker'. With only an honesty box for transactions, it was classic Tassie.

Lured by this beautiful, small-town sense of trust, not to mention some mid-winter loaf-lust, I wheeled my fully loaded bicycle onto the little car ferry. The 20-minute voyage would take me from Kettering on the mainland to Roberts Point, on North Bruny, my gateway to three days of gravel roads, wild beaches – and the promise of sourdough.

Bruny comprises two parts, the North and the South, joined by a skinny isthmus known as the Neck. It's also a foodie's paradise. On completing the steady bitumen climb away from the ferry, I reluctantly skipped the northern gravel loop on this occasion, wary of incoming weather, and instead pedalled towards a different indulgence on North Bruny, the Bruny Island Cheese Company.

I arrived to a roaring firepit and the chatter of rugged-up visitors enjoying paddles of frothy local beer and cheese platters: a far cry from my usual bikepacking rations. I sat under wintry skies sampling tangy pickles and warm bread, washed down with a fiery Tasmanian ginger beer. A hopeful magpie hopped around as I cheekily stashed leftovers into a plastic bag for later.

Sarah Pendergrass

Back on the island's sealed main road, I ducked into Bruny Island Honey, which offers tastings, in a shop where beeswax products glow golden on the shelves alongside all manner of honey (native flora, manuka, fennel...). I resisted, reminding myself I was leaving space for the real prize – sourdough bread.

By late afternoon, storm clouds rolled over the Neck. The elevated Truganini Lookout, reached by a steep wooden staircase, offered sweeping views of the isthmus and, ominously, the dense sheet of rain heading straight for me. Winter in southern Tasmania is notoriously fickle: one moment clear skies and the chance of Aurora Australis, the Southern Lights; the next, sideways rain. That weekend I saw countless rainbows. At first a gift, vivid arcs over the ocean, they soon became an omen of another downpour.

My plan for the first night was to camp in a national park campground near to the lookout and return at dusk to watch little penguins waddle ashore. But the storm hit fast, and with little cover I pushed on, hunched against the rain. By the time I reached Adventure Bay, I was drenched. At a caravan park, I pitched my tent and dried out by the fire.

Morning brought respite. The sweeping sands of the bay stretched long and white, framed by turquoise water and forested hills beneath a soft sunrise. Day two began with the longest and steepest climb of my trip, across the Mount Mangana Conservation Area. A sign announcing '4WD recommended' hinted at what was to come. It wasn't long until I was off the pedals, hiking and pushing my loaded bike up a rough gravel road, through cloud-wreathed forest. As tree ferns unfurled and towering gums disappeared into mist, a small car bounced over the hill, its passengers laughing gently at my slow progress. I laughed back and kept pushing. The crest arrived with little fanfare, but great satisfaction.

Carefully picking my line on the descent, the steepest of the trip too, I flew back to sea level, cold fingers and toes tingling, my eyes streaming. In the village of Lunawanna, a homemade pie beside the community hall's fireplace delivered the perfect warm-up before the undulating road to the Cape Bruny Lighthouse. Despite the potholes, the trail revealed panoramas of steel-grey seas and flashes of sun on whitecaps. A short detour took me out to the lighthouse itself, perched high on cliffs where daffodils bent in the wind and the ocean crashed below.

From the majestic lighthouse I rolled back down to Jetty Beach, the most idyllic campsite on my trip. This being winter, I shared it only with one couple, and a bold pademelon, who

Sarah Pendergrass

SWEET ON SOURDOUGH

The 'Bruny Baker', real name John Bullock, is a legend in these parts. With no storefront or staff, Bullock delivers his loaves every morning to three retro fridges tucked down a gravel road. He leaves fresh, woodfired sourdough daily, but the menu is subject to change, or certainly tweaks; from classic loaves to fruit-bread, and even Anzac biscuits. Both locals and visitors make pilgrimages for a loaf, proving that simplicity and good baking are timeless drawcards.

Left to right: the 'bread fridge' on Sheepwash Rd; lunchtime; the Neck; quiet gravel roads. Previous spread: heading towards Cape Bruny lighthouse

repeatedly tried to sneak into my tent. I cooked dinner on the white sandy beach, the air salty and sharp, and fell asleep under the gumtrees, to the sounds of the surf.

My third and final day, when it arrived, was the long-awaited 'bread day'. I traced Bruny's coastline on a patchwork of gravel and bitumen, fighting headwinds. I passed fields of cows and sheep, grazing quietly beneath stormy skies, and then, finally, I saw it, a weathered wooden sign nailed to a gum tree: 'Bread'. I turned a final corner and there they were, three retro fridges standing sentinel in the sun, just as I had seen them.

Opening one fridge excitedly, the smell of sourdough wafted out. I pulled out a squashy loaf, slipped notes into the honesty box, and grinned. A local islander rolled up and pointed at my bike. 'Hope you've olive oil in there.' I chuckled, somewhat regretfully, aware of the basic nature of my bikepacking supplies.

Retracing my journey along the coast, the last miles crawled by, the wind reminding me of every pedal stroke. At the ferry, a lone road cyclist zipped past. I rolled on board behind him, satisfied, mainly thanks to the bread and cheese tucked into my backpack. Next time I'd pack the dipping oil. **SP**

Sarah Pendergrass

TOOLKIT

Start/finish // Kettering Ferry Terminal
Distance // 83 miles (134km)
Getting there // The ferry is a 19-mile (30km) road ride or a 30-minute drive from Hobart.
When to go // Year-round. Winter in Tasmania (June to August) means harsher conditions but quieter roads in what can be a (very) popular summer tourist destination, both for Hobartians and the rest of the world.
What to wear // Sunscreen, but be prepared for four seasons in one day.
Where to stay // Options include low-cost campsites, with no pre-booking available (The Neck Campground, Jetty Beach Campground). Captain Cook Holiday Park (Adventure Bay) is a caravan park with facilities, including basic cabins. The Bruny Baker offers self-contained accommodation at Sheepwash Bay (sheepwashbay.com)
More info // www.brunyisland.org.au

Opposite: Trousers Point on Flinders Island; a common wombat on Maria Island

MORE LIKE THIS
ISLAND RIDES ON LUTRUWITA AND BEYOND

MARIA ISLAND TRAVERSE

If you've always wanted to see a wombat in the wild, Maria Island will deliver. Catch the passenger ferry from Triabunna to this car-free, national park paradise. Offering convict history, coastal wilderness and abundant wildlife, multiday rides typically head south from Darlington, via the basic bunkhouse accommodation at the Penitentiary. Ride past the striking Painted Cliffs, down to Frenchs Farm and Point Lesueur, with campsites along the way. Gravel roads and grassy tracks make for variable riding, with sandy patches and creek crossings to keep things lively. The super-adventurous can take a fat bike and cross the notoriously sandy McRaes Isthmus, to Haunted Bay. With no shops or services on the island, you'll need to be self-sufficient. Nights under starry skies, with wombats grazing around your tent, make it unforgettable.
Start/finish // Darlington
Distance // 22-45 miles (35-72km), depending on detours

FLINDERS ISLAND CIRCUIT

Rugged and windswept, Flinders Island is a bikepacking gem of granite peaks, sweeping bays, coastal lagoons, quiet gravel roads and sandy singletrack. A classic circuit links Whitemark with the west and east coasts, combining climbs towards the Strzelecki Peaks with long stretches of coastal riding past Trousers Point, Patriarch Inlet, and Killiecrankie Bay. The pace of island life is slow, with services sparse outside of Whitemark and Lady Barron, so careful resupply planning is essential. Camping options include secluded beach sites and designated campgrounds, while self-contained accommodation is sprinkled around the island. Expect ever-changing Tasmanian conditions, from wild seas and headwinds to serene sunsets over empty beaches. A truly rugged adventure ride at the bottom of the world.
Start/finish // Whitemark
Distance // 106 miles (170km)

THE LORAX ROUTE

If you need a little more, and are perhaps looking to complete a loop from Devonport or Launceston, consider this tour of the Tarkine and the wider northwest created by Tyla Bickley in order to draw attention to the ecological threats facing the takayna/Tarkine region of Tasmania. With the major exception of the Road to Nowhere, this route runs predominantly on sealed highways and well-kept back roads. Before you enter the Tarkine, you'll pass through the sub-alpine highlands at the foot of Cradle Mountain, one of Tasmania's scenic calling cards. The northern continuation includes a loop around more upstream forest reaches of the Arthur River, and a close track of the north coast and its small towns. The temperate rainforest remaining from the Gondwana supercontinent that you'll pass through is a global wonder.
Start/Finish // Launceston
Distance // 524 miles (843km)
More info // www.desirelinescc.com.au

Martin Pelanek /Shutterstock; Alex Cimbal/Shutterstock

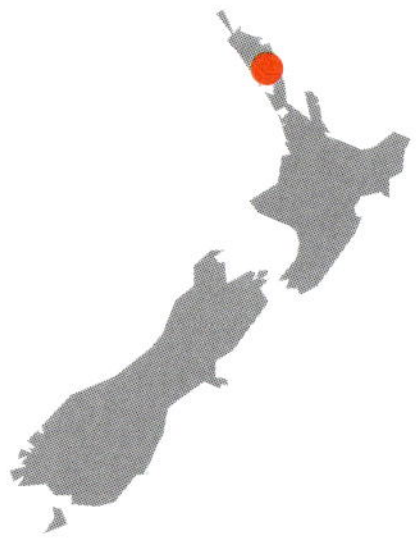

THE HEART OF THE OCTOPUS

The Heart of the Octopus is a five-day (or more) bikepacking loop along the east and west coasts of Northland, discovering giant trees and beautiful beaches.

Before each solo bikepacking trip my mind is a whirlwind of increasingly irrational worries: what if I can't fix a mechanical problem? What if I'm chased by a pack of wild dogs over a cliff? Prior to embarking on this loop of Northland's east and west coasts, these anxieties were compounded by the conveyor belt of El-Niño-fuelled storms that were hitting New Zealand's North Island for weeks. On most days the rain and the trees were horizontal in the wind. I'd decided to start from near Opua on the east coast, because it was close to Russell in the Bay of Islands, a place I knew from my childhood. But, from the comfort of my Airbnb near Opua, the skies were dark and the wind was difficult to stand upright in.

The route I wanted to follow was developed by New Zealand's mountain biking pioneers, the Kennett brothers: Jonathan, Paul and Simon. They've been devising bike races and routes since the 1980s and were project managers on the Ngā Haerenga New Zealand Cycle Trail. The Kennett's Heart of the Octopus bikepacking route follows the Pou Herenga Tai – Twin Coast Cycle Trail, one of New Zealand's 23 Great Rides, from the east coast of the North Island's northern tip to Horeke near the west coast. Then it turns south onto the Kauri Coast Cycleway and passes through the North Island's kauri forests, one of the world's arboreal wonders. After returning to the east coast via farm roads, the final stretch hugs the coast back to the Bay of Islands.

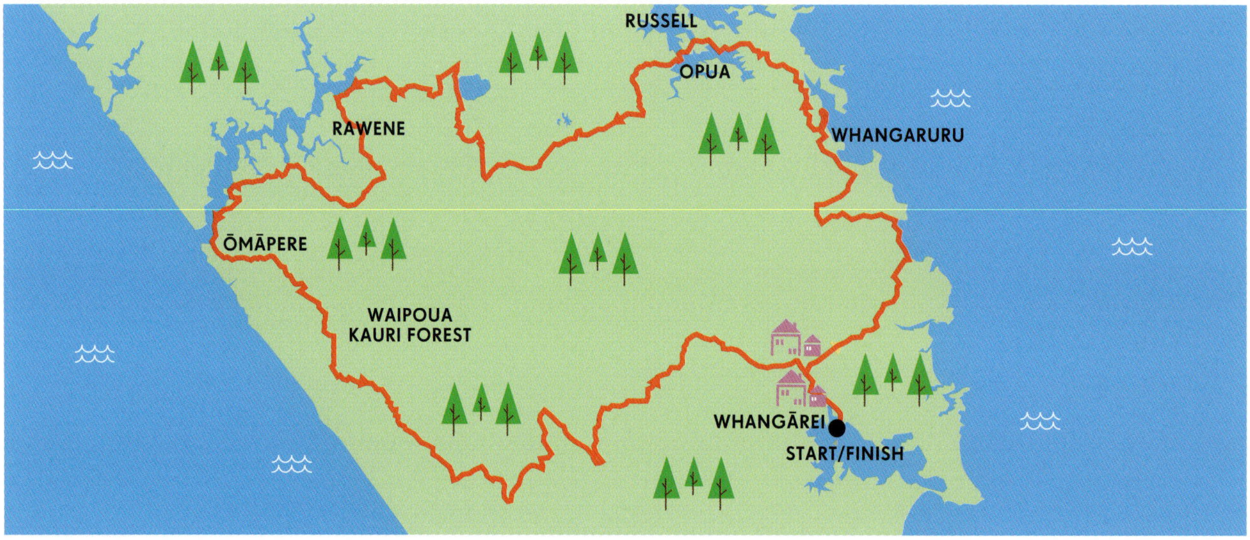

Robin Barton

'You'll see two sides of Northland,' my Airbnb host Jarrad assured me. 'Extreme wealth and some of the most deprived communities in the country.' The east coast of Northland is where billionaires and celebrities, such as Dame Kiri Te Kanawa, buy beachfront property. But the communities of the wild west coast have long lacked investment.

When a day dawned with sunshine instead of storms, I set off. As always, once I was on the road for 30 minutes, every anxiety dissipated. Life got very simple: if I kept pedalling, I kept moving forward. Soon, I'd joined the gravel bike path that forms most of the Pou Herenga Tai / Twin Coast Cycle Trail. The total distance of this Great Ride is 54 miles (87km) to Horeke so I'd planned to do that leg in one day and stay at the only hotel in Horeke, a hamlet on the shore of huge Hokianga harbour. From here, riders only wanting to ride the cycle trail need to book a shuttle van back to their starting point, which defies the point of being independent on a bicycle. A better schedule would be to break the journey in the township of Kaikohe, skip the hotel in Horeke, which is difficult to recommend, and continue to Rawene.

Regardless, I followed the largely flat and straight cycle trail across the top of Northland. Towards the end of that first day, the storms returned. Wind and rain bombarded me before I made the strange sanctuary of Horeke's hotel. The forecast didn't look great for the following day but there was little option but to commit and continue. So, I pulled on my waterproofs and set out towards the west coast under a heaving sky. Squalls of rain stung my skin but once you're wet, you're wet, and I dried quickly under the hot sun before the next drenching. This was an enjoyable day on quiet roads. I ate some excellent fish and chips at the takeaway in Opononi with views of sand dunes across the harbour mouth, before Haraena refilled my water bottles.

TĀNE'S TALE

Ranginui, the Sky Father, and Papatūānuku, the Earth Mother, clasped each other tightly, such was their love. Not a shaft of sunlight squeezed between them. But their children tired of darkness and their son, Tāne, used his broad shoulders to prise his parents apart. He pushed Ranginui upwards until light and life flooded throughout, creating the world. The rain that falls from the sky is Ranginui's grief but Tāne, the god of the forests, is still braced against Ranginui and Papatūānuku.

Clockwise from top: an audience with Tāne Mahuta; post-ride relaxation at the Wild Forest Estate; fish and chips in Opononi; riding the gravel roads of the kauri forest

Joanna Wickham; Robin Barton; Shaun Jeffers/Shutterstock

The Heart of the Octopus now adopts part of the Kauri Coast Cycleway as it heads south into Waipoua Kauri Forest, where the giant tree Tāne Mahuta stands just off the road. I chatted to the warden who ensured that visitors disinfected their shoes. Kauri are among the world's largest and longest-lived trees and Tāne Mahuta is 2000 years old and the largest of his kind at around 167ft (51m) tall and a chunky 45ft (13.8m) in circumference.

This is a sublime section of riding, especially on an off-season weekday. My overnight stop in a hut at the Wild Forest Estate, hosted by Joanna and Nigel, was just as glorious. I bathed outside and listened out for kiwis calling in the dusk.

The next stretch took me back across Northland to Whangārei on a mix of gravel and tarmac roads. A navigational error sent me along State Hwy 14 but, with a breeze behind me, the detour was over quickly. After a night in Whangārei, I rejoined the Heart of the Octopus for two more legs up the east coast. This was another fantastic couple of days' riding. I passed through Glenbervie Forest on mountain-bike tracks, into highland farming country, then reached the coast at Helena Bay before pitching up at the Whangaruru Beachfront Camp for the night. That section was harder and hillier than expected but I spent my last evening swimming and beachcombing at Whangaruru. The final stretch back to Opua was a short one at just 30 miles (48km) but it took me past several Māori marae and along the Russell-Whakapara Rd high into a cloud forest. Is the Pou Herenga Tai / Twin Coast Cycle Trail by itself a great ride? Not in my opinion. But the full Heart of the Octopus loop is a fine experience. **RB**

Joanna Wickham

Previous spread: overlooking a beach near Woolleys Bay on Northland's east coast

TOOLKIT

Start/Finish // Opua (or anywhere along the loop)
Distance // 450km (280 miles)
Getting there // The standard start is from Whangārei, which is about a 2hr drive from Auckland. You should be able to take a bike on the InterCity bus service if it has both wheels removed, the handlebars turned and the chain covered but check in advance.
Where to stay // Airbnb can offer options for most schedules, such as the Wild Forest Estate (www.wildforestestate.com) in the Waipoua Kauri Forest.
What to take // Tools, spares and navigation kit – you won't pass many bike shops. A gravel bike is perfect.
When to ride // Northland has a mild climate so it's possible to ride the route all year round. Some of the gravel roads might become muddy in winter.
More info // www.kennett.co.nz has maps and route directions in their *Bikepacking Aotearoa* book.

Opposite: Ninety-Mile Beach in New Zealand's Far North; cross Kaipara Harbour on the Missing Link route

MORE LIKE THIS
NORTHLAND RIDES

GLENBERVIE FOREST

A tentacle of the Heart of the Octopus reaches out to Glenbervie Forest via the Old Coach Road just northeast of Whangārei but doesn't linger. If you wish to explore the mountain bike trails here more deeply, you'll need to budget an extra day in the area. You'll find a network of old-school, slippery singletrack trails through tight-spaced trees, but don't expect signposting or other amenities – local knowledge from the Whangārei Mountain Bike Club goes a long way. Glenbervie Forest is rideable from town (in 30 to 40 minutes) but most people will drive to ride. Gravel forest roads link the off-road trails so riders can piece together longer routes.
Info // www.whangareimtb.nz/trails-glenbervie

FAR NORTH CYCLEWAY

This route is a key component of the Tour Aotearoa, the once-in-a-lifetime ride along the length of New Zealand. The well-travelled cycleway starts from Cape Reinga, the country's most northern point, complete with a lighthouse and endless beaches. It bears south along Ninety-Mile Beach towards the charming historic town of Rawene, sitting on the south bank of the Omanaia River, where it joins up with the Twin Coast Cycleway and the Heart of the Octopus extended loop of Northland. To reach Rawene you will take a ferry across the river from Kohukohu. It's a fine end to a wind-swept 100-mile (160km) ride. Rawene has good options for food and accommodation and actually it makes a better base than Horeke on the Heart of the Octopus for several reasons.
Info // www.nzcycletrail.com

KAIPARA MISSING LINK

If you've ridden half of the Heart of the Octopus from the east coast but would prefer to ride all the way to Auckland rather than complete the loop through Whangārei, then this is the cycle route for you. You'll need to continue a little further south down the Kauri Coast to Dargaville rather than turn east to Whangārei. Then you pick up the Kaipara Missing Link from Dargaville and follow it for 75 miles (120km) to Auckland across fertile farmland and through some Victorian-era towns to New Zealand's largest city. A highlight is a lengthy boat trip across beautiful Kaipara Harbour from Pouto Point to Parakai. Many riders opt to spend a night in historic Helensville nearby.
Info // www.nzcycletrail.com

Martin Vlnas/Shutterstock; Henri Martin/Shutterstock

THE MAWSON TRAIL

This 560-mile (900km) bikepacking odyssey through the Outback, from the Flinders Ranges to Adelaide, mixes gravel, grit, wind farms, wineries and wonder.

'Guess where this guy is taking his kids on holiday?' the service-station mechanic in the tiny town of Hawker shouts to his wife. 'Adelaide... on a bike. Lucky kids!'

I have to laugh. He's just let me pump up four sets of tyres in his workshop, and runs the general store, the first shop we've seen in two sleeps and 89 miles (144km). The joke at our expense is totally worth it.

The daily stages of our 560-mile (900km) Mawson Trail trip were months in the planning, especially over this first week in the Outback when help could be too far away to think about. In the first phase, route length depends solely on the distance between towns or, in their absence, hamlets and campsites with any type of food. After the fresh blast of air at Hawker, we experience our first headwinds as we turn away from the central Flinders Ranges' huge variety of hills towards flatter, dustier country and the pub in Cradock, population 13, with only five full-time residents according to the tourist sign.

Next morning, we start a 53-mile (85km) transition from the wide-open red-and-brown landscape into arid sheep-grazing land. We pass through the ruins of Simmonston, a town that started to be built in the late 1800s but was never finished, because it was too far from anything useful, and have lunch at the grave of the son of an earl, who drowned in a flash flood in 1852.

There's no sign of any water today, until we reach the green farms on the edge of Quorn. It's the first time we all think we might just make it to our destination in Adelaide, having become familiar with the packing and long days of decreasing

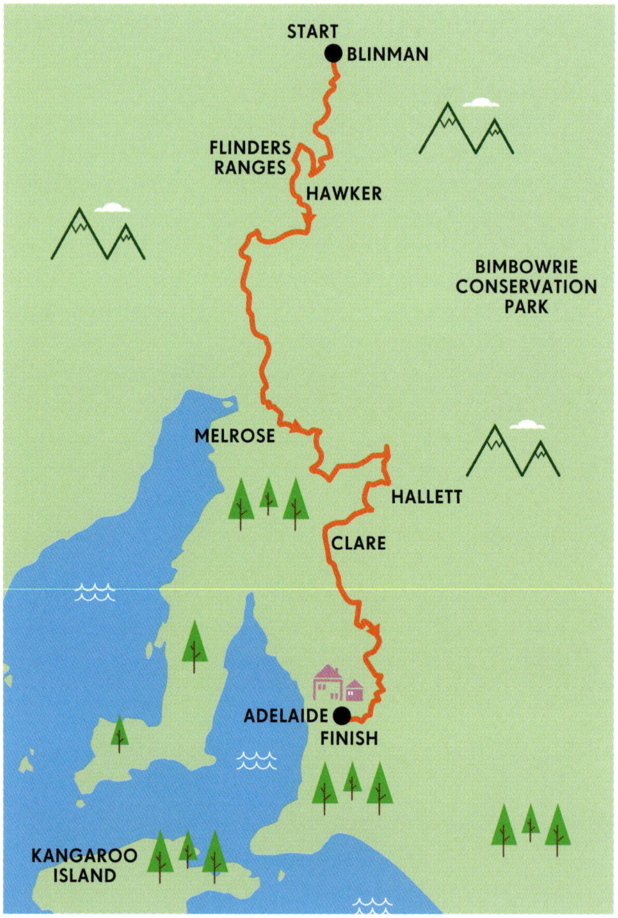

Southern Lightscapes-Australia/Getty Images

worry and increasing fun. From tomorrow, if we have a mechanical, someone will see us within an hour.

We had started the north-south version of the trail in Blinman, a former copper mine and South Australia's highest town, dug deep into the rugged Outback with the stunningly brutal Flinders Ranges in every corner of the background. Attempting our 15-day version of the route was a way to show our daughter and son, both young teenagers, different parts of the country and open their eyes to new realities – and adventures.

The route is named after Sir Douglas Mawson, an Australian geologist best remembered as a brave Antarctic explorer, and we spotted the first of the many well-placed trail signs near the Blinman Pub. A group of riders who had just finished the south-north route waved us off, and when they tooted their car horns later as we descended towards the first stretch of dirt, we thought of the cyclist camaraderie we'd share over the next few weeks. We didn't see another bike for three days.

Instead, our four-person peloton travelled with wedge-tailed eagles, brown falcons, echelons of emus, and squawks of corellas and galahs through the valleys and gorges. The profile on day one drew some groans from the teens, with 3610ft (1100m) of climbing over almost 43 miles (70km) into Wilpena Pound, the most elevation until the penultimate day. On the plus side, it had the Bunyeroo Rd, a gravel surface winding down to the base of the Pound, and a mountainous backdrop to the best descent of the trip. It was a shame the tour's Instagram highlight came so early, but if we didn't ride another day we'd already have banked something spectacular.

Each morning begins with a stage overview, often in the mode of Eurosport commentator Carlton Kirby. There are many starts when pretend Carlton can't contain himself, such as the drop from Wilpena Pound into Rawnsley Park on stage 2: 'What a treat we have today, forget the sprinters, take in the vistas.'

Over the first three days there was Outback eye candy everywhere, including on all sides of the Moralana Scenic Drive back to Wilpena Pound, or west to the Elder Range. We were glad to be on mountain bikes on the rough trails and often spiky rocks, although this changed for the final two weeks when we wished we owned gravel bikes.

Melrose, where we have our first rest day after six stages and 220 miles (360km), has a dedicated mountain bike park – and a bike shop. After a midday sleep-in, I ask my daughter if her legs are sore. 'Yes.' Where? 'Everywhere.' I can't convince anyone else to try the trails.

Overnight, it rains, and it's still drizzling when we re-start, dreading the upcoming Mawson mud. In a couple of spots, thick gloops of red muck stick onto everything, forcing a cleaning stop every 50m or so, just to get the wheels moving. Nobody is allowed to think of the damage to their components. It's only day eight, and there's still about 500km (310 miles) to go. In a place where water is precious, it takes some courage to ask the caravan park owners in the small town of Laura if we can hose down four bikes. They say yes. They also give us scones with jam and cream.

The Mawson often intersects with the Heysen Trail, a 1200km (756 mile) walking track named after the artist Hans. The ruined settler cottages dotted across the canola country outside Laura create views that will hang in our memories forever. If you squint at the yellow blossoms, you can imagine sunflowers and riding through a French summer instead of a shivery headwind. The wind farms on the peaks around here are perfectly placed.

Peter English; woodgnomefotos/Shutterstock

Today, the sun is out and we cross the Mt Lofty Ranges for the first time before descending towards Spalding, avoiding our first two snakes, and passing through a gauntlet of gates that make us grumpy. Nobody needs to stop this often near the end of a hilly 50-mile (80km) family ride.

Across the hills to the northeast is Hallett, which has a general store and a cafe. A road sign tells us Adelaide is only 115 miles (186km) away. Sorry kids, on the zig-zagging Mawson there's still double that to go. Our trip motto has been 'adventure, not torture' and so far there's been plenty of the first and not enough of the second to bother either of the teen activists. But it's during another Mt Lofty Ranges crossing that my daughter sums up her version of the tour. 'The hills are nice to look at,' she says, 'but I don't like riding up them.' She never asks if she can give up.

By stage 12, when the scenery changes in the riesling wine region of Clare, both children are realising their fitness gains. 'I'm almost faster than you, Dad,' my boy says as we climb up through more sheep and canola fields in the Camel Hump Range. He was only partly right – sometimes he's quicker. His main daily concern now is whether the next place will have wi-fi.

Happily, the tour has reached the indulgence phase, and we have no doubt we'll make it to the end. This is cycling mini-break territory, and we are only a handful of bumps from the Barossa Valley. Whether a day off spent wine tasting there should be followed by a 46-mile (74km) uphill traipse into the Adelaide Hills is still up for debate.

As we slog up our last real climb, a 820ft (250m) gravel rise through more vineyards, my boy is waiting for everyone again, barely puffing when we reach him. 'I didn't need to stop,' he tells us. While we snuggle at the Cudlee Creek Tavern, I wonder how long us parents will be able to ride with both kids? Will he and his sister still let us?

Adelaide and the promised hotel-with-pool are on the horizon, along with our finish line. We cruise down the appropriately titled Gorge Rd, finding the final trail marker, then soft-pedal on a bike path towards the city's North Terrace, where we pose for a treasured family holiday photo in front of the bust of Sir Douglas Mawson. **PE**

Hans Wismeijer/Shutterstock

BEFORE THE DINOSAURS

Wilpena Pound, in the Ikara-Flinders Ranges National Park, dominates the view at the northern end of the Mawson Trail. A bowl created by a circle of spectacular peaks, the Pound is popular with walkers and wildlife. The area is also a geological marvel, containing fossils dating back hundreds of millions of years to the Ediacaran Period. The Wilpena Pound entrance is almost at the start (or end) of the ride, so it might be best to return another day.

Left to right: Flinders' gravel roads; one of several abandoned cottages; the welcoming town of Laura. Previous spread: Wilpena Pound

TOOLKIT

Start/finish // Blinman/Adelaide
Distance // 560 miles (900km)
Getting there // Adelaide's airport is a 15-minute drive from the CBD. The official trail starts at the base of Gorge Rd, on the edge of the city. Blinman is roughly 500km (310 miles) by road north of Adelaide.
When to go // Avoid January to March, when there is danger of heatwaves and bushfires.
What to wear // Weather conditions vary considerably.
What to pack // Long-sleeve hiking shirt, raincoats, thermals, neck warmers, suncream, first-aid kit, GPS emergency beacon, bike tools, pump and spare tubes.
Where to stay // Pubs, motels, caravan parks, cabins, Airbnbs, camp dongas, walking huts...
Things to know // Be prepared to be self-sufficient. Carry extra water, up to 4 litres, in the northern sections.
More info // www.southaustraliantrails.com

Opposite: Kangaroo Island's Remarkable Rocks; bottlenose dolphins surfing off Kangaroo Island

MORE LIKE THIS
SOUTH AUSTRALIA FAMILY RIDES

KANGAROO ISLAND

This is a choose-your-own route, not an official trail, but if riders want a memorable experience on Australia's third-largest island, there are many rewards. The highlight is Flinders Chase National Park, tucked in the southwest corner and recovering from the horrendous bushfires of 2020. If there's one stretch to aim for, it's Cape du Couedic Rd, bumping its way through the regrowing bush on the way to cliffs overlooking the Southern Ocean. Watch the seals at Admirals Arch, stare at the lonely lighthouse, and remove your cleats to clamber over the Remarkable Rocks. One idea involves starting at the Penneshaw ferry and looping the island anti-clockwise – 220 miles (360km) in six days of riding. Fun rest-day sights and activities include Seal Bay, Stokes Bay, swimming with the wild bottlenose dolphins off Kingscote and spotting penguins at night in Penneshaw. This trip is best on gravel, touring, or wider-tyre road bikes, but careful planning is required for the western and southern sides of the island to avoid running out of supplies.
Info // www.tourkangarooisland.com.au

LAVENDER CYCLING TRAIL

A useful practice trail if building up to the Mawson, this links the wine region of Clare, through farming land and small country towns, with the plains of the Murray River, Australia's longest. While best ridden over four to six days, the route still requires considerable planning because of the distances between food and accommodation, variable phone reception and the remoteness east of the Mt Lofty Ranges and Barossa Valley. Look out for old farmhouses, grain silos, wildlife and churches along the mostly gravel roads and variable singletrack. The elevation in Clare is almost 1300ft (400m) higher than Murray Bridge, which might be a factor in route selection.
Start // Murray Bridge
Finish // Clare
Distance // 185 miles (300km)
Info // www.lavendercyclingtrail.org.au

THE RIESLING TRAIL, BAROSSA TRAIL & JACK BOBRIDGE TRACK

Not ready for a multiday trip but still want to ride with the family on holiday? The Clare and Barossa valleys both have dedicated tracks with lots of distractions. The Riesling Trail is a section of the Mawson, along an old rail route from Auburn to just north of Clare. Pass a string of cellar doors and enjoy the well-packed path with gentle gradients, making it suitable for the whole family. Further south is the Barossa Trail and Jack Bobridge Track, connecting Gawler and Angaston in the heart of the wine region. The sealed path, which has some steep pinches not so suitable for younger children, travels through some of the area's most famous wineries.
Distance // Riesling Trail: 20 miles (33km); Barossa Trail and Jack Bobridge Track, 25 miles (40km)
Info // www.southaustraliantrails.com

MUNDA BIDDI

Head off-road for more than 620 miles (1000km) through the sky-scraping southern forests of Western Australia, on one of the continent's longest dedicated cycling trails.

In the forests around Nannup in southern Western Australia, the canopy is a raucous chorus of red-tailed black cockatoos. Kangaroo-paw flowers as large as my hand bend under their own weight, and the earth is a colourful constellation of other wildflowers. Through it all, I'm approaching the Munda Biddi Trail's midway point, pedalling south from the hills behind Perth towards the southern coastal city of Albany, almost predominately off-road. I've been in the saddle for eight days, and there have been so many of these moments gifted by nature: a wedge-tailed eagle lifting silently off a branch just above my head; large monitor lizards scurrying up trees at my bike's approach; emus sprinting down the trails as though I'm chasing them.

Created to mirror the walkers' Bibbulmun Track – itself a 620-mile (1000km) journey from near Perth to Albany – the Munda Biddi is predominantly a ride on fire trails, dirt roads and singletrack, shunning sealed roads and highways as it hops between 12 national parks. In the local Noongar First Nations language, Munda Biddi means path through the forest', though it is in effect a ride in three parts: the dry bush of the Darling Range behind Perth; then the taller, lusher karri and tingle forests (among Australia's finest) between Donnelly River and Denmark; and, finally, brief but brilliant brushes with the coast and beaches at the ride's southern end.

I've started my ride in the north, at the trailhead in Mundaring, covering the Munda Biddi's most difficult sections in the first few days. The Darling Range is disliked by many Munda Biddi cyclists for its deep patches of pea gravel, which are as soft as sand and plentiful across the first few days of the trail. Through each pit of gravel, wheel tracks betray where bikes have fishtailed, and footprints betray where cyclists have dismounted and pushed. And yet I find that this stretch's reputation is far worse than its reality – even on a gravel bike, I drift through each section without harm – and I'm quickly immersed in the joy of motion as the early miles tick slowly by.

My first day is short – just 27 miles (43km) to Carinyah Hut, the first of 12 purpose-built huts interspersed between the towns through which the Munda Biddi passes. Each hut features sleeping platforms, tables and benches, undercover bike racks, water tanks and tent sites. As I settle into my bush-wrapped

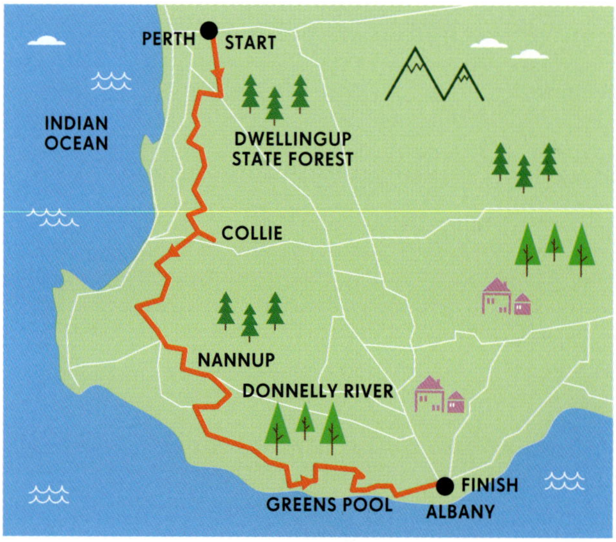

Andrew Bain

> *"The trail passes not around one of the largest tingle trees, but tunnels straight through its hollowed trunk"*

campsite at Carinyah, I already feel entirely removed from the world. The notion that Perth's CBD is just 19 miles (30km) away feels fanciful.

Four days pass before I roll into Dwellingup, the first significant town along the trail, and even the Munda Biddi's dedicated app is spruiking better things ahead: 'If you started in Mundaring you're going to be delighted at how much nicer the trail is south of Dwellingup.'

For the first time I can roar downhill without worrying about the possibility of coming to a hard stop in a trap of pea-gravel. There are also the first swims (with plenty more to come), as the trail dips across the Murray River in Lane Poole Reserve.

But it's at Donnelly River that I know I'm entering cycling greatness. The former logging settlement, 310 miles (500km) from Mundaring as the bike rolls, marks the point at which this forest path reaches its forest best. Suddenly, karri trees line the trail, rising as straight as rods, their white trunks almost like alabaster.

They're trees that are matched only by the remarkable tingles still ahead in the so-called Valley of the Giants. It's a tough morning of riding out of Walpole to reach the Valley of the Giants, first along the bank of the Frankland River – another day, another swim – and then through the torture of a succession of thigh-stripping climbs.

A TRINITY OF TREES

Three tree species endemic to Australia's southwest corner all but define the Munda Biddi Trail. Among the drier bush, it's the jarrah tree, growing to 160ft-plus (50m) in height, but it's the karri and tingle trees that are the true stars of this cycling show. The tallest tree species in WA, the karri can grow up to 300ft (90m) in height (the King Karri, just off the trail near Donnelly River, is the fourth-largest-known karri), while tingles are most impressive for their girth. Their enormous trunks can reach a circumference up to 80ft (24m).

Clockwise from top: crossing Warren River; staying overnight at Karta Burnu hut; the King Karri tree at Donnelly River; Quinninup caravan park

Andrew Bain

Tingle trees grow only in a small area around the Valley of the Giants, their buttressed trunks so wide that visitors once used to park their cars inside the burnt-out trunk of one particular tree. It's a short detour off the trail to walk through the forest canopy on the Valley of the Giants Tree Top Walk, but the Munda Biddi has its own private tingle treat – a few miles from the Tree Top Walk, on perhaps the most flowing and fun section of the entire ride, the trail passes not around one of the largest tingle trees, but straight through it, tunnelling through its hollowed trunk.

The tall forests stretch east, to Jinung Beigabup Hut, the Munda Biddi's final hut, set within a ring of lofty karri trees. From here, I'm two days' ride from Albany, with the trail about to begin its spectacular dismount along the coast.

From Jinung Beigabup, I plunge to the shores at Greens Pool, one of WA's true coastal beauties, its turquoise waters dotted with rounded granite boulders. Wriggling past beaches, cliffs and copious wildflowers, I enter the town of Denmark beneath the turning arms of its wind turbines.

A day later I will pass through a wind farm again on the Munda Biddi's final approach into Albany, though there's one final, cruel climb to reach the turbines. I've now climbed more than 12,000m since leaving Mundaring 18 days ago, and I feel like Don Quixote charging at his windmills as I battle my way up the steep climb. Parrots fly ahead of me like escorts, and soon Albany, the Munda Biddi's sprawling finish line, rises into view. I pause, reluctant to finish after this short but full life on a bike, but bakeries and beer beckon. I ride on. **AB**

Andrew Bain

Previous page: riding beneath the canopy of karri trees

TOOLKIT

Start // Mundaring
Finish // Albany
Distance // 666 miles (1072km)
Getting there // Mundaring is a 40-minute drive from Perth. Suburban trains run to Midland, 9 miles (15km) of uphill cycling from Mundaring.
When to go // Spring, when forests bloom with flowers.
What to pack // Sleeping bag, mat and all cooking gear are needed, even if bunking down in the shelters. Perth-based About Bike Hire offers packages that include rental of suitable hardtail mountain bikes.
Where to stay // The 12 trail huts are interspersed between towns, allowing stops (and restocks) in Jarrahdale, Dwellingup, Collie, Boyanup, Donnybrook, Nannup, Donnelly River, Manjimup, Quinninup, Pemberton, Northcliffe, Walpole and Denmark.
More info // www.mundabiddi.org.au, also the app.

Opposite: the Daintree River region on the National Trail; watch for saltwater crocodiles

MORE LIKE THIS
AUSTRALIAN LONG-DISTANCE ROUTES

MAWSON TRAIL

Go from urban to outback on this off-road trail from Adelaide into the desert fringes of the Flinders Ranges, South Australia's major mountain range. The toughest moments are at the very start, as it climbs steeply into the Adelaide Hills, but rewards come on the other side as you pedal through the vineyards of the Barossa Valley. The Mid North can be dry and hot, making spring a good time to be on the trail, with lingering water sources from winter rains. At its northern end, the ride scoots beneath the mountain walls of Ikara-Wilpena Pound before threading its way through the northern limbs of the Flinders Ranges into Blinman Gorge. Though the trail is at times remote, it's feasible to stay in towns each night, though camping brings greater freedoms. See page 280.
Start // Adelaide
Finish // Blinman Gorge
Distance // 560 miles (900km)
Info // www.southaustraliantrails.com/trails/mawson-trail

TASMANIAN TRAIL

This multiuse mountain-bike trail runs almost the length of Tasmania. Handily, it begins in Devonport, on the north coast, where ferries from the Australian mainland arrive on the island state. Befitting a mountainous island, this is no ride in the park – the terrain is varied and at times challenging and there are plenty of climbs and descents, especially beyond Deloraine as you climb into Tasmania's highlands; though remote, it's possible to sleep in a bed each night if you plan ahead. There are several locked gates along this rugged route, the keys for which can be obtained from the Tasmanian Trail Association (which also publishes a trail guidebook in pdf form) – you'll need to become a member of the association and allow up to three weeks for delivery of the keys.
Start // Devonport
Finish // Dover
Distance // 298 miles (480km)
Info // www.tasmaniantrail.com.au

NATIONAL TRAIL

First developed as the Bicentennial National Trail to commemorate 200 years of European settlement, in 1988, the National Trail is one of the world's longest marked cycling routes. A multiuse trail, it was created with horse riders in mind, but has been equally adopted by hikers and mountain-bike riders (the website offers a pdf of notes for cyclists to help them navigate around the most rugged sections). Ultimately, the trail runs the length of the Great Dividing Range, the long string of mountains behind Australia's east coast, utilising a range of roads and tracks. As you'd anticipate across such a distance, the terrain is highly variable – rainforest to alpine meadows, mountains to gorges – and the trail has been broken down into 12 sections, each 250 miles (400km) to 300-plus miles (500km) in length, if you don't have the time and legs for a full traverse.
Start // Cooktown
Finish // Healesville
Distance // 3312 miles (5330km)
Info // www.nationaltrail.com.au

Ewen Bell for Lonely Planet

THE NEW ENGLAND HIGH COUNTRY 1000

A route atop the Great Dividing Range might be dubbed 'Outback lite' but expect high country and high mileage, through dusty paddocks and ancient rainforest

Everyone has a favourite terrain and top of my list is big-sky country. Where you can see not just your next hour of riding but see it all at once. A layer of dirt on my skin, a sandwich that's hard to swallow and the sun all but inescapable. That, for me, is the best kind of bike-touring; which is precisely why the New England High Country 1000 (NEHC1000) was created.

Put together by a few knowledgeable locals, myself included, the route is a circumnavigation of the highest plateau on Australia's Great Dividing Range, a 621-mile (1000km) journey around 'New England': not the Ivy League-rich region of northeast America but its lesser-known namesake, in the Australian state of New South Wales; and 'High Country' because the plateau is located at 3300ft (1000m) above sea level. It's an area of Australia that experiences extreme changes in weather throughout the year, as does the route that bears its name (and I've ridden it in all seasons).

My upcoming trip has some of my pre-requisites. It's the height of summer, so the heat will be impenetrable, our water bottles the temperature of tea. The ride will be part of a local event called the Super Jambo Grom Pre, not so much a race as a bikepacking/touring ride. First staged in 2022, it traverses the landscape and townships of New England, is self-supported, and most riders aim to complete the circuit in 10 days.

I'm riding with two friends, Jack and Izzy. With other participants joining at different points around the route, we start where I always begin my NEHC1000 rides, in Walcha, the southernmost point on the circuit. The town itself is neat and humble, its main strip lined with Land Cruiser utility vehicles, or 'utes', many with crop-spraying booms attached, or else dogs barking from cages on flatbeds. The men and women start their working days with a coffee and quick yarn. It's a small town, clearly they all know each other.

Walcha skirts the edge of the plateau and, as we head west on our first day, we are treated to misty-blue views, from the Great Dividing Range to the sweltering lowlands below. The next few days are easy, as we ride through rolling farmland and along quiet country roads. It's the type of terrain I like best on the NEHC1000, what I like to call 'Outback lite'. Ideal for when the Outback proper is too nerve-wracking, this less-extreme

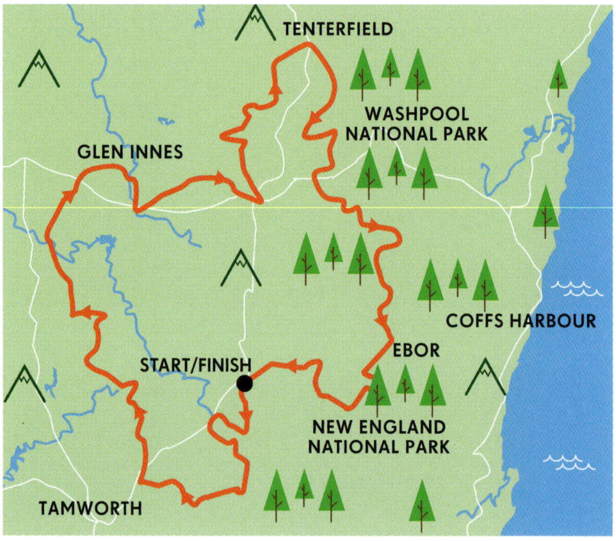

Bourne for nature/Shutterstock

version runs along the flat, dusty roads on the western side of the plateau. It's extremely scenic; the roads are wide and the traffic scarce. It's 'working' territory, where sheep are rounded up by quad bikes and dogs. We pass tractors kicking up dust in the paddocks, while my own, skinnier tyres do the same along the roads. In this vast landscape, a simple wave 'G'day' requires an exaggerated gesture.

With gradients of up to 11%, the western portion of the route is the perfect place to warm up the legs. In my experience, it always takes the first few days of any bike tour for your legs to show up. A rattling ute or truck hauling cattle pass from time to time, as we chew up the miles on our way to the rockier territory of the NEHC's northern section. For now, the terrain is a mix of gravel country roads and unmaintained Crown-land tracks. We come across old homesteads and cattle stations; galloping horses are occasional companions.

After Glen Innes, the route becomes steeper and progress slower. We face our first significant climb as we follow along Pyes Creek, pedalling over the granite-littered ridge to drop into Tenterfield, our halfway point. Located at the route's northern pinnacle, Tenterfield shades us beneath its willow trees, while we take stock of supplies and massage our waning legs. After 329 miles (530km) we've found our rhythm – and fatigue has found us. The last few days have given us a chance to understand just how much food and water we need, especially in summer. We decide Tenterfield is a good place to resupply, aware we won't get another chance until Ebor – three days' riding away.

"From Armidale, the highest city in Australia, there are several more landscape changes until we feel the grit of Walcha's dirt stuck in our teeth again"

With few sightings of any other participants, it seems everyone must be riding at the same, steady pace. Next up for us, however, is to navigate the eastern escarpment of the Northern Tablelands. With spectacular gorges, rainforests, and waterfalls, much of this region is protected by national parks, including a portion of the Gondwana Rainforests of Australia, a UNESCO World Heritage Site and the planet's largest area of sub-tropical rainforest.

We enter Washpool, one of those national parks, by way

William Edge/Shutterstock; Jorja Creighton

CATTLE COUNTRY

Over the year, farmers in New England must cope with extremes of climate. As well as hot summers, working stations are no strangers to cold, dark winters – even snow. As you ride past these farms on the NEHC1000, you'll see cattle known as Speckle Park. Distinguished by black-spotted colouring, the breed was imported from Canada, where it was first bred in Saskatchewan. Versatile Speckle Parks can cope with the Northern Tablelands' droughts and deep winter.

From left: Speckle Park cattle; ready for adventure; dirt tracks in the New England High Country. Previous spread: the Guy Fawkes River cascades over Ebor Falls

of fern-lined tracks. The sun blinking through lush rainforest canopy provides a stark contrast to dusty farm-roads. Despite the rainforest, it's a section with limited resupply opportunities; it requires careful planning and ensures our water-purification systems get a good workout. The riding is rough, the climbs testing. From here, Ebor is still 166 miles (267km) away, a distance that includes 19,000ft (5802m) more climbing. Back-to-back days of riding like this are hard and though there are by now more regular sightings of other participants, the words between the three of us become fewer, as we save our energy for the ride.

In Ebor we take a breather, popping to the nearby Ebor Falls to admire the Guy Fawkes River, as its plunges 328ft (100m) over two waterfalls. By the time we are back on the road, on our way back to Armidale, we can smell home. By this point, my body has succumbed to the idea that it's destined to spend every day in the saddle for the rest of its life. From Armidale, the highest city in Australia, there are several more landscape changes until we feel the grit of Walcha's dirt stuck in our teeth again. As ever, the NEHC1000 proves a challenging but rewarding experience that pushes me to my limits both physically and mentally. **JC**

TOOLKIT

Start // Walcha/Armidale
Finish // Armidale/Walcha
Distance // 644 miles (1037km)
Getting there // The New England High Country is a five-hour drive from Sydney, six hours from Brisbane. Also rail links from Sydney or Brisbane. Flights into Armidale.
When to go // Early March or November. Wilderness experience essential, check conditions in advance.
What to wear // Local conditions are changeable; bring light, breathable gear for the heat, as well as apparel for cold and rain, eg base layers, shell and insulated jackets.
What to pack // A bike set up for rough off-road sections. Expect days without phone signal or resupplies of food and water: minimum 2.5-litre water capacity (in summer 3.5 litres) and a water-purification system. Camping gear.
More info // www.jambijambi.com

Jorja Creighton

Opposite: riding the Sandstone Wilderness 600 route

MORE LIKE THIS
BACKCOUNTRY BIKEPACKING

SANDSTONE WILDERNESS 600, QLD

Sarah Pendergrass's Sandstone Wilderness route through Outback Queensland came about in part from a desire to visit friends who had relocated to the region's unofficial capital, Longreach. And the name, 'Sandstone Wilderness', was born from the landscapes of the many national parks in the area, with views of rugged sandstone cliffs appearing on the horizon, towering over the vast, barren plains below. Kick off the route from the lovingly restored railway station in Emerald, which is on the Spirit of the Outback's schedule route from Brisbane to Longreach (and will be your route back from Longreach, or take the Greyhound bus at the end of your adventure). Sections of this ride involve days without resupply of food and water, or phone signal. Full research and experience in arid wilderness areas is essential.
Start // Emerald
Finish // Longreach
Distance // 435 miles (700km)

KAHURANGI 500, NEW ZEALAND

Arguably the southern hemisphere's most exciting bikepacking circuit, this lovely loop leads riders on a 300-mile (500km) route around Kahurangi National Park at the top of New Zealand's South Island. The multiday off-road odyssey incorporates several iconic smaller routes, including the Rāmeka and Heaphy tracks, and the Old Ghost Road. Most bikers begin in Tapawera and go anticlockwise towards gorgeous Golden Bay, before lapping up the fabulous flowing singletrack trails encountered on the Rāmeka and Heaphy tracks. You have to earn your turns first, however, by sweating up Tākaka Hill. After the Old Ghost Road the route rises over the mountains to reach Lyell, before rolling through Buller Gorge to Murchison and then tracing the Braeburn Track to Lake Rotoroa and closing the circle with a spin up Tadmor Valley to Tapawera. There are campsites and facilities at regular intervals, and opportunities to plunge into the ocean.
Start/finish // Tapawera
Distance // 310 miles (500km)
Info // www.nzcycletrail.com

THE TASSIE GIFT, TASMANIA

A route thought up in 2019 by long-distance, all-terrain cycling enthusiast Emma Flukes, the Tassie Gift may or may not be fated to become a regular event, but it's already legendary by its very nature. At almost 1120 miles (1800km), with more than 98,000ft (30,000m) of climbing, the route represents a serious undertaking. The figure-of-eight loop traces two butterfly wings towards the northwest and northeast corners of the island, hinging at Miena in the centre. The Tarkine figures strongly, but so too do the mountains around Queenstown, the Bay of Fires, Cradle Mountain Rd, the surroundings of Hobart, and countless more places that show the diversity of Tasmania. The precise route includes some portions on private land, with permissions given for specific events, but at other times you will need to make modifications to skirt inaccessible spots.
Start/finish // Hobart
Distance // 1100 miles (1780km)
Info // www.bikepacking.com

Sarah Pendergrass

THE OLD GHOST ROAD

Despite the name, the Old Ghost Road will keep your spirits high with its epic singletrack through native New Zealand forest, open tussock tops and forgotten valleys.

Floss-dipped forest, jagged ridgelines and great, grumbling gorges rest beneath us as we stop, perched on the wafer-thin trail at Heaven's Door. At 4777ft (1456m) above sea level, Tāwhirimātea (the Māori god of wind) wields his power without remorse. Suddenly, swathes of dense fog and frigid clouds billow and swell around us, smothering the trail and erasing the sun and all its warmth from the sky.

Visibility is reduced to mere metres, as nerves are put to the test. The group is quiet now. All attention is turned to getting through the fog unscathed. One slip, one misjudged line or lapse in concentration, and we risk falling through the fog to join the spirits already haunting the Old Ghost Road.

Running above the West Coast of the South Island, the Old Ghost Road is the longest continuous singletrack route in New Zealand, and it's a trail-building triumph. Until 2015, it was a forgotten gold-miners' road, but now the 51-mile (85km) multiday trail is an outdoor enthusiast's dream. In the summer of 2021, my partner Bec, our friend Tom and I decided to tackle it fully loaded, as part of our year-long tour of NZ.

As quickly as it appeared, the fog rolls over us, leaving bright blue skies and a clear trail in its wake. With almost 19 miles (30km) of climbing and the high point of the route in the bag, Ghost Lake Hut is a welcome sight. As a southerly begins to blow, we rush inside and hover around the heat of the fire like sandflies on a nudist beach. 'You made it, guys, great effort!' a man with a four-foot smile yells. It's Phil, a hut warden we met at the trailhead earlier that morning. 'Your bunks are in the next room there. It's not quite the Hilton, but you should get a

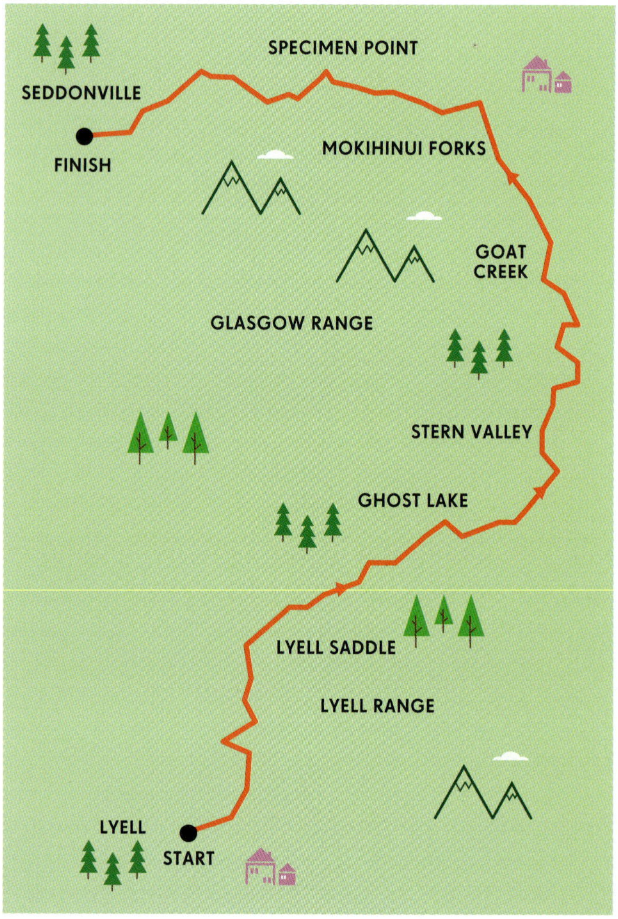

Sam Rice

good night's sleep after all that climbing today.' We unravel our sleeping bags in preparation for our forty winks.

The next morning, the wakening hut booms to the sound of Phil's voice, as he waves off the first set of early risers. Semi-conscious, I reach for my coffee kit and begin the daily grind. As the coffee blooms, Tom rushes over, distressed.

'You won't believe it, mate. Someone's stolen the head torch and protein bars from my frame bag!' He heads outside and shows me the crime scene. As we inspect the frame bag for clues, I catch a swish of movement in my peripheral vision.

'Over there, Tom – is that your head torch?' I ask, trying desperately to hold back my laughter. 'Come back, you little bastard!' Tom cries out, as a thieving weka retreats into the bush, Tom's head torch flailing around its speckled neck. The next 10 minutes feel like something out of a Monty Python sketch, as we try to catch the feathered bandit. After a few bumps (and bruised egos) we admit defeat, retreating to the hut. I pour Tom a coffee to help cushion the blow and we set about packing the bikes, ready for day two.

'This is epic! I feel like I'm riding in the European Alps,' Tom screams out as he negotiates a series of tight, off-camber switchbacks in the subdued morning light. Down 984ft (300m), we plummet through the morning mist and the landscape changes in an instant. Gnarled beech forest lines the trail, with long branches bowing under the strength of the wind. Burnt oranges, rusty yellows and lurid greens pop from the forest canopy as we snake our way down the beautifully treacherous trail ahead.

HUT-PACKING

Complete with fully equipped kitchens, campsites and even helipads, the huts of Old Ghost Road are almost as impressive as the trail itself. Don't miss a night's sleep at the Ghost Lake Hut: sitting at 3940ft (1200m) above sea level, its spectacular views are a highlight of the trip. From a standard self-supported bikepack, to a leisurely multiday cruise with chopper drops of cheese and wine, the huts make almost anything possible.

Clockwise from top: Ghost Lake hut; packing for the day on the trail. Previous spread: expect some water crossings on the route

Sam Rice

At Skyline Ridge, the trail dances its way through towering rocks, which stand like ancient sentinels guarding the onward path. Tāwhirimātea is with us once more, as he peels back the cloud cover to reveal the expanse of the Lyell and Glasgow Ranges that dominate the landscape. Down the infamous Skyline Steps, we drop another 328ft (100m). Under the rainforest canopy, the mottled sun casts a warm hue, punctuating the trail with bursts of golden light. It feels never-ending. Pedalling becomes a thing of the past, as laser-focused fun, childlike yelps and screams of pure elation fill the forest.

Stern Valley Hut comes and goes as our adrenaline-fuelled second wind carries us onwards. With full exposure, we soak up the harsh UV rays and sweat as the temperature soars to 32°C (90°F). We begin the climb through the earthquake-scarred Boneyard as the searing midday sun continues to sap our energy. Progress is slow, but we grind on through the lunar landscape, draining our water bottles until we taste their plastic.

One final pinch climb to crest the Solemn Saddle and we're fading fast. 'That's the last climb of the route, guys. It's pure downhill from here to pizza!' Bec announces, as she shovels peanut butter in her mouth. 'We've got plenty of light left, so I vote we go for it,' Tom gushes as the promise of pizza ignites the fabled third wind and we set off for one final flurry.

The group dynamic is at an all-time high as we pull into Rough & Tumble Lodge. Laughter fills the air as we replay the morning's antics with the naughty trail weka and tuck into our pizzas. After two months riding the South Island together, this would mark the end of our time with Tom. With new friendships forged on the trail, we part ways, thankful that our last ride was the Old Ghost Road. **SR**

Sam Rice

TOOLKIT

Start/finish // Lyell/Seddonville
Distance // 52 miles (84km)
Getting there // The best way to get to the Old Ghost Road is to use one of the round-trip van services, usually running out of Westport. There are also some great services that will drive your vehicle from the start to the end of the trail, with key-drop boxes at each end. Another option is to ride a loop from Westport.
When to go // October to April. February traditionally has the best weather.
What to wear // Be prepared for cold and wet weather. Long sleeves and trousers are essential as the sandflies can be pretty treacherous.
What to pack // Bug spray and wet weather gear are vital, along with some essential bike tools. Emergency kit items are also important as the ride is technical.
Where to stay // You can either choose huts or basic tent sites along the trail. Book your stays in advance, as it's a very popular ride year-round.
Good to know // We suggest starting at Lyell and riding in a south-to-north direction. Due to the technical nature and gradient of 2.5 miles (4km) of trail north of Ghost Lake, this section is easier to descend than ascend.
More info // www.oldghostroad.org.nz

Opposite: descending the Paparoa Track in New Zealand

MORE LIKE THIS EPIC MOUNTAIN BIKING

ALL-MOUNTAIN TRAIL, NEW SOUTH WALES

Thredbo is Australia's best year-round alpine destination. In winter, it's home to the country's longest ski runs and its only alpine gondola. In summer, the resort switches into MTB gear – it has Australia's only lift-accessed mountain-bike park, and more than 22 miles (35km) of trails, including downhill, flow and cross-country, plus a pump track and skills park. The trails are tucked into the side of Kosciuszko National Park, weaving around the highest peak in Australia, Mt Kosciuszko (7310ft/ 2228m). With beginner, intermediate and advanced level trails, bike rental and even an MTB school, Thredbo has something for every rider no matter your skill level. The All-Mountain Trail is an intermediate-level descent in two parts, running 5.5 miles (9km) from the topmost lift station back down to the resort.
Start/Finish // Thredbo, Kosciuszko National Park
Distance // 22 miles (35km)
Info // www.thredbo.com.au

THE PAPAROA TRACK, SOUTH ISLAND

Tucked away on the same coastline as the Old Ghost Road, the Paparoa Track showcases more of what riding the wild west coast has to offer. The first new Great Walk in 20 years, the track is a 34-mile (55km) purpose-built hiking and mountain biking route. Weaving its way past mine sites and through some of the most remote and untouched parts of Paparoa National Park, it stitches together an area that was inaccessible for 150 years. Lurid green ferns, spiky tropical nikau palms and northern rātā crowd around this epic trail, with abundant flowing singletrack and views that stretch across the Tasman Sea.
Start // Blackball
Finish // Punakaiki
Distance // 34 miles (55km)

AUSTRALIAN ALPINE EPIC TRAIL, MT BULLER, VICTORIA

The Australian Alpine Epic Trail is both tough and thrilling, with some calling it the jewel in Mt Buller's crown. Offering 25 miles (40km) of unique riding in the Australian Alps, the trail is the first in the Southern Hemisphere to be designated 'epic' by the International Mountain Bicycling Association (IMBA). You'll wind through a thick green canopy, showcasing terrain and landscapes that exist nowhere else in the world. With huge vistas, flowing singletrack and juicy descents galore, the Alpine Epic is a trail-building masterpiece – living up to its name as the 'best trail in Australia'.
Start // Mt Buller Alpine Village
Finish // Mirimbah
Distance // 25 miles (40km)
Info // www.ridehighcountry.com.au

Sam Rice

FLASHPACKING THE VIC DIVIDE 550

Want to make a backcountry ride from Melbourne to Albury even better? Then leave your tent and cookset behind and try 'flashpacking'.

It was some friends who suggested it might be possible to 'flashpack' the Vic Divide. That is, to tackle this 340-mile (550km) bikepacking route from Melbourne to Albury by travelling light, staying in accommodation each evening. A route that passes variously through the lands of the Woiwurrung, Taungurung and Pallanganmiddang people, we specced an itinerary of five days, each averaging a little over 68 miles (110km) and 8202ft (2500m) of climbing.

Crucially, flashpacking meant no boxing bikes, no camping gear, just long rides through incredible country with mates. And cool swims and made beds. And hot showers and pub meals... Andy, Adam and I chose to ride in late March, when the summer rush was over but the weather still favourable. 29er MTB hardtails were our bikes of choice: big tyres, low gears and limited luggage of food, water, and emergency provisions.

There is something special about starting a big ride from your front door. Leaving before dawn as the city awakens, you have the sense of being in a parallel universe. The ride proper starts at Wurundjeri Spur, on Yarra Blvd, a piece of bushland a mile or so from the city. Andy had ridden from his own front door too, so we met like a couple of kids who'd wagged school.

After following gravel tracks along the Yarra River for the morning, we stopped for a coffee in Warrandyte, where the route leaves civilisation behind. The rest of the day's riding consisted of quiet gravel roads, stunning doubletrack through State forest and some tricky singletrack around Smith's Gully, to remind us the route was technically challenging.

I'd earmarked this day as one of the easier ones but, after 77

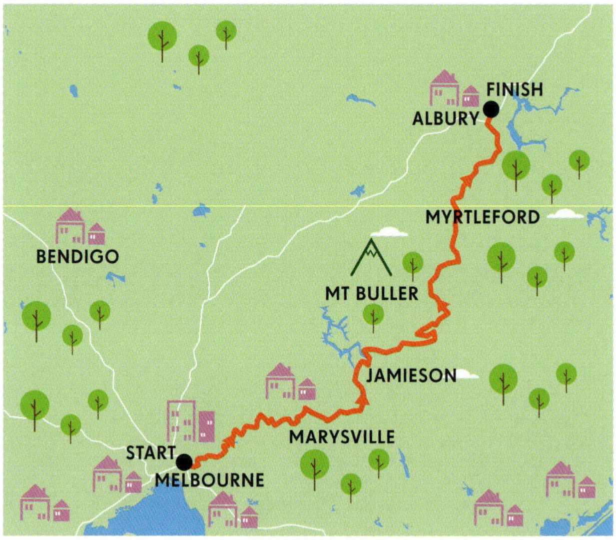

Andy White

miles (124km) and 10,500ft (3200m) of climbing, I was cooked. Following nine hours of riding, we dropped into Marysville to be greeted by Adam's beaming face – he'd ridden from his place, in Victoria's Alpine region.

The advantage of having booked accommodation at the Marysville Holiday Park was that, after introducing the other guys to my recovery-drink of choice – the 'Diesel', a 50-50 mix of beer and Coke – we could simply collect our key and retire to our cabin.

Next morning, with no opportunity to resupply during day two, a Marysville supermarket was our one-stop shop for breakfast, lunch and snacks. Fuelled by iced coffee and Vegemite scrolls, the fun started immediately, with fern-lined singletrack, followed by a long, gradual climb on doubletrack to the highest point of the day. Big River Rd is an absolute cracker, and we were lucky to be riding when it was just about 4WD-free.

The heat was oppressive but the frequent river-crossings kept our water supplies topped up, and our core temperatures in check. Late in the afternoon came an extended climb but the fast descent into Jamieson made up for it. Our accommodation that night, the Courthouse Hotel, was exactly what I think of when picturing a pub in an isolated hamlet; a wrap-around bar with a cubbyhole behind the counter, where locals keep (and help themselves to) stubby-holders. The rooms were basic, and all the other bikes in the shed had engines, but the hospitality scored 10/10.

While day three was the shortest, we also knew it would be the hardest. At 58 miles (93km), but again with 10,500ft (3200m) of climbing, it began, brilliantly, with a delicious cooked breakfast containing a day's worth of carbohydrates. The first few miles felt like a 'transfer stage', to where the real action started, the Howqua Inlet trail; 9 miles (15km) of incredible singletrack, much of it perched precariously, in some cases more than 165ft (50m) above the Howqua River in a narrow valley.

The riding was exhilarating, the views stunning, the stakes as high as the trail. One mistake, and you'd find yourself in serious trouble. Adam reminded us to keep each other in sight, and also to keep emergency beacons on our person, not on the bike – a satellite phone isn't much help if it's out of reach at the bottom of a ravine.

Despite being mountain biker at heart, I'm ashamed to admit that, by mid-afternoon, I was willing the singletrack to stop, to make faster progress. After a final dip in the Howqua, the last 17 miles (27km) of the day climbed 3281ft (1000m), up to Mt Buller Village. Above the snow line the surface deteriorated to chunky blue stone, some of which I was not too proud to walk.

Andy White

Andy White

LEADBEATER'S POSSUM

One forest resident you probably won't spot along the Vic Divide is the Leadbeater's Possum. Also known as the 'fairy possum', this mini-marsupial fits easily into the palm of a hand and is one of the world's most endangered creatures. Previously believed extinct, the species was rediscovered, near Marysville, in 1961. The mountain-ash forests of Victoria's Central Highlands are its habitat, where the possum makes its home in hollow trees.

From left: take refreshing dips in rivers; overlooking Lake Eildon near Jamieson; mountain ash forest along Monda Road, Murrindindi. Previous spread: Flagstaff road near Beechworth; Ritchie's Hut on the Howqua River

Ahead, our room was booked but dinner was no sure thing, as we watched the sun go down on our approach. Thankfully, with the kitchen still open at Arlberg House, the parmas were served with views to die for, including a thunderstorm as it rolled through the valley.

The profile for the next section, day four, suggested it would be all downhill, but that's not how it turned out; it was mid-morning before we even got off the mountain. The glorious singletrack on Mt Buller, however, including both Trigger Happy and Stonefly trails, elicited whoops of delight, but the maintenance tracks strewn with boulders made us thankful for our mountain bikes.

The rest of the day was spent revelling in glorious countryside, with long stretches of smooth gravel, and quiet tarmac through broad valleys. After a mid-afternoon resupply at Cheshunt, we pushed on through the sweltering heat to Myrtleford, rewarding ourselves with our fanciest dinner yet, at Tu Vietnamese.

The final day started with a magnificent climb, before six miles (10km) of hand-made trails, complete with berms and table-tops as we rode the Indigo Epic Trail, into Yackandandah. After lunch, the ride back to Albury was a gentle re-entry to city life. Completely exhausted, Andy and I barely spoke on the long train-ride back to Melbourne. I guess that, on the Vic Divide, everything had been said. **HV**

TOOLKIT

Start // Melbourne
Finish // Albury
Distance // 340 miles (550km)
Getting there // Start a mile outside Melbourne's CBD. Return train from Albury; some services require bike-boxes.
When to go // Late spring, or late summer to early autumn; avoid midsummer, when bushfire-risk is high, with limited water. Impassable in winter.
What to wear // The weather is unpredictable, so even in summer, take warm clothes and basic wet-weather gear.
What to pack // Emergency spares and tools (pads, cables). Water-purification system, emergency beacon.
Where to stay // Accommodation for a range of budgets, depending on location.
Where to eat // Flashpacking ensures breakfast and dinner, but plan daily fuel for riding eight to 12 hours.
Things to know // This is definitely a mountain-bike ride.
More info // ridewithgps.com/routes/45639381

Opposite: green tree ferns in the Great Otway National Park; riding the Goldfields Track between Ballarat and Creswick

MORE LIKE THIS
BIKEPACKING BEAUTIES IN VICTORIA

HUNT 1000

The Hunt 1000 was developed as a bikepacking race, in 2016, by Dan Hunt, founder of Australian bike company Hunt Bikes, as a way to cycle mainly off-road between Victoria's state capital, Melbourne, and national capital Canberra. Australia's southeast corner is quite high and cool, often with snow in winter. It's across this High Country that the Hunt 1000 weaves its way, a beautiful and emotive landscape that includes the national parks of Kosciuszko and the Yarra Ranges, plus the stark Jagungal Wilderness Area. The route is mostly via 4WD dirt tracks and the occasional township or shepherds' hut. The race stats are sobering: 73,000ft (22,250m) of ascent over 621 miles (1000km). Rough and remote, fewer than half the starters finish, most taking around a week. Training and bush-craft are required. If you're not racing, you can break this ride down into discrete sections, each spectacular, such as that between Melbourne and Mt Hotham.
Start // Melbourne
Finish // Canberra
Distance // 621 miles (1000km)

GOLDFIELDS TRACK

Some Australian off-road bikepacking routes require experience and expertise. Not so the Goldfields Track. It's not easy but it is accessible, fun and fairly forgiving, making it an ideal route on which beginner bikepackers can practise the basics of navigation. You'll be riding between some of Victoria's biggest country towns and cities, places built upon the money generated by the gold rush. In the 1850s, when 'gold fever' hit the region west and north of Melbourne, people from around the world trekked here in the hope of finding their fortune. This route follows in their tracks and consists of four other trails connected end to end: the Eureka Track, from Mt Buninyong to Creswick; the Wallaby Track, from Creswick to Daylesford; the Dry Diggings Track (Daylesford to Castlemaine); and the Leanganook Track, from Castlemaine to Bendigo. Most riders break their journeys two or three times, for example at Daylesford and Castlemaine.
Start // Ballarat
Finish // Bendigo
Distance // 130 miles (210km)

OTWAY RIP

Discover the beaches of the Great Ocean Road and the gorgeous forests of the Otways on this three-day tour along mostly quiet roads and shady forest tracks. The Otway Rip was developed in 2020 (and revised in 2025), to be a relatively accessible and highly enjoyable exploration of this region southwest of Melbourne. You'll start from the flat and fertile farmland around Camperdown, but it's not far until more interesting territory as you reach the tourist town of Port Campbell, then follow the Great Ocean Road past the Twelve Apostles limestone stacks. At Princetown, turn inland on gravel roads through the Great Otway National Park. Here, giant ferns and mountain ash trees conspire to make you feel minuscule. The route ascends into the Otway Ranges but waterfalls and lakes offer refreshing stops, as does the brewpub in Forrest, before you zoom down to Colac and its train station.
Start // Camperdown
Finish // Colac
Distance // 163 miles (262km)

CENTRAL OTAGO'S RAIL TRAIL

Take a virtual pub crawl along New Zealand's first and most famous rail trail, packed with history, barren landscapes, gentle gradients and an assortment of character-filled hotels.

Outside the Otago town of Alexandra, the landscape is straight from a spaghetti western. Across the bare schist hills, the earth is serrated with rock and old rail lines have been repurposed as fenceposts. Ahead, largest of all, is the scarily named Tiger Hill, the toughest climb on the Otago Central Rail Trail, although 'toughest' here is relative. It is the trail's steepest section, but Tiger Hill has an average gradient of just 2%. I later hear a cyclist mock it as 'Pussycat Hill'. There's nothing to fear here.

Australasia's love of a good rail trail was born on this ride. When a trail through this largely forgotten tourist region, pinched between Dunedin and Queenstown, was first mooted, the idea was met with opposition and indifference. But from the moment it opened as New Zealand's first rail trail in 2000, it was a hit, attracting more than 10,000 cyclists every year and resuscitating towns, pubs and accommodation providers along its horseshoe-shaped route. It's the kind of trail that a seasoned cyclist might attempt in a day, but it's just as friendly to those who come with little or no cycle-touring experience.

At its western end, the ride begins in the town of Clyde, cut into the bank of the Clutha/Mata-au River, which, during the Central Otago gold rush in the 1860s, was the richest gold-bearing river in the world. What gold remains as I set out riding is in the colour of the seasons. It's autumn, and every tree-lined waterway is a meandering yellow line through the bare landscape, as though a child has scribbled across this part of New Zealand with a crayon.

There's a symmetry to the Otago Central Rail Trail, which ascends gently for the first half (whichever direction you begin), and descends just as gradually through the second half. The climb is barely noticeable, ascending only 1480ft (450m) across

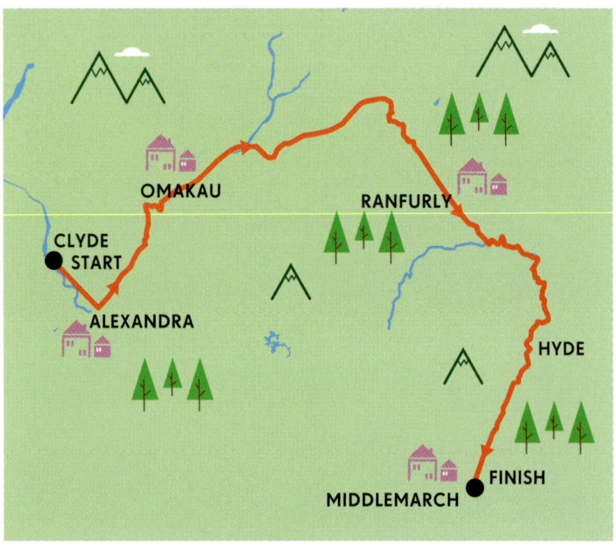

Janice Chen/Shutterstock

more than 44 miles (70km), even if somebody gave part of it a name as falsely fearsome as Tiger Hill.

The Tiger is quickly tamed, however – I pedal up the hill beside a newcomer to cycling who doesn't even change a gear for the entire climb – and the land beyond opens out into a broad, bucolic valley, with the frayed schist slopes of the well-named Raggedy Range to one side and the taller Dunstan Mountains to the other. Pinched between them is my first night's stop, Lauder, a settlement so small that it seems more of a glorified pub than a town. It's a common feeling on the Otago Central Rail Trail, which is dotted with so many hotels – about one pub every 7.5 miles (12km) on average – that it's also been christened the Ale Trail.

The one thing that outnumbers pubs on this trail is bridges, with the ride crossing almost 70 old railway bridges. The most spectacular of these – coupled with the trail's most dramatic section – are through skinny Poolburn Gorge, outside Lauder. To enter the gorge, I cross the 360ft/110m-long Manuherikia Viaduct, while inside the gorge is the Poolburn Viaduct, the ride's highest bridge, poised a heady 120ft (37m) above the creek.

Around these bridges, the hills and cliffs of the Raggedy Range close in to create a spectacularly narrow and rugged gorge. The tenacity of the Otago Central Branch Railway builders becomes clear as I ride over bridges and through a pair of 650ft/200m-long railway tunnels so dark that I hear another bike crash into the wall ahead of me.

Through the gorgeous Ida Valley, the ride begins to make its long, slow turn for home, swinging south and crawling up to

MAKE A GAME OF IT

A popular detour along the Otago Central Rail Trail is the Southern Hemisphere's only indoor curling rink. Located in Naseby, the Olympic-standard rink is a 8-mile (13km) side trip from Ranfurly (one of the logical stops on the second night along the rail trail). Hotels can often arrange shuttles if you don't fancy the extra ride. Book a sheet and deliver a few stones, or come in winter to try out the adjoining, 1180ft/360m-long ice luge through the Naseby Forest.

Clockwise from top: riding the Otago Central Rail Trail; truck outside a railway shed on the route; the Wedderburn goods shed; Previous page: cycling along the Poolburn Viaduct

Photos BrianScantlebury/Shutterstock; Janice Chen/Shutterstock

a subtle pass that is the trail's highest point at 2028ft (618m) above sea level). Along the way, I twice cross the 45th parallel: for these two brief moments, I am exactly halfway between the Equator and the South Pole. As cyclists universally like to chant (usually erroneously, though correctly in this case), 'It's all downhill from here.'

On a day of strong northerly winds, I blow south like a hurricane, moving quickly to my day's end in Ranfurly, before setting out the next morning on the final stage to Middlemarch. For the first hour of this new day, I cross the wide Maniototo Plain, a flat land of sheep and tussocks, wool and wind, before wriggling into the second of the trail's gorges: the Upper Taieri.

Fighting its way through this gorge is New Zealand's fourth-largest river, the 124-mile (200km) Taieri River. Fighting along beside it were once those 19th-century railway builders, carving another section of line where no line rightly belonged. Where the cliffs intruded, the workers built more viaducts and blasted a 490ft (150m) tunnel. As I ride through the darkness of a tunnel again, I listen for bikes hitting rock, but there is only the crunch of tyres on the earth. Things are improving.

A quick stop in Hyde brings the railway's darker history into focus, for it was here in 1943, midway through the Otago Central Railway's eight decades of operation, that a train derailed, killing 21 passengers. A memorial marks the site of what was New Zealand's second-deadliest railway disaster.

It's not the only late reminder of the trail's railway origins. Along this last afternoon into Middlemarch, there are lone railway sleepers beside the trail, sections of old railway track and, as I coast to a finish at the Middlemarch train station, a railway turntable. My ride is done; I'm off the rails. **AB**

"I twice cross the 45th parallel: for these two brief moments, I am exactly halfway between the Equator and the South Pole"

TOOLKIT

Start/finish // Clyde/Middlemarch
Distance // 94 miles (152km)
Duration // 2-4 days
Getting there // Clyde is a 2.5-hour drive northwest of Dunedin, and little more than an hour east of Queenstown. Middlemarch is an hour's drive northwest of Dunedin, and three hours southeast of Queenstown. Buses run from Dunedin and Queenstown to Clyde.
When to go // Autumn is the most colourful time on the trail, while winter rides offeran often crisp, frosty difference to the scenery.
Where to stay // There is accommodation along the trail's length. The official trail website has full listings.
Tours // Of the many tour operators along the trail, try Adventure South NZ (www.adventuresouth.co.nz), Trail Journeys (www.trailjourneys.co.nz) or Central Cycle Trail Co (www.centralcycletrail.co.nz).
More info // www.otagocentralrailtrail.co.nz

Opposite: shades of autumn on Lake Dunstan Trail

MORE LIKE THIS
CENTRAL OTAGO ROUTES

LAKE DUNSTAN TRAIL

Launched in 2021, the Lake Dunstan Trail spins off the Otago Central Rail Trail at Clyde, making it now possible to cycle almost 124 miles (200km) from Middlemarch to Cromwell purely on bike paths. Even as a standalone ride, there's a lot to like about the Lake Dunstan Trail, which follows the shores of its namesake lake for the entire journey between Cromwell and Clyde. At times it does so on sections of boardwalk clipped onto cliffs, while also crossing an 290ft/89m-long suspension bridge. This trail is more remote than the Otago Central Rail Trail – there's a 16-mile (25km) section with no road access – and your thighs can anticipate a greater workout, with 1900ft (580m) of ascent along the journey. But then there are the appeasing pleasures, such as the wineries around Bannockburn, and a floating cafe on the lake at Cairnmuir Gully.

Start // Cromwell
Finish // Clyde
Distance // 25.5 miles (41km)

ROXBURGH GORGE TRAIL

Another ride that branches off the Otago Central Rail Trail, the easy Roxburgh Gorge Trail clings to the Clutha/Mata-au River as it scores a deep gorge through the Otago landscape. The ride breaks away from the Otago Central Rail Trail in Alexandra (5 miles/8km along the trail from Clyde), following the river as it wraps around bluffs rising up to 1150ft (350m) above the river and old gold diggings. Schist huts remain as relics of the golden days, as does the thyme that was planted on the slopes – sniff the breeze to catch a scent. One unusual aspect of this ride is the need to break it with a jetboat transfer; book ahead (www.clutharivercruises.co.nz; www.beaumontjet.co.nz) to meet the boat at Doctors Point, taking a 40-minute spin to rejoin the trail eight miles (13km) downstream at Gorge Creek. The boat ride provides a whole new angle and perspective on the miners' huts and rock shelters inside the gorge.

Start // Alexandra
Finish // Roxburgh Dam
Distance // 13 miles (21km)

CLUTHA GOLD TRAIL

Continuing the journey along the Clutha/Mata-au River from Roxburgh Dam is this trundle deeper into Central Otago. From New Zealand's largest gravity-fed dam, it makes a gentle journey downstream. Pause just beyond Roxburgh town for a cooling dip at Pinders Pond, a rare tranquil moment on the Clutha/Mata-au (keep an eye out later for the sunken gold dredger in the river). Detour out to the Lonely Graves – unmarked graves from the gold rush – and Horseshoe Bend Bridge, an impressive, century-old pedestrian suspension bridge straddling the river, before climbing to Big Hill Tunnel, a 1444ft/440m-long railway tunnel that also marks the trail's highest point. The descent that follows brings you to the trail's end at Otago's very first gold-rush town, Lawrence.

Start // Roxburgh Dam
Finish // Lawrence
Distance // 45 miles (73km)

David Wall/Alamy

INDEX

K

L

M

N

P

R

Epic Bike Trips of the World
September 2026
Published by Lonely Planet Global Limited
www.lonelyplanet.com
10 9 8 7 6 5 4 3 2 1

Printed in Malaysia
ISBN 978 183 75 8758 2

Publishing Director Piers Pickard
Illustrated & Gift Publisher Becca Hunt
Senior Editor Robin Barton
Editors Mark Mackenzie, Vicky Smith
Art Direction Taylor Miles Hopkins
Layout Design Jo Dovey
Index Vicky Smith
Print Production Nigel Longuet

Lonely Planet Global Limited
Digital Depot, Roe Lane (off Thomas St),
Digital Hub, Dublin 8,
D08 TCV4
Ireland
(EU authorised representative)

STAY IN TOUCH lonelyplanet.com/contact

Writers Alex Crevar (AC), Andrea Sachs (AS); Andrew Bain (AB), Betsy Welch (BW), Cally Silberbauer (CS), Christina Palassio (CP), Edward Pickering (EP), Eileen Schwab (ES), Emma Osenton (EO), Ethan Gelber (EG); Huw Vellacott (HV), Jorja Creighton (JC), Julian Sayerer (JS), Kristina Vackova (KV), Lael Wilcox (LW), Maggie Slepian (MS), Mark Bailey (MB), Mark Watson (MW), Matt Swaine (MS), Oliver Bridgewood (OB), Oliver Smith (OS), Miles Arbour (MA), Nate Cavalieri (NC), Nicolas D'Hoedt (ND), Peter English (PE), Riley Missel (RM); Sam Rice (SR), Samuel Jones (SJ), Sarah Pendergrass (SP); Stefan Amato (SA), Virginia DiGaetano (VD);

Illustrations by Ross Murray (www.rossmurray.com)

MIX
Paper | Supporting responsible forestry
FSC™ C021741

Paper in this book is certified against the Forest Stewardship Council™ standards. FSC™ promotes environmentally responsible, socially beneficial and economically viable management of the world's forests.